Relational Missionary Training:

Theology, Theory and Practice

Enoch Wan & Mark Hedinger

Urban Loft Publishers
Skyforest, CA

Relational Missionary Training
Theology, Theory and Practice

Copyright © 2017 Enoch Wan & Mark Hedinger

Urban Loft Publishers
P.O. Box 6
Skyforest, CA 92385
www.urbanloftpublishers.com

Senior Editors: Stephen Burris & Kendi Howells Douglas
Copy Editor: Michelle Munson
Graphics: Amber McKinley & Elisabeth Clevenger

Scripture for the book taken from the HOLY BIBLE, NEW INTERNATIONAL VERSION®. Copyright © 1973, 1978, 1984 by International Bible Society. Used by permission of Zondervan Publishing House. All rights reserved

ISBN-13: 978-0997371765

Made in the U.S.

Table of Contents

Part One: Theology

Part Two: Theory

Part Three: Practice

List of Tables

List of Figures

SERIES PREFACE

Urban Ministry in the 21st Century is a series of monographs that addresses key issues facing those involved in urban mission whether it be in the slums, squatter communities, *favelas*, or in immigrant neighborhoods. It is our goal to bring fresh ideas, a theological basis, and best practices in urban mission as we reflect on our changing urban world. The contributors to this series bring a wide-range of ideas, experiences, education, international perspectives, and insight into the study of the growing field of urban mission. These contributions fall into four very general areas: 1. the biblical and theological basis for urban mission; 2. best practices currently in use and anticipated in the future by urban scholar/activists who are living, working, and studying in the context of cities; 3. personal experiences and observations based on urban mission as it is currently being practiced; and 4. a forward view toward where we are headed in the decades ahead in the expanding and developing field of urban mission. This series is intended for educators, graduate students, theologians, pastors, and serious students of urban mission.

More than anything, these contributions are creative attempts to help Christians strategically and creatively think about how we can better reach our world that is now more urban than rural. We do not see theology and practice as separate and distinct. Rather, we see sound practice growing out of a healthy vibrant theology that seeks to understand God's world as it truly is as we move further into the twenty-first century. Contributors interact with the best scholarly literature available at the time of writing while making application to specific contexts in which they live and work.

Each book in the series is intended to be a thought-provoking work that represents the author's experience and perspective on urban mission in a particular context. The editors have chosen those who bring this rich diversity of perspectives to this series. It is our hope and prayer that each book in this series will challenge, enrich, provoke, and cause the reader to dig deeper into subjects that bring a deeper understanding of our urban world and the mission the church is called to perform in that new world.

Dr. Kendi Howells Douglas and Stephen Burris,
Urban Ministry in the 21st Century Series Editors

Part One:
Theological and Scriptural Understanding

Chapter One
Introduction

Enoch Wan and Mark Hedinger began to work together on the Trinitarian paradigm in 2006;[1] yet this book is the first time collaborating on "relational paradigm" which was developed by Enoch Wan in the publication of several pieces since 2006. [2] Our

---

[1] See the two items below:
Enoch Wan serving as dissertation chair, Hedinger, Mark R. *"Towards a Paradigm of Integrated Missionary Training."* Unpublished dissertation, Doctor of Missiology. Western Seminary. Portland, 2006.
Wan, Enoch and Hedinger, Mark, "Missionary Training for the Twenty First Century: Biblical Foundations," *Global Missiology* (July 2011), <http://ojs.globalmissiology.org/index.php/english/issue/view/56>. (accessed October 21, 2016)
[2] Sample works by Enoch Wan on "relational paradigm" are listed below:
  • Wan, Enoch, "The Paradigm of 'Relational Realism'." *Occasional Bulletin* 19:2 of Evangelical Missiological Society, (2006), Relational Theology and Relational Missiology https://www.westernseminary.edu/files/documents/faculty/wan/Relational%20realism-EMS-OB-Spring2006.pdf. (accessed October 21, 2016)
  _____."Relational Theology and Relational Missiology." *Occasional Bulletin* 21, no. 1 (n.d.): 1–7. https://www.westernseminary.edu/files/documents/faculty/wan/Relat_theol_missio_OB_21_1.pdf.
  _____ and Johnny Yee-chong Wan. "Relational Study of the Trinity and the Epistle to the Philippians." *Global Missiology*, April 2010. www.GlobalMissiology.org./
  • _____. "A Missio-Relational Reading of Romans: A Complementary Study to Current Approaches." *Occasional Bulletin of the Evangelical Missiological Society* 23, no. 1 (Winter 2010): 1–8.www.GlobalMissiology.org.
  • _____ and Narry Santos. "A Missio-Relational Reading of Mark." *Occasional Bulletin of the Evangelical Missiological Society* 24, no. 2 (Spring 2011): 1–26.

plan is having this volume as a foundational piece, to be followed by another one that is practical.

Purposes of the Book

This book is more foundational in nature, introducing the theological, theoretical and practical aspects of "relational paradigm." It has been written with two purposes as follows:

1. to describe the Trinitarian and relational paradigm;
2. to develop contemporary missionary training program accordingly.

Definition of Key-Terms

In this book, several key terms are used and are defined as follows:

<u>Andragogy:</u> one subset of adult education with roots in the behaviorist school of education. Andragogy is not a synonym of the more general term "adult education."

<u>Disciple:</u> a person following Jesus Christ (being), being changed (becoming) to be more like Jesus and eager to bring others to Jesus with a Kingdom-orientation (belonging).

<u>Intercultural Leader</u>: Guided by the character of God and the will of the Father, a genuine disciple of the Son, Jesus Christ who models, motivates and mobilizes others towards spiritual maturity (i.e. being, personhood and character) and ministerial fruitfulness (i.e. doing, performance, and career) by the empowering of the Holy Spirit (both individually and institutionally) in kingdom service for God's glory within a cross-cultural context.

Missionary Training: the preparation of individuals, families, and groups of people toward the goal of developing in them the skills, knowledge, attitudes, relationships, wisdom, and maturity for effective intercultural Christian ministry.

Paradigm of Relational Realism: a conceptual framework for understanding reality based on the interactive connections between personal beings/Beings.

Pedagogy: the principles and practices of instruction. In this book, it is used to describe all instruction, regardless of the age of the intended learner. The specialized area of education that deals with adult learners is referred to simply as "adult education."

Relational Discipleship: the process of bringing others (people) to submit to the lordship (power and authority) of Jesus Christ primarily through vertical-relationship to the Triune God and secondarily through horizontal-relationship within the context of the Church/church in unity, mutuality and reciprocity.

Relational Missionary Training: missionary training developed from the perspective of the paradigm of relational realism.

Trinitarian Paradigm: a conceptual framework that understands reality to be primarily based on the vertical relationship between God and the created order and secondarily on the horizontal relationship within the created order.

Uniqueness of the Book

In terms of uniqueness of this volume, there are several points worth mentioning:

1. Theoretical framework: relational paradigm that is cross-cultural relevant
2. Practical element: with specifics as "who," "how" and "what"
3. Contemporary element: e.g. digital and virtual dimensions

Readership of the Book

This book is written with missionary trainers and institutional leaders in mind.

Organization of the Book

There are four parts to the book covering three areas: theological, theoretical, and practical. Part One (theological) has three chapters: Chapter 1 is introductory, Chapter 2 is on theological matters and Chapter 3 is on theoretical issues. Part Two has two chapters which consider general and specialized educational models respectively. Part Three has three chapters: Chapter 6 deals with seven key relationships within a relational paradigm for mission; Chapter 7 explains the connection between training models, training environment and relational paradigm; Chapter 8 covers training content and relational paradigm. Part Four includes Chapter 9 which is a summary of the contents of the book, and Chapter 10 includes a conclusion and recommendations.

Desired Results of the Book

It is the prayer of the authors that this book will expand the field of training for cross-cultural Christian ministry. In a world where Christian messengers travel "from everywhere to everyone"[3] the equipping and training of intercultural workers has never been so important.

We also pray that the Lord will use this book to build a generation of intercultural leaders. In our globalized world, those who have skill and understanding of intercultural life and ministry will be the leaders of Jesus' church. Our prayer is that one result of this volume is to equip those who, through a vital vertical relationship with Triune God, model, motivate, and mobilize others towards spiritual maturity and ministerial fruitfulness in kingdom service for God's glory within an intercultural context (see Definitions of Key-Terms for our full definition of leadership).

---

[3] Escobar, Samuel. *The New Global Mission: The Gospel from Everywhere to Everyone*. Downers Grove, Ill.: InterVarsity Press, 2003.

Chapter Two
The Trinity and Relational Realism Paradigm

Introduction

Reality is based on relationships between created beings and Creator Beings. Mission work is about human beings who are in relationship with God introducing yet other human beings to Him. God's purpose is relational. Our calling in mission is relational and training for mission also needs to be relational.

The theoretical framework of this book began with a 2006 article by Enoch Wan titled, "The Paradigm of 'relational realism'" in which Wan stated,

> Ontologically, 'relational realism' is to be defined as 'the systematic understanding that 'reality' is primarily based on the 'vertical relationship' between God and the created order and secondarily 'horizontal relationship' within the created order. [4]

---

[4] Wan, Enoch. "The Paradigm of 'Relational Realism.'"*Occasional Bulletin* 19, no. 2 (2006): 1–4. https://www.westernseminary.edu/files/documents/faculty/wan/Relational%20 realism-EMS-OB-Spring2006.pdf. (Accessed October 21, 2016).

At the outset of this book, we seek to systematically understand the paradigm of relational realism through a theological consideration of relationships within the Trinity and with created beings. The second section of the book will look at educational theory relevant to training for intercultural ministry. The third section of the book will develop introductory ideas of how these elements of relational study can be integrated into training for intercultural ministry. Finally, the fourth section will seek to draw conclusions that are at once practical and yet theoretically, theologically, and scripturally rooted.

Understanding Relationship

Jesus' followers had to be startled and probably confused when He said, "Now this is eternal life, that they may know you, the only true God, and Jesus Christ, whom You have sent." (John 17:3). Or maybe they were not confused or startled – if they were at all like me, they tucked that idea away to try to understand it later. Is life really about knowing God?

What about biology? Surely, according to atheistic scientists, life is more about biology than it is about a relationship with God. And yet, Jesus brought Lazarus back from the dead in a way that biology cannot explain; but divine-human relationship can.

What about defining life as experience, as taught by existentialists of the 1960s? Those who experienced their life situations in the 1800s are no longer with us in life. They certainly experienced things both good and bad, happy and sad; those experiences did not move them into eternity. "I am the way, and the truth, and the life," says Jesus (John 14:6). No one goes to the Father except in relationship with Him. Our experiences cannot by-pass that relational WAY.

Instead of starting with mechanisms or organizational structures, we could compare worldview, spirituality, etc. of cultures; we opt for a relational framework at macro level. We agree with the apostle Paul who gave high priority not to his credentials, accolades and accomplishments which had been considered as rubbish; knowing Christ is his supreme goal in life (Phil 3:8). It all comes back to relationship: first and foremost vertical then horizontal.

If we want to understand life, we must understand relationship. The starting point for that understanding is God who is Relational. He is first One then three and He is both One and Three. We begin by looking at the relational patterns between the Father, the Son, and the Spirit. The distinctive attribute of the Trinity is that He is "relational" horizontally among the Three and vertically with the created order.[5]

Creator/creature. The fundamental distinction

A starting point for understanding Trinitarian relationality is the idea that there are only two categories of existence: the

---

[5] Wan, Enoch. *Relational Theology.* (in Chinese) Hong Kong: TienDao Publisher. 2015. www.toelibrary.com.

Creator and the created order (i.e. angelic/human beings and the natural order). As Vern Poythress phrased it,

> According to the Bible, the Creator-creature distinction is fundamental. There are two levels of being, two levels of existence: the self-sufficient, original existence of God the Creator, and the dependent, derivative existence of creatures.[6]

This fundamental distinction between the Creator and created order at a macro level is shown in Wan's figure[7] below:

Figure 1: Creator and Creatures in Relation to Each Other

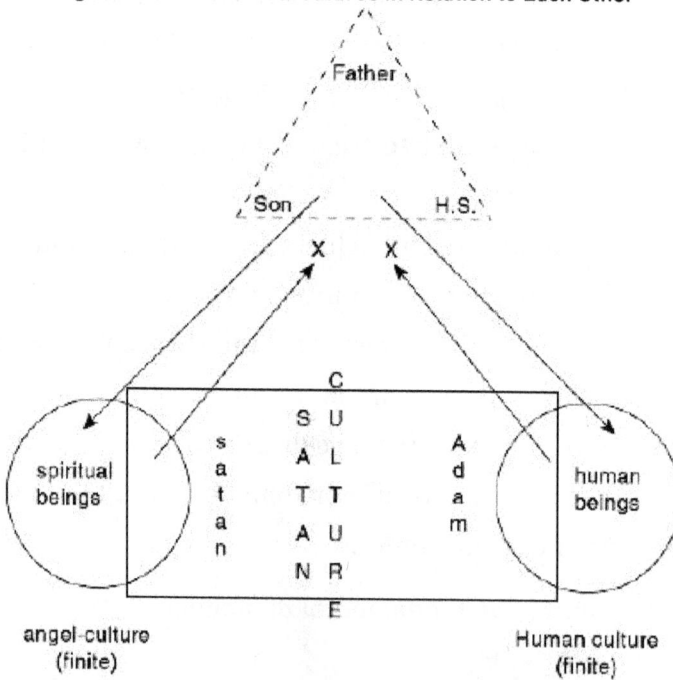

angel-culture
(finite)

Human culture
(finite)

---

6 Poythress, Vern S. "Reforming Ontology and Logic in the Light of the Trinity: An Application of Van Til's Idea of Analogy." *Westminster Theological Journal* 57, no. 1 (Spring 1995): 187.

7 Wan, Enoch. "Ethnohermeneutics; Its Necessity and Difficulty for All Christians of All Times."*Global Missiology*, January, 2004. globalmissiology.org.

How does that fundamental distinction between Creator and creatures impact the relationships seen in Figure 1? How do the members of the Trinity relate to each other? What does the Trinity tell us about relationships between people, and with other created spirit beings? The following pages will examine those questions.

Epistemology and Revelation: the creature knows only what the Creator reveals

Following close upon the fundamental distinction between Creator and creature is the realization that the creature only knows that which is revealed in some form or other by the Creator. As Ralph Smith phrased it, "The truth that defines a Christian as a Christian, our faith in the triune God, is *revealed* truth" (emphasis in the original).[8] That which we know of the Trinity is that which the Trinity has chosen to reveal. What, then, has the Trinity chosen to reveal about His/Their relational patterns?

God's Relationship: Immanent and Economic

Two frames of reference are used to capture the idea of the relationships within the Trinity and between the Triune Creator and creation. Theologians have coined the terms "Immanent Trinity" and "Economic Trinity" to refer to these two concepts.

---

8 Smith, Ralph A. *Trinity & Reality: An Introduction to the Christian Faith*. Moscow, ID: Canon Press, 2004, 13.

The phrase "Immanent Trinity" refers to the self-revelation of how the members of the Trinity relate to one another. The concept of "Economic Trinity" derives from the Greek word used to describe the organization of a household and, by extension, within the state.[9] To speak of the "Economic Trinity" is to speak of the interaction between God the Trinity and creation; it is God as revealed and active in the world.[10] The "Immanent Trinity" refers to the inner life of God within the relationships of the Trinity

In other words, there are elements of the relationship between the Father, the Son, and the Spirit which are not shared in God's relationships with human beings. There are some things that simply exist between the members of the Trinity. Yet other relational elements between the members of the Trinity are shared in one way or another by creation. J. Scott Horrell has helped to put that concept into words when he wrote that the economic Trinity gives an accurate though not necessarily complete representation of the immanent Trinity. In his words,

> We presuppose that the economic Trinity as revealed in the Bible *accurately* represents to finite creation who and what God is; but that the economic Trinity is by no means all that is God [emphasis in the original].[11]

---

[9] Gunton, Colin E. *The One, the Three, and the Many: God, Creation, and the Culture of Modernity.* Cambridge; New York, NY,: Cambridge University Press, 1993, 158.
[10] Cunningham. *These Three Are One: The Practice of Trinitarian Theology.* Malden, MA: Wiley-Blackwell, 1998, 37.
[11] Horrell, J. Scott. "Toward Clarifying a Biblical Model of the Social Trinity: Avoiding Equivocation of Nature And Order." *Global Missiology*, January 2004. www.globalmissiology.net. Accessed February 16, 2005, 2.

The nature of our knowledge of the Divine, that such knowledge depends on revelation, points toward Horrell's viewpoint. Though it is entirely correct to say that no contradiction or falsehood would corrupt the accuracy of God's self-revelation, at the same time we are nowhere given an indication that he has told us all that there is to know about himself. For these reasons, the economic Trinity and the immanent Trinity will not be seen as equal in this study. Rather, any given relationship between members of the Trinity will be depicted by the biblical revelation touching that relationship, realizing that any given relationship might go beyond what has been revealed.

Relationships within the Trinity

Essential Relationships within the Trinity: Equality and Mutuality

Perichoresis is a term coined by the Latin fathers to convey the idea that the members of the Trinity are mutually involved in personal and dynamic ways. Perichoresis was described by Gunton when he stated, "It would appear to follow that in eternity Father, Son and Spirit share a dynamic mutual reciprocity, interpenetration and interanimation."[12] An approximation of this concept can be seen in the indwelling of the Spirit in the life of a believer. In the same way, the Father, the Son and the Spirit are referred to as being in a mutually indwelling relationship.

---

[12] Colin Gunton, *The One the Three and the Many*, 163.

Ralph Smith provided a simpler definition of perichoresis and at the same time offered a helpful discussion of what that indwelling entails. According to Smith, "When biblical writers speak of being 'in' someone or something, they employ the analogy of physical space to convey the intimacy of covenant union."[13] Smith's explanation that perichoresis refers to a dynamic, mutually-intimate relationship is helpful. The Gospel of John, particularly (but not exclusively) the 17th chapter, demonstrates that the Son and the Father have this sort of mutually indwelling relationship.

A second relational element that is seen in the interaction between the members of the Trinity is what David Cunningham called "polyphony."[14] This concept reflects the fact that to pay attention to one member of the Trinity does not diminish the value of others. As harmony in music augments the beauty of diversity, so in Trinitarian studies there are indeed points of time where one member of the Triune God is in focus for a period of time; yet that focus on one member does not imply a diminution of the others' involvement.

Existential Relationship within the Trinity: Hierarchy and Subordination

Another significant aspect to the relationship between the members of the Trinity has to do with roles that are assumed by

---

[13] Ralph Smith, *Trinity and Reality*, 42.
[14] Cunningham, *These Three are One*, 127.

the various Persons. Horrell called attention to the fact that within the Triune God there are identifiable roles given to specific Persons when he wrote, "I define an eternally ordered social model as the social model that, while insisting on equality of the divine nature, affirms perpetual distinction of roles within the immanent Godhead."[15] This reality is seen for instance in the submission of the Son to the Father's will and his obedience, even to the point of death on the cross (Phil 2:1-8).

Ralph Smith called this differentiation of roles within the Trinity by the name "hierarchy" as seen in his explanation that, "Hierarchy in relationship means that the Father is greater than the Son in His *office* only, not in His *being*" (emphasis in the original).[16] The distinction of roles leads to an understanding of how the Father could send the Son, and how the Spirit could be sent to bear witness of the Son. Though equal in being, there are different roles for each member of the Trinity.

Another author who has recently written on theological implications of the Trinity is Bruce Ware. In his work, *The Father, the Son and the Holy Spirit; Relationship, Role, and Relevance,* [17] Ware added insights that are helpful for our study. He traced the twin themes of authority and submission, showing how those roles are not simply part of our human condition, but, in fact, are part of Divine Nature. There is an eternal hierarchy within the Trinity: the

---

[15] Horrell, *Toward Clarifying a Biblical Model of the Social Trinity*, 1.
[16] Ralph Smith, *Trinity and Reality*, 35.
[17] Ware, Bruce. *Father, Son and Holy Spirit; Relationships, Roles, and Relevance.* Wheaton, IL: Crossway, 2005.

Father eternally in authority over the Son, who is eternally submissive to the Father; at the same time, the Spirit is in submission to both the Son and the Father. The theological concept that describes the ordered nature of relationships within the Trinity, including levels of authority and submission, is called by the Greek word for arrangement or order: "taxis." What is amazing in Divine taxis is that all three Persons use their particular role of authority and/or submission to bring honor, joy, and glory to the Others. The eternal existence of loving and mutually honoring relationships between Persons who are in authority and submission relationships is so unlike human experience that it is startling, and yet it is an important part of the relationship that exists between the Father, the Son, and the Spirit.

Trinity as Personal Beings

Going back then, to our basic question, what is it that the Trinity can tell us that will help to build a paradigm of relational realism? We have seen four key relational elements that exist between the members of the Trinity: *Perichorisis*, polyphony, equal stature and yet diverse roles, and the issues of hierarchy and submission.

These four relational characteristics can be understood as the dynamic interplay between equality and mutuality. The Father, Son, and Spirit are all equally God, and all are mutually involved in One Another's existence. Yet there are other relational truths that refine our understanding of equality and mutuality: All Three are equal in honor and in standing as True God, but there are distinctions in role. All are mutually involved in One Another, yet they are truly separate.

Another way to see how the Father, Son, and Spirit interact is by looking at the key attributes which the biblical text ascribes to their relationships. Ralph Smith highlighted three of these attributes:

> If words describing the attributes of God require for their understanding both the notion of the covenant and interpersonal relationships, it is reasonable to conclude that at least some of God's attributes describe first of all the covenantal relationship of the persons of the Trinity.[18]

The attributes that Smith discussed are love, faithfulness, and righteousness. The Members of the Trinity, in their mutual relationship with one another, demonstrate these characteristics. The same attributes are also essential parts of the Triune God's economic relationships with created beings.

John Dahms considered the relationships between members of the Triune God from the perspective of feelings. He focused on love, joy, and peace, concluding with the statement that "If, as we have stated, the feelings of love, joy, and peace are

---

[18] Ralph Smith, *Paradox and Truth*, 85.
[19] Dahms, John V. "Biblical Feelings And Emotions." *Global Missiology English 2*, no. 2 (29-30, 2010). http://ojs.globalmissiology.org/index.php/english/article/view/91.Accessed October 21, 2016.

eternal and fundamental, they must characterize deity, quite apart from His relation to what He has created."[19]

Another important element remains to be noted in this discussion of the immanent Trinity. The point bears repeating that the three are personal Beings. These are neither simple forces nor manifestations of one another. They are truly personal beings, distinct from one another and yet intimately, dynamically related as well. The personal nature of the relationships between the members of the Trinity led Horrel to write that the three members of the Godhead are "genuinely personal in relationships."[20] This highlights once again the fact that the three are each unique, distinct persons.

How do those personal Beings relate to One Another? In his classic systematic theology, William Shedd answered that question with Scripture:[21]

1. One person loves another (John 3:35).
2. Persons dwell in one another (John 14:10, 11).
3. One person suffers for another (Zech 13:7).
4. One person knows another (Matt 11:27).
5. Persons address one another (Heb 1:8).
6. One person is the way to another (John 14:6).
7. One person speaks of another (Luke 3:22).
8. One person glorifies another (John 17:5).
9. The persons confer with one another (Gen 1:26, 11:7).

---

[20] Horrell, *Toward Clarifying a Biblical Model of the Social Trinity*, 1.
[21] Shedd, William G. T. *Dogmatic Theology*. Nashville, TN: T. Nelson, 1980, 279.

10. The persons make plans with one another (Isa 9:6).

11. One person sends another (Gen 16:7, John 14:26).

12. One person rewards another (Phil 2:5-11, Heb 2:9).

We have briefly seen, then, how the members of the Trinity relate to each other. We now shift to another topic. How can we describe the relationship between God and created order?

Understanding the Relationship between God and Creation

We now move into a review of Economic Trinity: God in relationship with created beings. This is the watershed issue: this is the defining line by which all other reality must be measured. There is God, and there is creation.

Creatures know what they know by revelation that is always accurate and sufficient, though we have no reason to believe that it is total and complete (given the infinite nature of the Creator and the finite nature of the creature).

This fact leads to an important relational issue: humans come to God on the basis of faith. One mark of a healthy vertical relationship is that humans believe what God has said; it is a relationship of trust, belief, faith.

A second and related reality that is made plain by the vertical relationship between believing humans and Triune God is that God invites us to come to him through his chosen paths. Where human religions try to say that "all roads lead to Rome" as a way of saying all worship is acceptable to God, in fact, Jesus is THE WAY, and no one comes to the Father but through Him

(John 14:6). The Old Testament stories of unacceptable worship that used innovative forms of incense give an illustration of the importance of this fact (Ex 30:34–38 cf. Lev 10:1–3). God invites his creation into relationship; but that relationship is governed by him, not by his creatures.

A very brief survey of Scripture will confirm that God's desire is a healthy interpersonal relationship with people. Just as the Persons in the Trinity live in relationship with one another, so too the Trinity seeks personal involvement with creation as part of that vertical relationship.

In Eden, the first people walked with the Lord in the cool of the day (Gen 3:8).

In Deuteronomy, God used relational terms to set the Mosaic Law in its right context: Deuteronomy 6:5, "Love the Lord your God with all your heart and with all your soul and with all your strength."

David and other psalmists called upon people to "Delight yourself in the Lord" (37:4). "Trust in the Lord" (for example, Psalm 37:3), and "commit your way to the Lord" (for example, Psalm 37:5).

The Prophets called Israel to a relational depth with the Lord described, for instance, in Jeremiah 9:23–24, "Let not the wise man boast of his wisdom, or let the strong man boast of his strength, or let the rich man boast of his riches; but let him who boasts boast about this, that he understands and knows me, that I am the Lord who exercises kindness, justice and righteousness on earth, for in these I delight," declares the Lord.'

Micah wrote a relational-based appeal to Israel: in Micah 6:7–8, the prophet compared cold performance to relational depth when he discounted the value of burnt offerings of thousands of rams and rivers of oil and even of the first born of a supplicant. Rather than a "contract" that offered emotionally distant fulfillment, Micah said that God seeks those who act justly, love mercy, and walk humbly with God. To walk humbly with God is to be in a relationship with him.

Moving to the New Testament, Jesus' objection to the Pharisees was not in their zeal to complete technical elements of the law. His criticism of the Pharisees was their belief that God was pleased with what they did quite apart from their trust, love, and faith to the Lord. "Away from Me," he will say even to those who did great acts like prophesying, casting out demons, and performing miracles. The rejection of these apparently great people is on the relational basis that "I never knew you." (Matthew 7:21–23).

Jesus told us that fruitful ministry activity is impossible if we do not abide in him. The life of Jesus must flow through us with the same freedom as the life of a grape rootstock flows through the vines and into the growing fruit. Without that depth of relationship, there is neither Christian life nor fruit from Christian ministry (John 15).

Paul's hope was neither in his heritage nor his accomplishments: it was his desire, "I want to know Christ and the power of His resurrection." (Phil 3:10). The life he lived, he said, was not based on works he had done; but rather, "by faith in the Son of God who loved me and gave himself up for me." (Gal 2:20).

The point of this very brief review of Scripture is that God himself described what is an appropriate vertical relationship. It is personal. It is based on faith, trust, and love. It is genuinely warm and emotionally engaged. It seeks to obey not as some cold exercise to gain benefit, like a workman whose sole interest is to receive a paycheck. Rather the vertical relationship that God has ordained is one of obedience as a display of love (John 14:15ff).

When we consider the foundational truth that reality is about relationship, we see that God is relational as the Three interact with One Another. That same God then describes the vertical relationship that is pleasing to Him: it is a relationship with the living and loving God. We return to Jesus' words that the essence of life is to know God and Jesus Christ whom God sent (John 17:3).

Other authors have contributed to this relational understanding of the vertical relationship. Ralph Smith called attention to the relational nature of the covenants of the Bible, noting that "Covenant means relationship, and the essence of the covenant relationship is love."[22] This relational, personal nature of the Trinity is not simply an element that allows us to apprehend God in analogy to human relationships. The personal nature of the members of the Trinity stands in stark contrast to ideologies which consider the divine to be impersonal. As Colin Gunton phrased it:

---

[22] Ralph Smith, *Trinity and Reality,* 38.

32

The doctrine of the Trinity replaces a *logical* conception of the relation between God and the world with a *personal* one, and accordingly allows us to say two things of utmost importance: that God and the world are ontologically distinct realities; but that distinctness, far from being the denial of relations, is its ground. Such relation as there is is personal, not logical, the product of the free and personal action of the Triune God [emphasis in the original].[23]

The authors discussed so far have examined the Trinity in terms of the Trinity's relationship with creation. Other authors focus on the revealed relationship patterns of each individual member of the Trinity with creation. An example is Ajith Fernando who considered the role of the Father, of the Son, and of the Spirit individually in relationship with the created order.[24] God the Father is presented in Scripture as the Source, Originator, and End. He draws people to the Gospel message, and His characteristics and attributes bring blessing to all generations and all nations. [25] Jesus is both the message itself and the model of what ministry is all about.[26] The Spirit is the One who implements mission as He gives power, gifts, truth, companionship, and holiness to His people. [27]

As we consider vertical relationships, another important implication is that not just any relationship is acceptable to God. There are good relationships and there are bad relationships –

---

[23] Gunton, *The Promise of Trinitarian Theology*, 72.
[24] Ajith, Fernando. In *Global Missiology for the 21st Century*, Pasadena, CA: William Carey Library, 1999, 189 - 254.
[25] Ibid, 191 – 198.
[26] Ibid, 207 – 221.
[27] Ibid, 223 – 236.

whether between creation and Creator, or simply between created beings. David Cunningham spoke to this point when he suggested that relationships are not arbitrarily good; they require content, and in some cases that content can be pathological.[28] The question is not simply if one is in relationship with the Creator, but if one has a healthy, appropriate relationship.

This healthy relationship includes the theme of salvation. Writing in a devotional, pastoral style, A.W. Tozer used the vocabulary of relationship to discuss salvation when he wrote, "Essentially salvation is the restoration of a right relation between man and his Creator, a bringing back to normal of the Creator-creation relation."[29]

The Bible speaks of both acceptable and unacceptable forms of relationship between man and the Triune God. God demonstrates faithfulness, love, provision, and forgiveness in his relationship with humanity. Man in turn is expected to demonstrate such characteristics as faith, love, obedience, faithfulness, and dependence.

Looking at another element of the vertical relationship, it is not only defined by God, but also empowered by His indwelling presence. Within the immanent Trinity there exists a dynamic mutual indwelling between the persons. By dynamic we refer to a continual mutuality among the Three as they interact. Relationships between the Trinity and creation also have that

---

[28] Cunningham, *These Three are One*, 192.

[29] Tozer, A. W, and Samuel Marinus Zwemer. *The Pursuit of God;* Harrisburg, PA: Christian Publications, 1948, 99.

dynamic interchange; yet it is different in at least two respects from relationships between members of the Trinity. One difference is that our creaturely relationship with the Triune God is marred by sin, whereas relationships between the three members of the Trinity are not. The effects of sin speak not only of the act of sin; but also the impact that sin has on human character and the consequences of sin on both human/human and human/divine relationships.

The other difference between the perichoresis within the Persons of the Trinity and the indwelling of the Spirit in humans is seen in human need to grow and develop. Relationships which include humans will inevitably involve progress, growth, and dynamic change. As physical maturity brings about changes, so too spiritual and relational maturity is accompanied by change. Thus, for instance, John wrote of some Christians as "little children," and others as "fathers" in the faith (1 John 2:12-14). Peter exhorted believers to "grow in the grace and knowledge of our Lord and Savior Jesus Christ" (2 Peter 3:18). Within the Trinity, relationships are dynamic; when humans are involved, relationships may be both dynamic and progressive.

Another comment about the economic Trinity comes from the work of Enoch Wan. Wan's model of anthropology began with the Trinity and then followed into the realm of created beings. This all-encompassing model gave appropriate attention to the distinction between Creator and creature, and also allowed humanity to be understood as being related to the Triune God.

This model (see Figure 1) gave an elegant description of the types of relationships between Beings and beings.[30]

The fact that Wan's chart included all divine Beings along with all created beings (spirit and physical) is important to this discussion for at least two reasons. Wan illustrated the fact that relationship can occur across that fundamental Creator/creature division. Secondly, he also demonstrated how all creation is united in some ways and yet not in others. The unity in diversity motif can be seen, for instance, by noting that all Creator Beings and all creatures fit into one chart; and yet, there is true distinction between Creator and creation, as well as true distinction between redeemed and unredeemed creation.

The issue of unity in diversity brings with it a cognitive challenge when we consider the Trinity: when is it that the One is in focus, and when are the Three in sight? To put the question a different way, how do we resolve the apparent contradiction between Deuteronomy 6:4 "Hear O Israel, the Lord our God, the Lord is one," and the equally clear call to worship and trust and believe in the Father, the Son, and the Spirit?

Wan brings to this question the practical help of primary and secondary levels. In the case just mentioned, the primary truth about God is that He is Unified. However, it is also true, though in secondary form, that He is Three. The pre-eminent truth is God's Unity.

---

[30] Wan, "Ethnohermeneutics," 3.

That primary/secondary distinction helps to keep a both/and thought pattern even in issues that appear to be contradictory. The primary/secondary distinction is of great help in developing the relational paradigm.

That primary/secondary reading is, in fact, key to a right understanding of reality and relationship. As Wan phrases it, "Ontologically, 'relational realism is defined as 'the systematic understanding' that 'reality' is primarily based on the 'vertical relationship' between God and the created order and secondarily 'horizontal relationship' within the created order."[31] Any true and correct understanding of reality must start with the reality of God the Father, the Son, and the Spirit, and then move towards observation and interpretation of created order. The implications of that statement in our modern, materialistic worldview are as obvious as they are revolutionary. In fact, in a follow-up to the article just quoted, Wan constructs a relational missiology on the theoretical basis of relational realism. "The key," he writes, "of Christian doctrine is 'relationship.'"[32]

In his relational paradigm reading of Paul's Epistle to the Romans[33] Wan leans on Christopher Wright's observation that

---

[31] Wan, *Occasion Bulletin* vol 19: no. 2 of the Evangelical Missiological Society, 1.
[32] Wan, Enoch. "Relational Theology and Relational Missiology." *Occasional Bulletin* 21, no. 1 (n.d.): 1–7 .https://www.westernseminary.edu/files/documents/faculty/wan/Relat_theol_missio_OB_21_1.pdf.
[33] Wan, Enoch. "A Missio-Relational Reading of Romans: A Complementary Study to Current Approaches." *Occasional Bulletin of the Evangelical Missiological Society* 23, no. 1 (Winter 2010): 1–8 .www.GlobalMissiology.org. (April, 2010).

relationships can be either vertical or horizontal.[34] The primary touch point for a correct understanding of reality is that <u>vertical relationship</u> (God and man within the divine-human relational network) is the fundamental issue of life: <u>horizontal relationship</u> (between created beings) is secondary. The Great Commandment is vertical and primary: to love God. The second greatest commandment is horizontal and secondary: love your neighbor.

Kinds of Relationship between Creator and creature

How can we analyze a topic as broad as the relationship between the members of the Trinity and the created order? In this section we will begin to build a model of relational mission. We start out by identifying and describing the vertical relationships that are part of the Economic Trinity, which we will then simplify. The simplified version will include seven relationships that are key to intercultural Christian ministry.

We begin by considering relational pattern possibilities. Within the universe of Beings/beings, what are the range of possible categories? Table One is helpful. Looking at Table One, we can identify the particular relational pairings (dyads) between Triune God and creation. Table One is an attempt at identifying 11 different relational dyads:

---

[34] Wright, Christopher J. H. *The Mission of God: Unlocking the Bible's Grand Narrative.* 1st edition. Downers Grove, IL: IVP Academic, 2006, 208 – 211.

Table 1: Eleven Different Relational Dyads

First member of dyad	Second member of dyad	Relational Pairings
Member of the Trinity	Another member of Trinity	Father/Son Father/Spirit Son/Spirit
Trinity	Redeemed human beings	Father/redeemed human Son/redeemed human Spirit/redeemed human
Trinity	Unredeemed human beings	Father/unredeemed human Son/unredeemed human Spirit/unredeemed human
Trinity	Unfallen spirit beings (angels)	Trinity/Angels
Trinity	Fallen spirit beings (demons and Satan)	Trinity/Demons and Satan
Redeemed human beings	Unfallen spirit beings (angels)	Redeemed humans/angels
Redeemed human beings	Fallen spirit beings (Satan and demons)	Redeemed humans/demons and Satan
Unredeemed human beings	Angels	Unredeemed humans/angels
Unredeemed human beings	Fallen spirit beings	Unredeemed humans/demons and Satan
People group	Another people group	These could include a wide variety of redeemed/unredeemed as well as cultural dynamics
Angels	Demons	Angels/demons or Satan

These categorical dyads could each be considered theologically and sociologically, with other categories added to better understand many issues of life. Since our interest in this study is relational training for mission work, though, we will simplify this chart to better identify the key categorical dyads that are important in the sending and preparing of intercultural workers. For our purposes, we will consider the relational dynamics between:

1. members of the Trinity
2. God and the gospel messenger (vertical)
3. God and the audience (vertical)
4. the messenger and the audience (horizontal)
5. the gospel messenger and the culture from which he/she comes (horizontal)
6. the audience and the culture from which he/she comes (horizontal)
7. demonic interaction with all other relationships

Figure 2 is a tool to help visualize the seven relationships that will become a key guide to our discussion of training missionaries for intercultural ministry.

Figure 2: Relationships within Intercultural Ministry

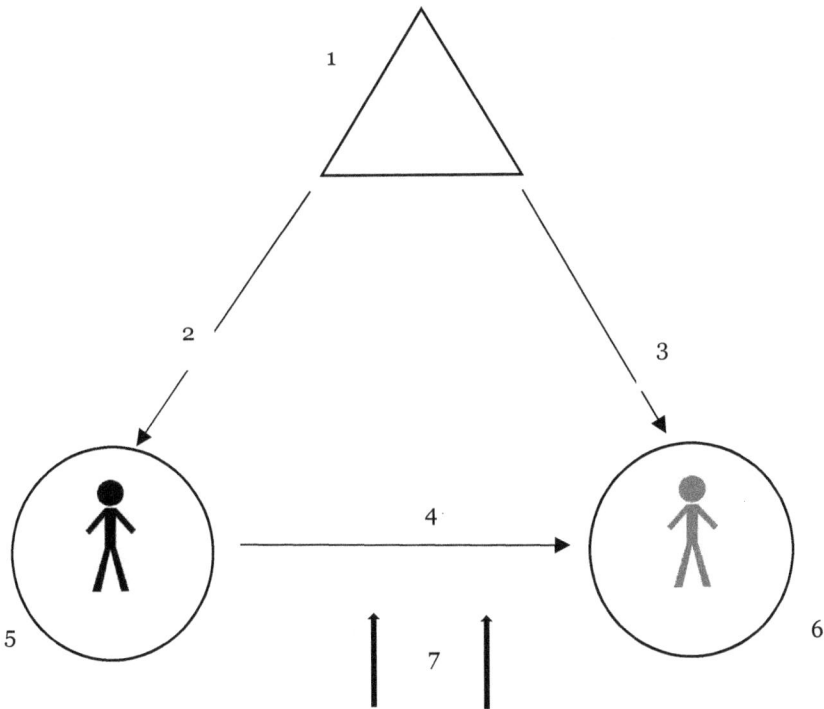

1. Relationships between the Members of the Trinity
2. Relationship between God and the gospel messenger (vertical)
3. Relationship between God and the audience (vertical)
4. Relationship between the messenger and the audience (horizontal)
5. Relationship between the gospel messenger and his/her home culture (horizontal)
6. the audience and his/her home culture (horizontal)
7. demonic interaction with all other relationships

Missionary Relationship One: Between Members of the Trinity

We considered this topic in the previous sections "Essential Relationships within the Trinity" and "Existential Relationships with the Trinity."

Missionary Relationship Two: Between God and the Gospel Messenger

Any sort of ministry depends on a variety of vertical relationships, including the relationship between God and the gospel messenger. The Triune God is active in the life of the people he sends. Fruitfulness in ministry relates to the relationship a Gospel worker has with the Triune God. "Neither can you bear fruit unless you remain in me" (John 15:5) is an important principle in ministry.

Relationship with the Triune God is fundamental to ministry fruitfulness as the apostle Paul stated it well: "I have planted, Apollos watered; but God gave the increase." (1 Cor 3:6 KJV) This vertical dimension generally is not highly valued in "managerial missiology" which can be humanistic and obsessive of productivity, effectiveness and outcomes.[35]

---

[35] Wan, Enoch. *Diaspora Missiology: Theory, Methodology, and Practice*. Portland, OR: Institute of Diaspora Studies of USA, Western Seminary, 2014, Chapter Two.

Missionary Relationship Three: Between God and the Audience of Gospel Ministry

As important as the relationship between Gospel worker and God is, though, there will be no fruit if the audience is not being drawn into relationship with God. Our dyad analysis includes looking for the relationship between an active God and those who hear the Gospel. "I will draw all men to Myself" (John 12:32) says the Lord. It is his voice, his activity that ultimately is effective, and this is for the simple reason that the point is to bring people into relationship with him. Human activity in and of itself will not bring someone into relationship with God. The Triune God must be in contact, drawing a person to himself if there is to be fruit.

Missionary Relationship Four: Horizontal between the Messenger and the Audience

In our normal ministry training, we very often start by thinking of a human messenger and a human audience. The two people are linked together by what we might call simple active ministry. It is the sense we get when we hear, "go into all the world and preach the Gospel" – a firm, clear, active statement that calls the hearer to go and do. This connection between the messenger and the audience is the focus of millions of pages of description of techniques, methods, and insights, and even more when the two people are from different cultural backgrounds.

Western ministry is enthralled with direct, active ministry effort. "Go and do" is not only a good fit with modernity and its love for technique, but it is also relationally clean and simple. Obedience to "go and do" is rightfully and appropriately given as evidence of love for the Lord. Passages such as John 14:15, "if you love Me you will obey what I command," show that "go and do" activity is indeed one evidence of a loving relationship.

The problem is that a mindset of "go and do" can also be cold and distant. In the absence of healthy relationship, cold obedience is not scriptural. The Lord said that fruit grows as we abide in him (John 15). Going and doing is important to the extent that the going and doing is within an abiding, significant relationship with the Triune God. This chart of vertical relations may include "doing;" yet that activity is important to the extent that one is in relationship to the Father, Son, and Spirit. In other word, appropriate horizontal relationships first of all require appropriate vertical relationships (as just one of many examples, see 1 John 4:19–21).

The coldness of technique is, in fact, a major contribution to post-modernity. In light of the failed promises of modernity, post-modernity understands life in the absence of method and technique.

We would suggest that it is not the technique or method *per se* that is questionable. It is whether technique exists within a context of relationship. Seen from a relational paradigm, the presence or the absence of technique, method, and structure is not a watershed issue. The bigger question is whether significant relationship is present and undergirding those techniques, methods, and structures.

Missionary Relationship Five: Between the Messenger and his/her own culture

This relationship area will be considered later in our study.

Missionary Relationship Six: Between the Audience and his/her culture

This cultural area will also be considered later.

Missionary Relationship Seven: Between all of the above and evil spirits

There is one last relational element to consider: Scripture speaks to the question of how fallen spirit beings interact with God and with man. To understand relational patterns with evil beings, it is important to recognize that relationships are not always positive and healthy. There are dysfunctional relationships; in contrast distinction with the excessive emphasis of "functionalism" on positive function of everything including relationships.[36] There are relationships with evil and perverse beings. Demons and Satan are relational, but it is relationship from which followers of Jesus need to flee. As relationships with the Lord cause us to seek him and obey him, so our knowledge of the evil one should warn us to recognize his wiles and flee. A scripturally appropriate understanding of evil will recognize that

---

[36] Wan, Enoch. "Critique of Functional Missionary Anthropology." *His Dominion (Canadian Theological Seminary)* 8, no. 3 (April 1982). http://www.enochwan.com/english/articles/pdf/Critique%20of%20%20Functio nal%20Anthropology.pdf.

Satan and other evil spirits want to disrupt the relationships between God and messenger, God and audience, and between people. Evil always seeks to disrupt the flow of relationship by lies, lawlessness, and murder. A scripturally appropriate relationship with evil beings will recognize them, and actively resist their schemes, depending on the Lord to rebuke them (Jude 9).

Figure 2 and the seven relationships of mission work make more sense when we use this idea to analyze a case study. Acts 16 reports on mission outreach from Asia to Europe, and it also gives a wonderful illustration of the different components of this relational paradigm.

The missionary is sent, and goes. There is activity. Paul and his band are en route to share the good news, to encourage the churches, and to open new areas to the Gospel. They are certain that their plan will take them to Asia; but the Spirit intercedes and says "No." And so they look to Bithynia, but again the Spirit denies that route.

And so the arrow (#2 on Figure 2) from the Triune God to the Missionary begins by closing the door to some activities that the missionaries thought at least likely, and perhaps as the goal of their travels. The Triune God, across this chapter, actively directs his sent ones in many ways: He closes doors to Asia and Bithynia; he gives a vision to go to Macedonia; he directs Paul and the others to the riverside prayer meeting. In one of the most breathtakingly beautiful verses of the Bible, Paul spoke a message, and the Spirit opened Lydia's heart to believe what Paul had said (Acts 16:14). In looking at how relational ministry takes place, this is a wonderfully clear example: Paul had to be present and preach the Word, yet it would have been in vain had the Spirit not opened Lydia's heart to receive that truth.

The Lord continued to be active in opening Europe to the Gospel in Acts 16: He gave spiritual discernment to Paul about the nature of the young fortune-teller. The Lord removed the evil spirits from that young woman. He sent Paul and Silas to the jail, and then he sent an earthquake to open the doors of the jail and to open the heart of the jailer.

In short, though Paul and his mission company were busy and active, yet God was also active both in Paul's life (#2 on Figure 2) and in the audience (#3 on Figure 2). Both of the two vertical relationships are filled with evidence of God's involvement.

There is another level of relationship in Acts 16: relationships that include the created evil forces of Satanic and demonic beings. The fortune teller was empowered by evil spirits, and when Paul spoke and the Spirit worked to remove those spirits, the hopes of the owners of the slave girl for profit were shattered.

Looking at Acts 16 from a horizontal perspective, we see that Paul and his mission company deliberately sought out interaction with other people; for example, with Lydia and the other women at the riverside prayer meeting. We can also see the horizontal relationship with the slave girl, and with the jailer and his family. Interestingly, in every one of those situations there is at once a horizontal relationship and a vertical relationship. It was not only Paul but also God who was actively involved in those peoples' lives.

Acts 16 alludes to one other horizontal relationship: the interaction between people and their cultural backgrounds. Paul, for instance, came to Macedonia with his Hebrew background and his Antioch background. His understanding of life was not exactly the same as what he encountered in Europe. At the same time, Lydia was living at that time in Philippi, but was not native to that place. Her cultural backgrounds and her situation as an immigrant to Macedonia may well have been part of God's preparation for her to receive the Lord.

That cultural sphere that surrounded the new church in Philippi would eventually include Christians who came from Thyatira (Lydia) as well as the jailer and his family. We have no information about their cultural background.

Table two puts these seven missionary relationships into a chart form, helping to further identify the relational categories that are important for understanding ministry from a relational perspective.

Table 2: Seven Key Missionary Relationships

#	Relationship Name	Description	Vertical or Horizontal	Acts 16 illustration
1	Within the Trinity Relationship #1	Revealed knowledge about the relationship patterns between Father, Son, and Spirit	Horizontal within Trinity	N/A
2	Trinity and Gospel Messenger Relationship #2	The relational patterns by which God provides, guides, corrects, sustains his children in ministry	Vertical	God's leading of Paul though Macedonia call. God's leading of Paul in such a way that led to jail where more ministry took place.
3	Trinity and Gospel Audience Relationship #3	God at work drawing people to himself	Vertical	God opening Lydia's heart; God drawing jailer to Himself.
4	Gospel Messenger and Audience Relationship #4	The human relationship where good thinking and preparation for ministry is part of human responsibility	Horizontal	Paul investigating to learn where people in Philippi pray. Paul singing in the jail: worship and testimony to other prisoners and jailers.
5	Gospel Messenger and his/her culture Relationship #5	The culture of the messenger; creates expectations and understandings of how life works	Horizontal	Timothy's circumcision, Paul's Roman citizenship.

#	Relationship Name	Description	Vertical or Horizontal	Acts 16 illustration
6	Audience and his/her culture Relationship #6	The culture of the audience; as the Kingdom of God enters a people there are challenges to the values, beliefs and feelings that govern the people	Horizontal	The slave girl whose freedom from demons decreased her social and economic value. Timothy's circumcision.
7	Evil beings and Gospel contexts Relationship #7	Demons and Satan offer relationship that is evil and dysfunctional, but is also relational	Vertical: between evil beings and God; horizontal: between humans and evil beings	The spirit of divination in the slave girl.

Understanding Horizontal Relationships

This study began by looking at the relationship between the Father, the Son, and the Spirit. After considering the revealed truth about those relationships, we moved into a consideration of the vertical relationships, especially between humanity and the Divine. Other vertical relationships also exist, as created order includes spirit beings known as angels and demons who are also vertically related to the Triune God. Yet our primary focus has been to investigate the vertical relationships between humans and God.

We now turn our attention to horizontal relationships, again with primary interest in the human/human realm.

The most basic horizontal relationships would be represented by two individuals in relationship with each other. These human/human relational patterns could include a practically unlimited variety of societal variables: Christian/non-Christian, man/woman, child/adult, husband/wife.

According to the definition of relational realism, this individual-to-individual relationship is a vital and yet secondary part of reality. These relationships have a level of truth inherent in them, and yet they can only be fully comprehended in light of the primary Creator/creature relationship.

This simple concept explains how it is that human understanding can lead to helpful suggestions for many human relational dyads, and yet those suggestions never seem to quite present the whole picture. A study of marriage, for instance, can uncover real truth that helps explain relationships within matrimony. However, those insights are faulty if they do not build upon the fundamental Creator/creature relationship.

Horizontal relationships go beyond one-on-one relationships. There are also group interactions. Thus Paul could tell Timothy to treat older men one way, and younger men another way (1 Tim 5:1). Timothy was likewise instructed to treat older women one way, and younger women another way (1 Tim 5:2). Peter tells believers to behave in a certain way towards government and social authorities (1 Peter 2).

Another significant issue concerning horizontal relationships is that God has revealed His evaluation of what makes for good and healthy and right relationships, and what does not. How people treat one another is, after all, a matter of great importance to God. So much so that the judgment of the flood was due to grossly improper horizontal relationships (the earth was corrupt and filled with violence according to Genesis 6:11–13). In positive terms, 1 John says that our actions toward other people give evidence of our relationship with God (1 John 3:14, for instance).

Once again, an illustration can help us to better see the kinds of relationships that exist in the horizontal realm. Returning to Acts 16, there are human/human relationships that we did not mention previously (see Figure 2). Consider the line that connects the gospel messenger to the audience (#4). That point on the figure, in fact, represents horizontal relationship. In Acts 16, we could look at the relationship between Paul and Lydia, or between

Paul and Timothy, or Paul and the Philippian jailer and family. Those all speak to horizontal relationships.

In light of Acts 16, and especially verse 14, it is important again to realize that a relationship with God does not exclude horizontal relationships. When Lydia heard the message given through her horizontal relationship with Paul, it made possible the vertical relationship in which, we read, "the Lord opened Lydia's heart to the things spoken by Paul." The horizontal relationships and the vertical are tied together.

Looking one last time at Acts 16 in light of Figure 2, there is a circle around the "messenger" and another circle that surrounds the "audience." Those circles represent distinct cultures, and human cultures are clearly an important element in understanding horizontal relationships.

The various fields of anthropology can list a very wide variety of distinct patterns of human relationships. Even a beginning catalog of the range of cultural variations that exist within horizontal relationships is beyond the scope of this book; but a few illustrations are here offered. The idea is to show the connection between human culture and relational realism.

Individualism/collectivism Across human cultures, one of the main cultural dynamics is between cultures that are individualistic and those that are collective. Those two words represent extremes on a continuum. In the collective extremes, people gain their identity, their protection, and their provision from the group to which they belong. Their horizontal relationships are dominated by fulfilling group values, beliefs, and prescribed activities. "I am because we are" might be the model thought form in a collective society. Horizontal relationships within collective cultures are flavored by the collective values, and those values differ from those found in individualistic cultures.

Individualistic societies prefer a model by which the individual decisions of thousands and millions of people will jointly create the best conditions for all, and the best possibility of good for each. And so the individualist child is taught at an early age to make his/her own decisions, and to value the rights, privileges, and contributions of individuals. Horizontal relationships in such cultures are shaped by the values of individualism.

Leadership models form another important cultural dimension. Some cultures prefer their leaders to be accessible and transparent. These cultures do not give special status to their leaders, but rather only cede temporary and limited rights and privileges so that the leader can accomplish certain goals. These are referred to as low power-distance cultures. Again, it is easy to see how that power distance cultural dynamic is a variable within horizontal relationships.

By the same token the high power-distance alternative, where leaders are assumed to have prerogatives that are not available to the common person, is another viable form for a horizontal relationship. Horizontal relationships exist between people and groups. Horizontal relationships exist between leaders and followers. Yet the actual cultural preferences that those relationships take can in fact vary widely.

Cultural dynamics that play into horizontal relationships extend to whether people are honored due to their achievements or their ascribed status. Cultures differ in which emotions are appropriately expressed in given relational situations, and which ones are repressed. Cultures vary in their tolerance of uncertainties, in their willingness to accept innovations, and in their values of just what represents "progress." In short, horizontal relationships across cultures are multiplied in their complexities, with wide variations in the range of expressions of any given cultural trait. Our point here is that the traits, no matter how expressed, are relational.

This will become an important element in later chapters when we begin to consider the connection between missions, mission training, and relationality In order to effectively minister within a given culture, one needs both an appropriate vertical and an appropriate horizontal approach to relationships. In other words, gospel workers need to rely on the power of the Triune source of their message while simultaneously growing in their ability to understand, adapt, and adjust to the cultural preferences of their host culture.

And yet, even as we appreciate the value and significance of cultural variables within horizontal relationships, we also now understand why it is that at times this is of seemingly little importance. Since the primary relationship is vertical, God can and does use faulty human efforts to make his message clear within a new culture. Should humans strive to be as clear as possible in representing God before other cultures? Yes, we should. Does everything depend on our cultural competence? No, God can and does bring his vertical relationship into sharp focus even where the human agents were woefully unsuccessful at bridging cultural gaps.

In summary, "Relational realism is to be defined as the systematic understanding that reality is primarily based on the vertical relationship between God and the created order and secondarily horizontal relationship within the created order." The systematic understanding of revealed relational patterns within the Trinity gives us insight into how the Father, Son, and Spirit interact; it also gives us insight into expectations for human relationships.

The main relational issues uncovered by our theological consideration of the Trinity are summarized in Table 3:

Table 3: Theological Principles for Understanding Relationality

Theological Principle	Description	Application	Comment
Perichoresis	Mutual indwelling of members of the Trinity	A close relationship among the Trinity is model for all humans.	Humans do not experience Perichoresis but we experience the indwelling of the Spirit
Polyphony	Focus on one Member of Trinity does not diminish Others	A mutually supportive relationship among the Trinity is model for all humans.	This trait is especially hard for competitive human cultures to grasp.

Theological Principle	Description	Application	Comment
Taxis	Ordered nature of relationships within Trinity 1. equality of position/ distinction of roles 2. authority and submission is part of Divine Nature	Within the Trinity the unity of the Godhead is not diminished by diversity of roles and authority.	Relationship can be healthy even with distinction of roles and different levels of authority.
Ontology	The Creator/creature distinction is the watershed for understanding reality	There is no "closed system" into which God cannot enter.	Humanism and Materialism have relegated God to non-existence or at least irrelevance. That is flawed thinking.
Epistemology	God reveals what He wishes of Himself.	God's self-revelation is accurate yet we have no reason to think it is exhaustive.	Faith and trust in what God reveals is essential for human relationships. We must believe what he has said.
Soteriology	Salvation is a relational issue.	God has graciously provided The Way to re-establish relationship between God and man.	Though shame, guilt, fear, or clean/unclean paradigms have levels of truth, in all cases the restoration of healthy relationship is thanks to God's grace.

Theological Principle	Description	Application	Comment
Sanctification	Humans grow and develop.	One who is in relationship with the Lord is meant to grow in the grace and knowledge of the Lord.	Understanding this principle gives patience and hope in both human/human and divine/human relationship.
Hamartiology	Mankind's ability to form relationships is marred by sin.	Both human/human and human/Divine relationships are hindered by human sinfulness.	Understanding this principle gives appreciation for God's grace and for our human need to forgive one another.
Worship	God directs how humanity may enter into relationship with Him.	Human relationship with God permits a wide variety of human expressions but always under the direction and authority of God.	There is One Way to the Father.
Human relationships	God gives direction as to how humans should interact.	For both our good and his glory, how people treat each other is important in relational theology.	God knows what is healthy for the humankind he created. He also knows what human relationships will glorify Him.

Theological Principle	Description	Application	Comment
Human relationships across cultures	Since the Tower of Babel, language and custom have separated peoples and formed cultures. Understanding cultural traits is part of relational paradigm as people interact both as individuals and as members of different cultures.	Understanding cultural dynamics has an important place in relational realism, yet always in light of the overarching God/creation relationship.	People do not only interact as individuals; relationships also include understanding of cultural variables.

A tool that arises from this chapter is what we call, "The Seven Missionary Relationships." By looking at the different sorts of horizontal and vertical relationships, these seven relationships give us both a tool for analysis and a tool for ministry. We will pick up on the use of this tool for analysis in the next chapter. The seven relationships are:

1. Relationships within the Trinity
2. Relationship between Triune God and the messenger
3. Relationship between Triune God and the audience
4. Relationship between the messenger and audience
5. Relationship between the messenger and his/her culture
6. Relationship between the audience and his/her culture

7. Relationship between demons/Satan and the human parts of this paradigm (messenger and audience)

Summary

The Paradigm of Relational Realism is the conceptual foundation that we understand to be at the root of reality. This chapter has introduced the theological basis for the Paradigm of Relational Realism, describing relationships within the Triune God while also describing the vertical relationships (between God and creation), and horizontal relationships (between created beings). The identification of seven key missionary relationships is one practical outcome of this concept. Those seven key missionary relationships will be developed further in later parts of this book.

Chapter Three
Scriptural Foundations

Introduction

The previous chapter looked at the question of theological foundations of a "paradigm of relational realism." Chapter Three will look at the concept of relational realism through the lens of Scripture. In this chapter we will look at how the Bible presents issues of relationship, mission, and the preparation of new generations of gospel workers.

Scriptural Examples of Relationship and Mission

The Bible deals with propositions, and it deals with relationships. Western theological reflection has tended to focus on the propositional to the exclusion of the relational. In fact, we would likely see relational themes in Scripture as the realm of mystics more than theologians or missiologists.

The point we wish to make in this chapter is that God goes about his work in relational as well as propositional ways. Truth, after all, is not an abstraction but rather a Person ("I am the way, and the truth, and the life," said Jesus in John 14:6). Seeing

Scripture through the lens of relationship will help us better understand the nature of mission.

We have chosen three simple illustrations to point to the power of seeing Scriptures through a relational paradigm. There are many, many other biblical passages that could have been considered; but we trust that these examples of God at work via relational patterns will deepen our understanding of mission in a relational paradigm.

In each of the following examples, after a brief introduction we will look at the seven key missionary relationships as they appear in that particular book. It is worth noting at the outset that not all books will contain explicit illustrations of all seven relationships.

Jonah

The Book of Jonah is not only a great missionary study, but also a great study from the perspective of the relational realism paradigm.

Relationship One – Relationships within the Trinity

Jonah does not give specific insight into the relationships between the Members of the Trinity.

Relationship Two – Relationships between God and the Messenger

Jonah gives a beautiful illustration of the fact that relationships are not neat and tidy. They are complicated and painful at times.

God sent Jonah (1:1) with very clear directions. The relationship took what appears to be a negative turn when the prophet rejected those directions and fled. In the face of that rebellion, God pursued Jonah by way of a storm, a crew of spiritually sensitive sailors, and a fish. God's reaction to Jonah's rebellion was frightening to sailors and Jonah alike. God's reaction to Jonah's rebellion was also deeply relational, bringing Jonah to a point of prayer and obedience. In fact, the capstone statement found in Jonah 2:8 demonstrates God's relational perspective: "Those who worship worthless idols forfeit the mercy that could be theirs." Mercy, after all, is experienced in relationship.

We live in a time when missionary work often speaks of the good that comes to the missionary as he/she/they go about their work. Many short-term programs emphasize the good that one will receive from being involved in ministry to the ends of the earth.

Jonah is a good example of the reality that God in fact DOES do great things in the life of those He sends into mission. Jonah grew to better understand God. The fact that people are growing, changing beings should prepare us for the reality that intercultural ministry will benefit the one being sent. Saying that does not diminish the fact that the primary purpose is not the growth of the messenger; but rather it is taking a message to the audience. A self-serving purpose is not how we see God's purposes fulfilled throughout Scripture. Yet, in His grace, the one who serves God will often benefit and grow as a result.

Jonah is also a good example of the reality that God's relational objectives in the lives of human beings are often met via tears and fears. As the story of Jonah unfolds, Nineveh hears the news of judgment and repents. God accepts Nineveh's turn from their evil and spares the city. Jonah, in turn, is angered and twice says that he would have preferred death to seeing God's mercy over the people of Nineveh. God ends the book by pointing out that his relationship with the children and animals of Nineveh led him to show mercy; with the clear implication that he would like to see a compassionate spirit growing in Jonah.

From this brief look at the relational patterns between God and the Messenger, we can draw some conclusions:

1. God directs His people.
2. God works IN the messenger even while he is working through the messenger.
3. God uses what appear to be difficult and painful moments to deepen relationships. Storms, fears, tears all can act to bring people into closer walk with God.
4. God's character shows up in his relationships: he shows himself to be merciful throughout the book of Jonah, for instance.

Relationship Three – God and the Audience

At the outset of the book, there is a relationship between the Ninevites and God. It is not a healthy relationship, and it does not meet the test of appropriate response by the created to the Creator. Still, there is a relationship simply by virtue of the fact that God is almighty and omnipresent. If his creatures are faithless, he himself is still always faithful.

In light of an unhealthy relationship, God calls Nineveh to repentance through the announcement of judgment. Far from being vindictive or punishing, God used the announcement of judgment as a way to invite appropriate relational patterns.

From a relational perspective, it is also worth noting that God's mercy in saving Jonah's life by sending the fish was not only relational with Jonah, it was also relational with Nineveh. The mercy that God gave to Jonah was extended, in that one same act, to Nineveh. When God saved Jonah's life, he saved the messenger he had sent to Nineveh. The interesting thing is that Jonah did not understand the extent of God's mercy. Jonah seems to have seen himself as the object of mercy (2:2), not realizing that the Ninevites also received through that gracious gift.

Relationship Number Four – The Messenger and the Audience

Jonah's relationship with the Ninevites was not personal; from all appearances he reacted to the people of Nineveh in the way one would expect from any Jewish person of that time period.

For that reason, we will look at this question in more detail under the heading of Relationship Number Five.

Relationship Five – The Messenger and his/her culture

Jonah identified himself as Hebrew (1:9) when he was talking with the sailors onboard the ship. That particular interaction, held during the storm at sea, is of interest to seeing relationships through the lens of the individual as well as the culture.

The multicultural ship's crew used all of their wisdom and experience to stay afloat during the storm. They called on their various gods to no avail. They sought information about their passenger, and expected him to call on his god for protection (1:6-8). As Jonah explained the facts of his nation and the God that he served, the sailors responded. By the end of the scene, the sailors "feared the Lord greatly." An appropriate, healthy relationship began to grow between the sailors and Jehovah as the God of Israel was made known to the sailors.

There is another cultural perspective in this Book: the relationship between Jonah's home culture and the culture of Nineveh. God called Jonah, a Hebrew, to take a message of judgment and an offer of repentance to what we would today call a terrorist state. When Jesus called on His people to love their enemy, it is hard to imagine a starker example of what He was calling us to do. Jonah was being called to carry news of repentance to people that he literally preferred to see dead. The rogue nation of Nineveh threatened Israel along with the other civilizations of that day. Jonah would have been seen as a national disgrace, a traitor to his people, for calling their enemy into the blessing of God.

And so when Jonah disregarded God's directions, it was rebellious in a personal way, yet he is also shaped by the culture from which he came. His response to God's call was shaped by his Hebrew background and by the culture of Nineveh. God intervened in all of that to call the nation of Nineveh to repent; that is to say, to healthy, appropriate relationship. Israel would have been shocked, thinking a relationship with God was something that they themselves should certainly enjoy, but that evil nations like Nineveh should have no access.

When we think of God and relationship, He is no respecter of persons.

Relationship Six – The Audience and his/her culture

In one sense, this story calls us to avoid having too narrow a focus on only one audience. Jonah thought that he had been sent to the Ninevites, but in spite of the rebellion of the messenger, it turns out that there was an audience called "sailors" which also grew in relationship with the Triune God. The culture of shipping and the multicultural nature of the ship's crew are a glorious context for seeing God at work in a multicultural scene.

The culture that is most clearly in view in this book would be the Ninevites. In our modern vocabulary, it was a terrorist culture. The city practiced cruelty that was infamous in its day.

"Nineveh was the capital of one of the cruelest, vilest, most powerful, and most idolatrous empires in the world."[37]

And yet, God called that nation into relationship. He did not overlook the horror of their actions, but He sought them through Jonah, calling them to repent of their national as well as personal evil. The call to repentance was in fact a call to healthy, appropriate, and good relationship.

Relationship Seven – The realm of Evil Spirits

Jonah made no explicit mention of the satanic or demonic. We do see idolatry and false gods, and we see the fruit of anger which in New Testament terms we recognize as potentially a tool of evil (Eph 4:26–27).

It is immensely interesting that Jonah is not called to directly confront the evil spirits. God does not even deal directly with the possible spiritual roots of the anger that beset Jonah (see verses 4:1, 4, 9). God's strategy for dealing with evil spirits in the book of Jonah seems to be to work toward healthy, appropriate relationships with all of the different people involved. As people move toward healthy relationships with God and with one another, the influence of evil is reduced.

In a previous career, I (Mark) worked in the area of agricultural research with special interest in some particular soil-borne diseases. One of the stock phrases that we used in that

---

[37] Walvoord, John F and Zuck, Roy B (eds.) *The Bible Knowledge Commentary, Old Testament*. (USA: Victor Books, 1988), 1494.

research was that the best way to protect the health of a plant is to have a healthy plant. It sounds like a truism, but it is really different. The idea is that the best way to avoid effects of negative influence is to maintain overall good, positive health. We see that as well in human health where an otherwise healthy person will have better ability to avoid disease.

That idea enters the relational study of Jonah. Rather than directly combat evil beings, Jonah is called to a healthier relationship with God; the sailors are not chided for idolatry or worshipping the wrong god and they are shown the path to a relationship with the True God. Nineveh is called to repent as a call to relationship; moving toward God will of necessity move them away from the Evil One.

Conclusion

The book of Jonah can rightfully be seen from many perspectives. In this current study we have seen it as a rich environment for seeing how a paradigm of relational realism can help us to see God at work in even deeper ways. We will turn our attention to a second example – the New Testament relationship between Paul, God, evil beings, and the Thessalonians.

Paul and Thessalonians

The books of 1 and 2 Thessalonians and Acts chapter 17 give a strong illustration of how a relational paradigm can help us to understand intercultural ministry. As in previous examples, this is not presented as an exhaustive study. In fact, only selected portions of 1 Thessalonians will be mentioned. The purpose of this study is simply to illustrate the power of seeing Scripture through a relational grid.

Relationship One – Between the members of the Trinity

Within the first five verses of I Thessalonians, Paul points to the Father, the Son, and the Spirit and the role of each in the lives of the Thessalonians. He goes on in verse 1:6 to show that the Spirit brings joy even in affliction, and that the message that Paul presented was in fact from the Lord.

Relationship Two – Triune God at work in the Gospel workers

The activity of the living God is seen in encouraging Paul and his team (1 Thess 2:2). Later in 3:11 Paul expressed confidence that God would permit a visit by Paul to the Thessalonians.

Relationship Three – The Triune God in relationship with the Thessalonians

Paul shows in many ways that the relationship between God and the Thessalonians was a two-way relationship, in which each party was involved with the other. For example, God chose the Thessalonians (I Thess 1:4). They received His message (2:13). One is active in choosing, the other in accepting. Both parties are relationally active.

One of the most beautiful relational phrases in these books is found in 4:1. Paul is talking about ethics, but his basis for reasoning is not simply to present a code of proper behavior. He calls the Thessalonians to live righteously "in order to please God." That relational motivation stands in stark contrast to the forensic or shame-based motivations of human ethics. God calls us to live a life that is pleasing to him; doing that will affect our behavior and lead to a "righteousness that surpasses the scribes and Pharisees" (Matt 5:20).

Relationship Four – The relationship between Paul and the Audience

Paul and the Thessalonians had a rich, warm relationship: Paul saw himself as one who lived among the Thessalonians as a child (innocent, unassuming 2:7), as a mother (caring 2:7), and as a father (diligent to exhort and encourage 2:11). He uses "brothers and sisters" as descriptions of his relationship with the Thessalonians (1:4). He worked for his own financial needs so as not to be a burden (1:3).

The Thessalonians, in the reciprocal side of the relationship, became imitators of Paul and of the Lord, not allowing suffering to discourage them from the Gospel (1:6).

Relationship Five – The Messenger in Culture

This book does not explicitly deal with Paul and his team in relationship to the culture from which they came.

Relationship Six – The Audience in Culture

The reaction of the Thessalonians to the message led them to receive the Word and then to boldly proclaim it within their spheres. First Thessalonians 1:8-9 is the relational answer to church growth from a mechanical point of view: "in every place reports of your faith in God have spread." The statement continues, "for people everywhere report how you welcomed us and how you turned to God from idols to serve the living and true God and to wait for his Son from heaven." Believers responded to a personal, relational invitation to know the living God, and then they made that relationship known throughout their society.

There is another interesting relational comment that has to do with the Thessalonians and their compatriots. In 4:13, Paul introduced an eschatological section of the Book with the instructions that Christian grieving should not be as those who have no hope. The reason, unfolded in the following verses, is that our relationship with Christians who have died is not over. The relationship will be restored once again after the return of the Lord. Even traditional theological divisions like eschatology can be seen through a relational lens.[38]

Relationship Seven – Evil beings and negative relationships

In spite of the healthy and caring relationships that this book demonstrated, there is also explicit mention of satanic involvement. Satan and his demons will seek to disrupt the relationships between God and people. In the case of 1 Thessalonians, he did that by thwarting Paul's plans for a visit to

---

[38] For a more complete theological treatment of the relationship between God and man, see Lister, J. Ryan. *The Presence of God: Its Place in the Storyline of Scripture and the Story of Our Lives*. Wheaton, IL: Crossway, 2015.

Thessalonica (2:18). Even something as apparently mundane as failed travel plans can be part of demonic opposition to the deepening of Christian relationships.

We have seen the relational paradigm and God's mission outreach in an Old Testament prophet and a New Testament epistle. We offer one further example of relational paradigm in mission outreach, this time from the narratives of the Acts of the Apostles.

Phillip and the Ethiopian Eunuch

Acts Chapter Eight gives us the setting for the final illustration of insight into intercultural ministry through the paradigm of relational realism.

Relationship One – between the members of the Trinity

This short passage does not give insight into the relationship of the members of the Trinity; but there is a picture of how God used angelic beings to do his will. Acts 8:26 tells us that the instruction to go to the Gaza road came through an angel. In this case, a personalized message was sent by personal courier.

Relationship Two – God and the Messenger

The gospel worker in this chapter, Philip, received a message from God by way of the angel. The relationship between Philip and the Lord is seen in obedience to the instructions to go to the Gaza road (8:27). After the Ethiopian official was baptized, the direct interaction between God and Philip continued and we see him taken up and delivered to Azotus, from where he later ministered to Caesarea. The point is that God was active in Philip's life, directing him once by way of angels and in other cases by physically moving him to other communities.

Relationship Three – God and the Audience

The Ethiopian eunuch had a relationship with the Lord even before he was able to understand the Gospel message. The eunuch had been in Jerusalem to worship, and was reading Isaiah. He did not understand everything ("how in the world can I know [what this means]?" is the NET Bible's colorful translation of his response to Philip's question in 8:31[39]). Still, there was a beginning relationship between God and the Ethiopian that grew deeper through the interaction with Philip.

The model of ministry that we see in Philip is a helpful corrective to the program-orientation that so easily invades Western Christian ministry. Philip was taken from a growing and successful ministry in Samaria, and was led to an audience of one. His role with that one man was to explain more deeply; to create an environment favorable to deepening the relationship between the Ethiopian and the Lord God. As soon as the Ethiopian had heard and responded – as soon as the basis for a healthy and appropriate relationship with the Lord was established, Philip was taken away.

---

[39] "NET Bible Online." Accessed October 22, 2016.https://net.bible.org/#!bible/Acts+8.

Christian ministry is not about the building of programs. It is about guiding people into a deeper and healthier, appropriate relationship with God. That can happen through organizational structures; but too often the organizational approach leads to a mechanistic confidence in methods.[40] Philip's one-on-one relational work led to a deepening relationship between God and the Ethiopian, a good model for ministry in all cultures.

Relationship Four – Philip and the Ethiopian

There are several relational themes visible between Philip and the Eunuch. The first point is that this was not a prolonged relationship.

The very word "relationship" brings with it varying connotations depending on the experiences and background of the person who hears the word. For many westerners, "relationship" is a loose synonym for "friendship" or perhaps, in an internet context, for "romantically involved." The more hierarchical cultures of the world, though, will understand a wide range of possibilities for the word. Included among those varying meanings is the idea that one can have a warm, true human interaction that does not continue for prolonged time. "Relational" does not necessarily imply a long-term relationship.

---

[40] Wan, Enoch, et al. Diaspora Missiology: Theory, Methodology, and Practice. Portland, Or.: CreateSpace Independent Publishing Platform, 2012, 148 – 149.

Philip and the Ethiopian were not in a long-lasting human relationship, yet nevertheless it was a significant and legitimate relational interaction.

The short interactions that humans have with one another can be seen as real relationships, or they can be seen as simply mechanistic interactions where business is transacted. One of the relational lessons of Acts 8 is that the relationship between the human actors does not have to be long-lived to be true and valid.

This is especially true because it is not the human/human relationship that is priority. The priority relationship always involves God himself. Philip was in relationship with God. That is a long-lasting relationship. God directed Philip to give instruction to the Ethiopian. Though the relationship between the two men was short-lived, it led to an eternal relationship between the Ethiopian and God. That Philip was only involved for a matter of minutes or hours misses the real story; the relationship that was built between the Lord and the Ethiopian was very long lasting, and crossed the essential Creator/creature division.

Relationship Five – Philip and his culture

There is not much about this relationship in the passage, but it is worth noting that Philip was led away from a growing, successful ministry in order to meet a single man in an isolated stretch of highway.

Relationship Six – The Ethiopian and his culture

The important role of the Ethiopian Eunuch is a key part in this chapter. The man who wanted to understand Isaiah was also a man of influence within the government and society of his people: a treasury official, he was without doubt in contact with the queen and with key leaders both within and outside of Ethiopia.

Though we can only speculate at this point, it seems clear that God directed Philip to this man as a way to bring him into a deeper and more appropriate relationship with the Lord, and also to bring that relationship into the networks of relationship that he already enjoyed. A deeper relationship between the Ethiopian and God led to a broader relationship as many Ethiopians also entered relationship with the Lord.

Relationship Seven – Evil beings

Acts Chapter 8 does not contain any explicit mention of interaction involving either Satan or demons.

Conclusion

We have looked at three Bible passages with an eye to see how a prophet from the Old Testament, an epistle in the New Testament and a narrative from the Book of Acts each display relationships. The seven relationships that were identified in Chapter Two have been useful in shedding further light into the relational realities of human life. The core focus of this study is that the goal of human ministry is to provide a relationship through which people can grow in their walk with the Lord. It is the deepening of relationships between people and God that is of primary interest to the Christian worker. Growing a ministry organization is only useful to the extent that real people are drawn into healthier, more appropriate relationship with the Lord. Rules, propositions, and guidelines are valuable to the extent that they lead to healthier, more biblically appropriate relationships between people and God. It is of little importance whether a human/human relationship is long-term or short term on this planet. The important issue is whether the people involved all grew deeper in relationship with the Lord.

We have now tried to better understand what is meant by "paradigm of relational realism" and we have looked at Scripture to see if indeed mission outreach as seen in the Bible can be seen through that lens of relationship. At this point, we turn our attention to Scriptural insight that specifically touches the issue of training for intercultural ministry.

Scriptural Models of Mission Training

Missionary training has long been seen as an academic exercise; an intellectual process that in its worst case taught intellectual facts and figures, and even in its best case added skills and attitudes to those facts and figures. I have laughingly said that one can learn missionary work in a classroom as successfully as one can learn to sky dive in a classroom. At some point the environment needs to change so that the learner is doing the real thing in the real context.

The kind of change in mission training that we suggest is to see it through the eyes of relationship in the first place, and only in secondary way to see it as knowledge, skills, and attitudes. At this point, it is important to ask whether the Bible itself supports that kind of relationship-oriented approach to mission training.

Paul as Missionary Trainer

Paul was not only a missionary, he also deliberately went about training others to be missionaries. An examination of Paul's ministry in the Acts of the Apostles and in the Pastoral Epistles gives insight into how he went about the task of training missionaries. That Paul was intent on the development of missionaries alongside his direct evangelistic and discipleship ministries can be seen in numerous passages. Three prominent examples are found in Acts 16:1-3, Acts 20:4, and 2 Timothy 2:2.

In Acts 16:1–3, Luke wrote about the beginning of Paul's second missionary journey. Paul left Antioch in approximately A.D. 50[41] in order to visit churches established during his first tour. He also entered new territories (Acts 15:35-41). Entering the region of Derbe and Lystra, he came in contact with a young man named Timothy (Acts 16:1). Paul desired that Timothy accompany him on the missionary tour (Acts 16:2).

---

[41] Many sources agree on this dating, but one key proponent is Homer A. Kent, Jr., *Jerusalem to Rome, Studies in Acts* Winona Lake IN: BMH Books, 1972, 106.

The story of Paul and Timothy will be considered in more detail in later sections of this study; the essential element at this point is that Paul deliberately invited certain people (in this case, Timothy) to join his missionary outreach. Paul was interested in inviting new people to accompany him as a way of preparing new missionaries. Timothy is one example of someone thus chosen.

What Luke wrote in Acts 20:4 builds further on the idea that part of Paul's ministry was to recruit and train missionaries. In this verse, Paul is said to be have been accompanied by "Sopater son of Pyrrhus from Berea, Aristarchus and Secundus from Thessalonica, Gaius from Derbe, Timothy and also Tychicus and Trophimus from the province of Asia." The next verse includes the phrase "These men went on ahead and waited for us. . ." (Acts 20:5). The reference to "us" is generally understood to point to the presence of Luke as a member of the missionary band.

Acts 20 shows that Paul traveled with a fairly large and well-defined group of missionary colleagues. It is instructive to see where these companions came from. The places named (Berea, Thessalonica, Derbe, and Asia) were all places where Paul had established congregations in his earlier travels. One gets the impression that Paul entered a town with the explanation of the Gospel message and stayed for varying amounts of time to teach the new Christians. When he left, he seems to have had the habit of inviting one or more young men to join him in his travels; in other words, Paul recruited and trained younger colleagues for cross-cultural mission. The training that Paul offered was through the highly relational form of inviting them to learn ministry by doing ministry together with Paul.

One passage that clearly draws attention to Paul's ministry of missionary training is 2 Timothy 2:2. As Paul wrote to his protégé Timothy, he pointed Timothy not only to a continuation of active ministry; but he also reinforced the importance of training still others to be messengers of the Gospel. Thus Paul instructed Timothy to "entrust to reliable people who will also be qualified to teach others." The picture that Paul painted is that Timothy not only was to have trained other people in the essentials of the faith; but he was also to have trained some of them to be able to teach still others. Paul was talking of a chain of missionary and pastoral training. Paul trained Timothy who was to train others in areas of Gospel advance and disciple-making, so that those Timothy trained could continue the same pattern and teach others as well. The point here is that not only did Paul train missionaries; but he trained missionaries (like Timothy) who were able to train other missionaries.

Paul's Writings as Missionary Training Literature

Paul wrote three books directly addressed to his young missionary colleagues. Those three books are 1 Timothy, 2 Timothy, and Titus. Any brief survey of commentaries on these three books will find them collectively referred to as the Pastoral Epistles. That nomenclature began in A.D. 1703 and was reinforced by Paul Anton in A.D. 1726.[42] As D. Edmond Hiebert pointed out, while that is a convenient and, in a popular sense, appropriate classification, yet at the same time it is not wholly correct either.[43] One of the weaknesses that Hiebert pointed out about calling these epistles "pastoral" includes the fact that in none of the books does Paul use the terms pastor, shepherd, flock, or sheep. Hiebert went on to write,

> Timothy was not the pastor of the church at Ephesus
> in the modern sense of that term; nor was Titus the
> bishop of the Cretan churches, as is sometimes
> thought. . . [Titus'] work may perhaps be likened to
> that of a modern superintendent of missions
> appointed over a group of native churches. . .[44]

That Timothy was not the "pastor" in today's technical sense of the word can also be seen by the fact that the church in Ephesus (where Timothy served when Paul wrote 1 Timothy to him – see 1 Tim. 1:3) had elders established nearly a decade before Timothy's arrival.[45] Based on Kent's chronology, the church in Ephesus had elders present sometime between the years of A.D. 53 – 55 (Acts 20:17), yet Timothy was sent to pursue his particular ministry in the year A.D. 62 – 63 (I Tim 1:3).[46]

---

[42] Hiebert, D. Edmond. *An Introduction to the New Testament, Vol. Two: The Pauline Epistles*. Revised edition. Chicago: Moody Press, 1977, 307.

[43] Ibid, 307.

[44] Hiebert, D. Edmond. *Titus and Philemon*. First Edition. Chicago, IL: Moody Press, 1957, 7.

[45] Hiebert, D. Edmond. *First Timothy*. Chicago: Moody Press, 1957, 9.

[46] Kent, Homer Austin. *Jerusalem to Rome: Studies in the Book of Acts*. Grand Rapids, Baker Book House: 1972, 106.

While the name Pastoral Epistles correctly draws attention to the fact that these three books examine issues important to the local church, at the same time it is misleading to consider them to be manuals for pastoral ministry. D. Edmond Hiebert suggested a broader term as more appropriate, preferring to call these the "Ecclesiological letters." He wrote that these three books "form a unit in that all of them give prominent consideration to the matters of church order and discipline. Hence they are properly described as the Ecclesiological group."[47]

In this "Ecclesiological" group there is strong evidence that Paul's intention was not only to give instruction on the proper working of the church, but also to instruct his younger missionary protégés in the nature of missionary work. Some have even suggested that rather than "pastoral epistles" or "ecclesiological epistles," these three books should be called the "missionary epistles."[48] The idea behind this suggestion is that these books were attempts by a veteran missionary at training younger missionaries. Whether or not the name "missionary epistles" is adopted is not as important as the realization that Paul wrote these letters with the intention of giving guidance and instruction to new intercultural missionaries.[49]

---

[47] Hiebert, D. Edmond, *Introduction to the New Testament*, 307.
[48] D. James O'Neill has used this phrase in numerous contexts.
[49] Our deep appreciation to Dr. D. James O'Neill and Dr. John Sherwood for the Bible study sessions in which these ideas were developed. It was a privilege to think together with Jim and John about how the writings of Paul might apply to missionary training in our day.

That Paul's intention in writing these three books was directly involved with instructing the addressees in their missionary endeavors can be illustrated in three passages, one from each of the three books. In 1 Timothy, Paul gave Timothy direct instruction that supports the idea that this is a missionary letter by nature. Paul instructed Timothy to "stay there in Ephesus so that you may command certain people not to teach false doctrines any longer or to devote themselves to myths and endless genealogies." (1 Tim 1:3, 4). Timothy's assignment was not permanent, but rather he was to minister alongside the established leaders of the church (see Acts 20:17 where elders were already present) in order to bring needed correction on specific issues. This ministry assignment appears to be missionary in nature as opposed to strictly pastoral.

The book of Titus contains a similar insight into Titus' role as an itinerant, temporary worker in the churches of Crete. Paul's direct instruction to Titus was to "put in order what was left unfinished and appoint elders in every town, as I directed you." (Titus 1:5). Again, the implication is that Titus was not assigned to form part of the permanent pastoral leadership of any given church but rather was charged with the goal of completing what had not been finished by previous evangelistic and teaching ministries, and establishing leadership in the churches of Crete.

Finally, missionary training implications arise from 2 Timothy, again related to the key instructions of 2 Timothy 2:2. The apostle, as he sought to finish his own life and ministry well (2 Tim 4:7), wanted to see in Timothy not only quality ministry (2

Tim 4:1-5), but also the habit of continuing to train yet another generation of cross-cultural and local ministers of the Gospel.

This review of Paul's ministry and the letters he wrote to Timothy and Titus leads to two conclusions: that Paul considered part of his ministry to be the training of another generation of cross-cultural gospel messengers; and that Paul wrote 1 Timothy, 2 Timothy, and Titus with the intention of instructing younger missionary workers for effective cross-cultural ministries. In essence, we can conclude that the Pastoral Epistles are to a large degree letters of instruction written to developing missionaries.

What did Paul teach to new missionaries?

An inductive study of 1 Timothy, 2 Timothy, and Titus revealed seven themes that Paul included in his training of missionaries. The list will be presented briefly in this section[50] with the goal of showing relational patterns inherent in Paul's interaction with his ministry protégés.

1. *Theme Number 1: The Missionary's Focus on Scriptural Truth*
   - Teaching on Sound Doctrine (1 Tim 4:6–16)
   - The Gospel Itself (1 Tim 1:12–17; 2 Tim 1:8–10; Titus 3:5)

---

[50] For more extended treatment of these topics, see Hedinger, Mark. "Towards A Paradigm of Integrated Missionary Training." Global Missiology, 2006. http://globalmissiology.org/images/stories/documents/hedinger_missionary_training_2006.pdf., 82 – 89. accessed 21, October 2016.

- Teachings on False Doctrine (Titus 1:10–16)
2. *Theme Number Two: The Missionary as a Person*
   - The Activities of a Missionary (1 Tim 1:3; 2 Tim 2:2; Titus 1:5)
   - The Attitudes of a Missionary (1 Tim 4:11–12; 2 Tim 2:15; 3:10–11)
3. Theme Number Three: The Missionary as Teacher
   - Content that the Missionary Should Teach (1 Tim 2:8; 6:17–18; Titus 3:1)
   - Content to Avoid Teaching (1 Tim 6:20; 2 Tim 2:23; Titus 3:9)
   - Relationship Patterns of the Missionary as a Teacher
     — In Relationship to All People (1 Tim 2:24)
     — In Relationship to Certain People (1 Tim 2:25; 5:1–2; Titus 1:12–13)
   - Who Should Teach (1 Tim 5:17; 2 Tim 2:2)
   - False Teachers (1 Tim 6:3–10; 2 Tim 2:16–18)
4. Theme Number Four: The Missionary as Developer of Church Leadership
   - Choosing Leaders for the Church (1 Tim 2:12; Titus 1:5)
   - Character of Leaders (1 Tim 3; Titus 1)
   - False Leaders (related to false teachers) (1 Tim 4:1–5)

5. Theme Number Five: The Missionary as Defender against Opposition
   - From False Teachers (1 Tim1:3; 6:20; 2 Tim 1:8)
   - From Persecution (2 Tim 2:9—10; 2:14; Titus 1:11)
   - From Desertion (2 Tim 4:16)
   - From Divisive Persons (Titus 3:10)
6. Theme Number Six: The Missionary and Specific Relationships
   - God/missionary (1 Tim 1:12—17)
   - God/unredeemed (1 Tim 2:4)
   - Missionary/old man (1 Tim 5:1)
   - Missionary/young man (1 Tim 5:1)
   - Missionary/old woman (1 Tim 5:2)
   - Missionary/young woman (1 Tim 5:2)
   - Man/woman (1 Tim 2:11—15)
   - Church leader/his family (1 Tim 3:4; Titus 1:6)
   - Missionary trainer/trainee (1 Tim 1:2; 2 Tim 1:5; Titus 1:4)
   - Slave/master (1 Tim 6:1)
   - Believers/government (Titus 3:1)
   - Believers/their families (1 Tim 5:8)
7. Theme Number Seven: The Missionary and Spiritual Warfare
   - Satan – the enemy (1 Tim 1:20; 5:15)
   - Profane babblings and oppositions of the knowledge (1 Tim 6:20—21)

- The snare of the devil (2 Tim 2:26)
- Godly in Christ Jesus shall suffer persecution (2 Tim 3:12)
- Evil men and impostors shall grow worse and worse
- Deceiving and being deceived (2 Tim 3:13)
- Enemy (2 Tim 4:10, cf. 1 Jn 2:15; 4:13)
- Ungodliness and worldly lusts (Titus 2:12)

Simply looking at the titles and topics of the seven themes leads us again to understand the central place that relationships have in ministry. Paul's content for mission training was relational. We saw earlier that Paul's teaching methods were relational as he invited young men from young churches to travel and learn with him. We can see the example of Paul as supportive of the idea of a relational realism approach to mission training.

In the beginning of this book, we mentioned the ease with which modern Western thought patterns can direct us towards "go and do" activism that misses the fact that our activity needs to be in a context of relationship, not active in a sterile, cold, unrelated way. Paul's instructions to a new generation of missionaries were relational as well as propositional.

Biblical Themes in Relation to Pedagogical and Theological Principles

This brief review of biblical data from what are known as the Pastoral Epistles is relevant to the development of a relational paradigm for the training of missionaries. The seven themes highlighted by inductive study are key areas that one expert in missionary training (namely, Paul) thought important to include in his approach to missionary training. While recognizing that these are not themes that carry the weight of command for our generation, wisdom would instruct us to develop the themes of the apostle Paul in our own missionary training.

One particularly important reason for deriving missionary training themes from the Scriptures themselves has to do with the essence of 2 Timothy 2:2. Paul considered the work of the missionary to include the preparation of other ministers of the Gospel. This network of missionary training which crosses cultures runs into obvious contextualization problems if the missionary trainer from one national context trains missionaries from other cultures based on the needs and expectations of the trainer, and not of the trainee. As long as missionary training content is derived from a trainer's point of view, it will almost always skew towards a reflection of the trainer, not the trainee and certainly not the culture in which the trainee might minister. However, if the content of missionary training is derived from the Bible, there is a cross-cultural validity and respect that will accompany it. The Bible is valid across all cultures (as an example, see the universal relevance implied in Matthew 28:19). Based on that intercultural validity of the Bible, a missionary training paradigm that builds upon biblical themes will have the advantage of relating to all human culture.

This leads us to another inductive study in order to answer the question: Considering 2 Timothy 2:2, what did Paul teach to Timothy in the presence of many witnesses?

What Timothy Heard from Paul in the Presence of Many Witnesses?

According to some chronologies, there were approximately 17 years between Acts 16 (where Paul met Timothy) and 2 Timothy (the last writing of Paul before his death). As Paul's earthly ministry came close to ending, he wrote to his younger protégé with the intention of encouraging Timothy to continue preparing new intercultural gospel messengers. The famous passage of 2 Timothy 2:2 leads to a rich and fruitful study: across Paul's writings, exactly what did Paul teach Timothy in the presence of many witnesses? These topics are the same kinds of things that Timothy was to teach to faithful men, and, by extension, become the topics that mission training today should also consider.

The list below gives specific items that Paul taught Timothy over their years of interaction:

1. Cultural Sensitivity (Acts 16:1)
2. Multi-ethnicity in the church as Jews and Gentiles came together (Acts 16:5)
3. Church growth (Acts 16:5)
4. The Spirit's involvement in directing missionary outreach (Acts 16:6)
5. Evangelism and baptism (Acts 16:15)
6. Recognition of and reaction to demonic activity (Acts 16:16)
7. Persecution, jail, beating and suffering for the gospel (Acts 16:22)

8. Strategy of who goes to new towns and who stays to disciples new believers (Acts 17:14, 15)

9. Preaching in difficult circumstances (Acts 18:5)

10. Missionary finances (Acts 18:5)

11. Missionary team formation (Acts 20:4)

12. Doctrines and their application to Christian life (Rom 16:21, 1 Cor 4:17, 1 Thess 1:1, 2 Thess 1:1, Philemon 1:1)

Based on that phrase in 2 Timothy 2:2 "the things you have heard from me," we see a rich curriculum of understanding relationship, life, doctrine, skill, and wisdom. Paul passed that curriculum on to Timothy and expected that Timothy would likewise commit those truths to others who would be able to teach still others. Moreover, Paul taught those relational topics through the highly relational methods of apprenticeship-like collaboration.

Paul's Missionary Training in Relational Perspective

Looking at the Bible's record of Paul's relationships leads to a number of insights that are relevant to mission training. Wan and Nguyen understood Paul to be following a variety of relational patterns as opposed to the "program" perspective that can so easily be the foundation for training. They conclude that missionary training in relational perspective will seek

"establish, verify and develop the connection between the trainee and God, and create an environment conducive to spiritual accountability and mutual development, and teach skills in this open, trusting and highly relational environment."[51]

Wan and Nguyen concluded that there are five guiding principles for mission training:[52]

1. Relationship is prominent before, during and after the training process.

2. The goal of training [is] to build up spiritual Christians who possess and display biblical values.

3. Trainers and trainees create a community of faith in which they fellowship, set examples for one another and for the world.

4. Spiritual maturity, the outcome of the vertical relationship between God and the trainer and trainees, is the primary objective of mission training. Holiness is the most important qualification of God's servants.

5. Only spiritual trainers can produce spiritual trainees.

Summary

In this chapter our focus has been on the training of missionaries, especially looking to see how a paradigm of relational realism interacts with Scriptural examples. The briefest of summary statements is that God is relational, and so is His

---

[51] Wan, Enoch, and Tin V. Nguyen. "Towards a Theology of Relational Mission Training - An Application of the Relational Paradigm Enoch Wan and Tin V. Nguyen." *Global Missiology* English 2, no. 11 (11–12, 2013). http://ojs.globalmissiology.org/index.php/english/article/view/1626.. 5 – 6. Accessed 22, October, 2016.

[52] Ibid, 11.

ministry. Those who minister are not simple technicians; we are in real human relationships that permit us to help others to grow in their walk with man and with God. Our review of the biblical story has led to an understanding that missionary training calls for content of relationship taught in a context of relationship through methods that are also relational.

Part Two: Theoretical Framework – Educational Models

We have considered the relational paradigm, and we have considered biblical and scriptural approaches to the training of missionaries within a relational context. This second major section of the book will now consider how educational theory relates to the relational paradigm model.

Chapter Four
General Pedagogical Theory and Andragogy

Introduction

In the first few pages of this book, we suggested a straightforward premise: Our calling in mission is relational. Training for mission also needs to be relational.

That premise is more complicated than it appears! It requires a multidisciplinary understanding of mission, and a multidisciplinary understanding of training. Disciplines as diverse as biblical studies, anthropology, intercultural studies, and educational theory are all involved. The first section of this book considered the concept of "relationship" from biblical, scriptural, and theological perspectives. In this second section, we now turn our attention to issues of educational theory. It is not enough for us to understand the concepts of relational ministry: somehow we must also be able to teach those concepts and skills to a new generation of "sent ones." We turn now to the topic of educational theory with special attention on how best to train people for intercultural gospel ministry.

Educational Theory

The question of how best to train missionaries is being developed in a complex environment that includes theological, biblical, and educational perspectives. In this section our focus will begin broadly, considering educational theory in general. We will move from that to a narrower perspective, understanding educational methods involved specifically in mission training.

The discipline of pedagogy is undergoing dynamic shifts. Over the last several decades not only the world of Christian academics but all realms of pedagogy have seen upheaval at foundational philosophical levels. Various philosophies, giving rise to numerous educational models, are competing for preeminence among the theoreticians and practitioners of education.

This general trend towards the development of diverse philosophies of education creates a particularly interesting situation for those who wish to educate under some type of Christian paradigm. In the specific case of education aimed at missionary preparation, how will scriptural principles interact with paradigms arising from these competing philosophies of education? The situation is highlighted by Sara Wenger Shenk in her appeal to traditional values as a foundation for the Anabaptist educator. She wrote, "As is characteristic of unstable, dynamic times, when basic assumptions about truth and how we know truth are open for reevaluation, attempts are being made to provide new conceptual frameworks to examine the questions."[53] The goal for this section is to understand the various philosophical schools of thought. Principles drawn from this review will later be incorporated into a relational approach to mission training.

General Pedagogical Theory

George Knight summarized the primary issues in contemporary educational philosophy, and his analysis will largely form the basis for this section.[54] The word "philosophy," as Knight used it, involves three realms: metaphysics (cosmology, theology, anthropology, and ontology), epistemology, and axiology (ethics and aesthetics). Those three realms of philosophy interact with contextual factors to provide direction for basic educational issues.

The first philosophy examined by Knight is that of "idealism." In this context, idealism does not carry its popular meaning of a focus on high-minded principles. Rather, the term refers to a philosophy which grows from an assumed primacy of eternal concepts (for instance, beauty, honor, truth) in the realm of education. This philosophical perspective dates back to Plato. Religious education often falls within this sphere as it, by nature, considers truth in spiritual, eternal terms.

---

[53] Shenk, Sara Wenger, and Nancy Murphy. *Anabaptist Ways of Knowing: A Conversation about Tradition-Based Critical Education*. Telford, Pa.: Cascadia Publishing House, 2005, 15.
[54] Knight, George R. *Philosophy & Education: An Introduction in Christian Perspective*. Berrien Springs, MI: Andrews University Press, 2006.

Knight's second category of educational philosophy is what he called "realism." This is another school of thought with roots in antiquity. Realism in education will react against the abstractness and otherworldliness of idealism.[55] Realists see reality as existing even if there is no mind present to form ideas about that reality. Aristotle wrote from this perspective when he distinguished between form and matter.[56] In Knight's summary of Aristotle's writing, form (which includes ideals) can exist without matter (as, for instance, a human's idea of love or beauty or the divine), but matter cannot exist without corresponding form. According to the realist, truth is known through observation, and education is all about helping people to understand reality through the use of their senses.

The final ancient model of educational theory that Knight identified is what he called "neo-scholasticism." This philosophy grew from the rediscovery of Aristotle's writings by medieval scholastics. Neo-scholasticism was made famous by Thomas Aquinas and sought to harmonize human reason and faith. In this model, human reason is the basis for understanding as much of life as possible and faith is the basis for understanding that which falls outside the scope of human reason.[57]

Each of these ancient views of education focuses primarily on the metaphysical realm. Epistemology and axiology take secondary roles, being understood as subordinate philosophical

[55] Knight, *Philosophy & Education*, 50.
[56] Ibid.
[57] Ibid, 54–60.

realms. The universe is understood to hold *a priori* truth which is objective and can be known. The teacher takes an authoritative role in explaining the largely cognitive facts and skills related to these self-existing truths.[58]

Knight identified a newer philosophical viewpoint, not rooted in antiquity, as the "pragmatic" philosophy. Where the previous paradigms understood metaphysical questions to be at the core of knowing and teaching, pragmatism began with the viewpoint that epistemology is foundational. William James was one of the fathers of this uniquely American contribution to the discipline of philosophy. He summarized the shift from metaphysics to epistemology when he described his approach to knowledge as, "the attitude of looking away from first things, principles, 'categories,' supposed necessities, and of looking toward last things, fruits, consequences, facts."[59] Pragmatic theory understands that truth is simply what works; there are no *a priori* starting points. Further, this school of thought has given rise to a distinction between knowledge and belief. While an individual may hold any personal beliefs, what one professes to know must be proven.[60]

The fifth school of philosophical thought identified by Knight is "existentialism." Whereas pragmatism put the emphasis on epistemology, existentialism shifted the focal point of

---

[58] Ibid., 61–62.
[59] James, William. *Pragmatism* Meridian Books, 1955. Originally published by Longman, Green and Co., Inc., 1907) 47.
[60] Knight, *Philosophy & Education*, 66 - 74.

philosophy from metaphysics to axiology. By this way of thinking, the individual is the focal point of the universe, and what he or she values is demonstrated through his or her choices in life. Answers to life's questions are not "right or wrong," and the processes of knowing and educating are focused on facilitating an individual's decision-making. [61]

In Knight's survey of philosophies, he also discussed postmodern thought as it relates to educational philosophy.[62] By the late 20th century, mankind had seen ample evidence to support the conclusion that scientific progress does not lead to utopia. The continuation of problems in human life, in spite of the hope that modern science and technology would provide solutions, yielded two responses: the despair of existentialism and postmodernism.

Knight understood a certain inherent lack of clarity and consistency in the post-modern message. However, the lack of clarity by no means implies a lack of impact.[63] His analysis saw postmodernity as a reaction against the sterility of modern, pragmatic, realism-based knowledge. Negatively, postmodernism rejects realism-oriented philosophies. Positively, postmodernism aligns itself with sensitivity to the limits of language as a means of understanding human thought, and also with the facts of diversity and interconnectedness of human life.[64]

---

[61] Ibid., 75–83.
[62] Ibid., 85–89.
[63] Ibid., 96.
[64] Ibid., 89–100.

Knight's analysis pointed out how knowledge in strictly cognitive terms is suspect in postmodern thinking. Such knowledge is at best untrustworthy, and at worst is a tool manipulated in the self-interest of the powerful. Teaching, in postmodern terms, is not a process of knowing and imparting facts, but is a process of transformation in which teachers are

> "generators of knowledge within the daily uncertainty of the classroom experience. The teacher must be a person who is able to respond within the context of ever-changing settings. Thus teacher training needs to produce "teacher thinkers" rather than technicists." [65]

Based on these philosophical perspectives, Knight went on to examine nine different models of education. While his analysis is useful, he focused to a large degree on the pedagogy of children. Instead of examining Knight's nine models of pedagogy we now look at models of education which specifically focus on the adult learner, since missionary training is aimed at the adult.

Adult Education

Any educational scheme, including the preparation of missionaries, begins with basic assumptions about the nature of learning and teaching. In her consideration of learning theories, Lois McKinney-Douglas wrote of three primary issues as being of interest to mission: Adult Learning Theory, Cognitive Style

---

[65] Ibid., 99.

Theory, and Moral Development.[66] In the next few pages we will consider two of these three issues: adult education and cognitive styles (to be considered as a part of the discussion of specialized training for mission).

Adult education is a fairly young discipline, dating largely to the work of Carl Rogers, Malcolm Knowles, and Paulo Freire.[67] Over the years since those authors wrote, seven primary philosophical foundations developed within the realm of adult education. These foundational schemes have been identified by Elias and Merriam[68] as the liberal arts, progressive, behaviorist, humanistic, radical, analytic /critical and postmodern schools of thought.

The "liberal arts" philosophy of adult education, according to Elias and Merriam's analysis, is based on liberal learning, organized knowledge, and the development of cognitive intellectual powers. This approach led to programs such as the Great Books program, and is seen in many of the liberal arts university programs.[69] Liberal arts education promotes an approach to teaching and learning that is rational and intellectual. Along with knowledge, liberal arts programs also frequently include teaching in the realm of values, spiritual or religious education, and aesthetics. Elias and Merriam suggested that

---

[66] McKinney, Lois. "Learning Theories." *Evangelical Dictionary of World Missions.* Grand Rapids: Baker, 2000, 568-569.
[67] McKinney-Douglas, 568-69.
[68] Elias, John L, and Merriam, Sharan B. *Philosophical Foundations of Adult Education.* Malabar (USA: Krieger Pub., 2005.)
[69] Ibid., 17–49.

liberal arts education is fulfilling to people who "search for truth, desire to develop their moral characters, strive for spiritual and religious visions, and seek the beautiful in life and nature." [70]

The second foundational philosophy of adult education was called the "progressive" school by Elias and Merriam. This philosophy seeks to use education as a tool in the promotion of political and social change. John Dewey, one of the philosophical fathers of progressive education, saw education as a life-long process. In that light, adult education became an important component in social reform and reconstruction movements.[71]

The third foundational philosophy of adult education is what Elias and Merriam called the "behaviorist school." In the words of Elias and Merriam, "probably no other system of psychology has had as much impact on general and adult education . . . as behaviorism."[72]

According to behaviorists such as John Watson and B.F. Skinner, human behavior can be understood, predicted, and controlled though scientific means. Education, accordingly, can be understood as the means of reinforcing some kinds of behavior and eliminating others. Behaviorist theory brought the following elements to adult education:[73]

1. Behavioral objectives in teaching, in which learning outcomes can be measured objectively and precisely.

----

[70]Ibid., 49.
[71] Ibid., 55.
[72] Ibid., 83.
[73] Ibid., 93.

2. Accountability of program administrators to fulfill the learning objectives that they propose at the outset.

3. Instructional methods which seek to produce change by repeated reinforcement of desired behaviors.

Behaviorist viewpoints are common in the realm of adult education. One clear illustration of this viewpoint comes from the volume *Adults Teaching Adults* which states, "the educator's basic job is to bring about some new and desired student behavior." That thought is followed by the statement that "Behavior, therefore, is the key consideration for adult educators as they carry out their professional duties, and learning (changing behavior) is the primary focus of the instructional act."[74]

Closely allied with the liberal arts approach to adult education is the approach that Elias and Merriam called "humanistic" adult education. This view stresses the values, freedom, and dignity of human beings. Humanistic learning seeks to elevate the human being, fostering environments in which self-actualization can occur. In this school of thought, learners cooperate actively in the learning process.[75]

Malcolm Knowles, one of the most influential of adult educators, was a key spokesman for the humanistic approach to adult education. Knowles coined the term "andragogy" to describe the teaching of adults. As Elias and Merriam phrased it, "with its

---

[74] Verduin, John R. *Adults Teaching Adults: Principles and Strategies. First Edition.* Austin, Tex: Pfeiffer & Co, 1977, 9.
[75] Elias and Merriam, 111–145.

emphasis upon the learner and the development of human beings, andragogy is basically a humanistic theoretical framework applied primarily to adult education."[76] They continued with an outline of four underlying assumptions which characterize andragogy.[77]

The first assumption basic to andragogy is that adult learners are self-directed and teaching is best achieved when that fact is taken into consideration. The importance of a positive self-image (since a feeling of inability to complete a task will create a formidable barrier to the learning process), cooperative rather than competitive environments, and the necessity for trusting and respectful relationships are all part of this foundational assumption about the adult learner.

Elias and Merriam's second summary statement about the nature of adult learners is that an adult identifies him or herself by the unique accumulation of life experiences.

The third assumption which guides andragogy is that the adult learner's readiness to learn is linked to developmental tasks unique to a specific stage of life. Learning, in other words, is based on relevance to the specific issues that an adult learner is facing or will be facing very soon.

Finally, with the fourth assumption, Elias and Merriam wrote that andragogy assumes that adults desire an immediate application of new knowledge rather than a postponed application that is common in general education.

---

[76] Ibid., 132.
[77] Ibid., 133–134.

Appendices 1 and 2 go into still more detail about the nature of pedagogy and the nature of andragogy.

Paulo Freire is the exemplar of the next form of adult education identified by Elias and Merriam. This approach, called "radical and critical adult education," began with the notion that society needs to be recreated. This philosophy of adult education may take powerful political overtones. The forms of adult education that have been considered up to this point assume the values of society, differing primarily in how to best transmit and foster those values. Radical forms of adult education, though, promote fundamental changes in society. Freire's approach to societal change through adult education included the process by which the oppressed are allowed to reflect on their social state and on ways to change that condition. Following that "conscientization," a problem-posing approach to adult education was suggested as a way to motivate learners to look for unique solutions to the problems that they face.[78] Freire understood the role of the teacher to be one who helps learners to find solutions rather than as a "banker" who makes "information deposits."[79]

Elias and Merriam's fifth philosophy of adult education is a fairly young approach to the discipline, one that they called the "analytical philosophy of adult education." This analytic approach seeks to define the key terms in a given discipline and, by developing analysis and definitions, to develop improved

---

[78] Freire, Paulo, and Bergman-Ramos, Myra. *Pedagogy of the Oppressed*. New York: Continuum, 1993. 79.
[79] Ibid. 71–72.

understanding of the issues. In the case of the analysis of adult education, analytical definitions have brought clarity of thought and expression to the discipline.[80]

Elias and Merriam's final approach to adult education grows from post-modernism. [81] Post-modern thought will approach the subject and process of adult education through a frame of reference which prefers the non-traditional and unconventional. It will reject overly planned events, preferring a more spontaneous responsiveness to immediate circumstances. It will applaud a wide diversity of goals, curriculum, procedures, and participants. It may also redefine and revise previously accepted expressions of truth. It will tolerate uncertainty and unpredictability in matters of authority and decision-making. Post-modern education will involve participants in the decision and control levels of a learning situation. Post-modern education places a premium on the educational experience. Finally, post modernity will not categorize as freely as modernity does; for instance, work and education will not necessarily be considered as distinct from each other. The lines are not so clear in post-modern thought.[82]

Besides identifying the underlying philosophies of adult education, it is likewise important to observe the practice of adult education over the past decades. Since much mission training has developed from adult educational principles, a review of common

---

[80] Elias and Merriam, 213-214.
[81] Ibid., 217–246.
[82] Ibid., 239–242.

trends in the praxis of adult education is also germane to this discussion.

Peter Jarvis highlighted nine axes upon which the practice of adult education has moved over the past decades.[83] Jarvis began with the perspective that adult education is an outgrowth of social movements of the early 20th century. In that modern world, adult education took on forms appropriate for its day. In light of current globalization and post-modernity, Jarvis pointed to the shifts within those nine axes so that adult education can continue to be relevant in its aims and its institutions.

The nine shifts that Jarvis discussed include the following:

1. A shift from recurrent education to continuing education. In the 1960s, a sense of entitlement was encompassed in the word "recurrent education" as that term was used in Jarvis' native United Kingdom. Yet the continuing education models of the early 21st century do not carry that expectation of social entitlement.

2. A shift from teacher-centered to student-centered education. Malcolm Knowles in particular developed a student-centered approach to adult education.

3. A changing status of knowledge. Whereas knowledge in the past took on a status of fact presented by authoritative instructors, Jarvis pointed out that knowledge is increasingly understood to be relative, contextually-

---

[83] Jarvis, Peter, "Adult Education – an Ideal for Modernity?" in Peter Jarvis, ed. *20th Century Thinkers in Adult & Continuing Education. 2nd ed. edition.* London: Routledge, 2001, 7–9.

determined, and narrative-based. Learning this kind of knowledge is quite different than learning about something that is assumed to be objective.

4. A shift from curriculum to program. Rather than promote a particular series of courses which should be studied, adult educators increasingly offer a selection of programs out of which students select that which interests them. This is in some ways due to management and marketing realities; but it also reflects changing views on the nature of knowledge.

5. A shift from liberal to vocational goals. Adult education in the past was aimed at a liberal education. Increasingly the goal is vocational expertise. The relevance of study is tied to the professional aspirations of the student.

6. A shift from face-to-face to distance learning. Education has traditionally occurred in face-to-face situations where either the students would travel to the instructor or the teacher would travel to the students. Increasingly, though, print, video, and electronic media allow for teacher/student interaction at a distance.

7. A shift from education/training to learning. Jarvis pointed out how the distinction of "education" as opposed to "training" is disappearing as a larger realm of "learning" is the new focus. Whether the learning is at a level that would have once been called education or at the level once known as training is not as important as that everyone learns the things that they need to know.

8. A shift from rote learning to learning as reflection. Previous practitioners of adult education could focus on the learning of facts, since knowledge and facts were synonymous. However, Jarvis showed how perceptions about the nature of knowledge have become more relative and so teaching and learning have become more process-oriented and reflective.

9. A shift from welfare needs to market demands. Whereas adult education in the past focused on meeting basic survival needs, Jarvis pointed out how it is increasingly tied to the ability to increase income. Rather than simply allow for minimal lifestyle standards, education is now seen as part of upward mobility. It has become a consumer commodity, subject to supply and demand market forces.

Educational Theories Particularly Relevant to the Paradigm of Relational Realism

So far our survey of educational philosophies has stayed at the general, broad level. It is apparent that there are numerous approaches to the very human tasks of learning and teaching. It is also apparent that some of those approaches are compatible with the paradigm of relational realism, and other models are inconsistent. In this section we will look at several authors or educational approaches that have special relevance to the idea of relational paradigm.

The first author is Jane Vella, who has made significant contributions to the field of adult learning.[84] Among other concepts that she has brought to the field, of special interest to us is her idea of Achievement Based Outcomes in adult learning situations. By this, she pointed towards the importance of specific activities which learners will "do to effectively learn [the] content."[85] She suggests teachers develop meaningful achievements that in fact require the learner to do things that will both help them learn and demonstrate that they have learned.

Similar to a shop class where one learns to use saws and drills by making a cabinet, so the concept of Achievement Based Outcomes suggests that learning intercultural ministry is best done by actually doing the activities that are part of intercultural ministry.

This Achievement Based Outcome approach has implications for relational reality paradigm. When Learner and Facilitator work together to achieve common goals, relationships can be fostered. Teaching and learning that is focused on simple information transmission can take place with minimal personal interaction. On the other hand, when a joint project that requires achieving real-world goals is part of the teaching environment, that environment readily fosters meaningful interaction.

---

[84] Vella, Jane. *On Teaching and Learning: Putting the Principles and Practices of Dialogue Education into Action*. 1 edition. San Francisco: Jossey-Bass, 2007, 41–42.
[85] Ibid.

A second approach to adult education with strong
relevance to the paradigm of relational realism is seen in the
practice of mentoring as a form of adult education. In an
unpublished evaluation of mentoring, Dan Anderson gave both a
useful definition and analysis of mentoring. He defined mentoring
as, ". . . an intentional relationship that involves a transfer of
resources from a mentor to one or more mentorees with the aim of
producing specific, and/or holistic growth toward maturity in the
mentoree."[86]

Anderson's definition continued with concepts that are
particularly helpful to a relational paradigm.

> Mentoring happens in the context of 'relationship,'
> specifically relationship between a mentor and the
> mentoree(s), and God, as an unseen, personal presence in
> every mentoring relationship, who is involved to the extent
> that he is welcome and/or the extent that he chooses to be.
> Christian mentoring is effective as a result of divine and
> human activity in the mentoring relationship, i.e. God's
> guiding and enabling in the life and relationship of the
> mentor and the mentoree."[87]

Anderson leaned heavily on the work of Stanley and
Clinton[88] who identified nine types of mentoring activities:
discipleship into the basic habits of Christian life and belief;
spiritual growth through insight and accountability; coaching to

---

[86] Dan Anderson, unpublished paper, "Missiological Implications of Biblical Mentoring for Mentoring Duna Youth," submitted to Dr. Enoch Wan, Western Seminary, Dec 19, 2014, 2.
[87] Anderson, 2–3.
[88] Stanley, Paul D, and J. Robert Clinton. *Connecting: The Mentoring Relationships You Need to Succeed in Life*. Colorado Springs, CO.: NavPress, 1992.

develop motivation and skill, counseling to provide timely advice to improve perspective and clarity; teaching to impart knowledge for specific life and ministry issues; sponsoring to protect and guide the movement of resources; modeling of life, ministry, and professional ability; historical modeling through examples of life stories; and divine contact as the mentor points the mentoree to God. These kinds of mentoring activities take place in varying time frames; there are intensive and deliberate activities in some cases, occasional mentor/mentoree interaction in the second group, and passive "teach by example" in yet others. Both vertical and horizontal relationships are clearly involved in all nine types of mentoring.

A third trend in adult education that relates to missionary training is the recognition of the cycle of action and reflection which lead to learning. Based on the concept that learning in adults takes place best in such a cycle of activity and reflection, Broucek [89] suggested that missionary training can be improved by involving church planters in dialog with one another. The building of relationships where this praxis cycle takes place has proven to be an effective part of missionary training.

The fourth school of thought in educational theory that is relevant to both relational realism and to mission training is the school of thought within adult education that is known as "transformative education." This school, growing from the

---

[89] Broucek, Dave. "An In-Service Training Idea for Church Planters." *Occasional Bulletin of the Evangelical Missiological Society* 10, no. 2 (Spring 1998).

foundational work by Jack Mezirow and Associates,[90] sees education as a much deeper process than most other educational philosophies we have considered. In this perspective, the learner will not only gain facts, attitudes, and skills but more importantly will reflect critically to validate and/or challenge their own beliefs, interpretations, values, feelings, and ways of thinking. As Mezirow phrased it, "Learning is understood as the process of using a prior interpretation to construe a new or revised interpretation of the meaning of one's experience as a guide to future action."[91]

Importantly, this transformation of beliefs, interpretations, values etc. does not happen in isolation. A strong element in the transformative education movement is the observation that these deep levels of change are, "not only rationally driven, but equally dependent on relational ways of knowing."[92]

An implication of Mezirow's insights can be seen in the work of Knud Illeris[93]. Illeris described learning as simultaneously occurring along two axes: acquisition and interaction. The acquisition line roughly corresponds to Bloom's traditional educational schemes that speak of cognition, psychomotor skill and affective domains. The interaction line, on the other hand, is not present *per se* in other schemes: it is the continuum between

---

[90] Mezirow, Jack, ed. *Learning as Transformation: Critical Perspectives on a Theory in Progress.* 1 edition. San Francisco: Jossey-Bass, 2000.
[91] Ibid., 5.
[92] Taylor, Edward. "Analyzing Research on Transformative Learning Theory," ch. 11 in Mezirow, Jack, ed. *Learning as Transformation: Critical Perspectives on a Theory in Progress.* 1 edition. San Francisco: Jossey-Bass, 2000. p. 306
[93] Illeris, Knud. *Transformative Learning and Identity.* 1 edition. London; New York: Routledge, 2013.

oneself and the social environment in which the learning occurs and is applied. Illeris explained this component of learning, "one process is the interaction between the individual and social and material environment. . . the criteria of this process are of a historical, geographical, and societal nature, depending on time and place."[94]

Ruth Wall has taken these concepts of transformative education, and especially of the relational nature of transformative education, into the Christian realm in her writing. In a short yet insightful article, she wrote, "Being able to learn and being able to relate are essential in Christian mission. Being able to learn and being able to relate are indivisible and together represent the process of whole person learning."[95]

Enoch Wan has also developed the concept of transformative education from a Christian perspective.[96] In describing the dynamic interactions that lead to adult transformative learning from a Christian perspective, he reminds us that relationships are more varied and complicated than is apparent in Mezirow's work. Figure 3 and Figure 4 graphically describe transformative education from the perspective of a relational realism paradigm.

---

[94] Ibid., 34.

[95] Wall, Ruth. "Equipping the Whole Person." *Bulletin of the International Mission Training Network*, January 2015.http://www.missionarytraining.org/mt/index.php/forum/bulletin-no-1-equipping-the-whole-person. Accessed October 22, 2016.

[96] Wan, Enoch. "Christian Adult Transformational Learning" (Transformative Andragogy within a Christian Context. Unpublished paper, April 24, 2016).

Figure 3: Christian Adult Transformational Learning

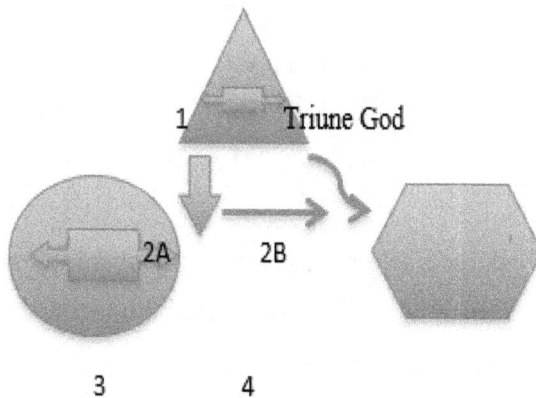

#1、#3 — horizontal relationship

#2、#4 — vertical relationship

#1 — Internal within the Triune God: perfect, infinite...etc. (horizontal)

#2A— External manifestation in teacher (special grace and appointment as teacher):
  regeneration, calling, endowment and empowerment (vertical)

#2B — External manifestation in learner (general grace and providential arrangement for learner): (vertical)

#3 — Internal within the faith community: *ecclesia, koinonia*, etc. (horizontal)

#4 — Interaction between teacher & learner (horizontal) leading to transformational change:

    a) Ontological convergence of spheres in reality (interplay and overlapping)

    b) Pedagogical confluence in dynamic interaction (interactive throughout)

    c) Transformational change
  - integrative: being + doing; belief + behavior;
  - Multi-dimensional change = cognition + volition + affection + action within a relational context
  - transformative change = divine aid + godly teacher's input + Christian learner's response, i.e. adults (willing to grow and change) by entering a relational community can experience positive change through interactive learning vertically and horizontally

Figure 3 is Wan's representation of the relationships through which transformative education takes place. The vertical relationship between Triune God and humanity carries strong transformative potential. These vertical relationships include Triune God's activity in the teacher as well as the learner.

Figure 3 also shows the transformative nature of horizontal relationships. Where Mezirow's approach correctly sees human relationship and dialog as fundamental to the process of change and transformation, Wan gives further definition to that concept. The horizontal relationships that foster transformative learning include not only teacher/student, but interactive relationship with a faith community as well. It is not simply a series of one-on-one relationships that foster transformation. Interaction with the larger group – the church, the Christian community – is also key to transformation.

Summarizing the contribution of Figure 3, then, Wan added complexity and accuracy to the concept of transformative education by reminding us that relationship with God is an important part of transformation, and that besides individual teacher/student relationships there is also the important and dynamic relational involvement of the "koinonia and ecclesia" – Christian fellowship and church. Wan's summary statement for Figure 3 is:

Transformative change = divine aid + godly teacher's input + Christian learner's response (i.e. adults who are willing to grow and change can experience transformation by entering a relational community).

Wan's Figure 4 moves beyond the relationships that foster transformative education, and proposes a representation of transformational process and progress. This process begins again with the active involvement of Triune God simultaneously in the life of the teacher, of the student, and of the faith community (church). These vertical relationships take place primarily between God and his people. His people act horizontally to bring the transformative Word into the non-Christian community. Some of that horizontal witness is through the gifted people within the church (teachers, evangelists, pastors, missionaries). Some of the horizontal witness is through the Christian community as a whole, acting as salt and light within the realm of human society.

Figure 4: Relational Transformation: Process & Progress

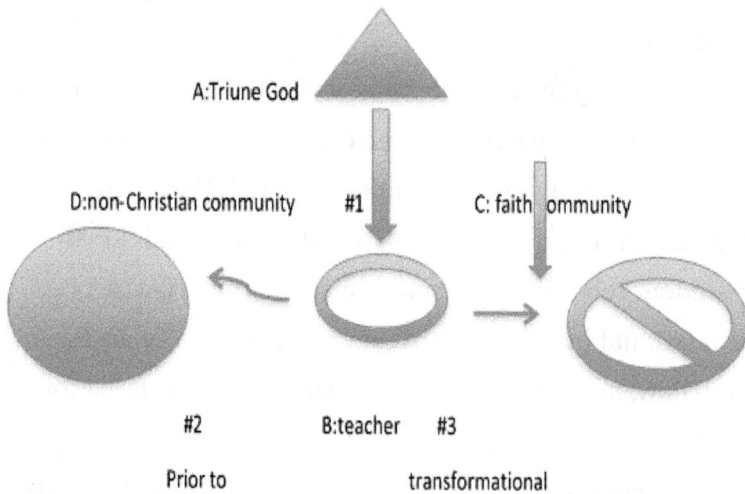

NOTE:
A: Triune God
B: teacher

C: faith community: *ecclesia, koinonia*, etc. (horizontal)

Operational process:
#1 — regeneration, calling, endowment and empowerment
(vertical)
#2 – Prior to learning
#3 – transformational change through interaction vertically and
horizontally
 ➢ Interaction between teacher and learner (horizontal)
    leading to transformational change
 ➢ transformative change = divine aid + godly teacher's input
    + Christian learner's response

Figure 4 can be summarized in the same equation that we saw in

Figure 3:

Transformative change = divine aid + godly teacher's input

+ Christian learner's response (i.e. adults who are willing to grow

and change can experience transformation by entering a relational

community). See Appendix 1 for more detail on transformative

andragogy.

We have now seen four educational theories that are

particularly relevant to the paradigm of relational realism:

Achievement-Based Outcomes, mentoring, action/reflection

cycles, and transformative education. The remainder of this

chapter will present transformative education within the

specifically Christian context of andragogy for discipleship.

Transformative andragogy within a Christian context

As previously stated, "education" is "a process in which a

learner comes to understand reality (vertical and horizontal relationships) and truth (Truth revealed vertically and truth communicated horizontally) with transformative changes (being & doing)." Christian educators and learners rely not merely on human reasoning nor expertise in pedagogy in order to produce new understanding in the learner; but on the spirit of God who leads all people into truth (truth – John 14:6; and truth - John 16:13 NIV) with dynamism for change (Phil 2:13 – "for it is God who works in you to will and to do..." and Rom 12:1—4 "...transformation...").

Transformative learning[97] is a matter of allowing the spirit of truth to transform the heart (Matt 15:10-2), as well as the mind (Rom 12:1—2) through relationship with God vertically and fellow Christians within the body of Christ horizontally (Eph 4:15, 25—32). It is our understanding that the philosophy of adult education (andragogy) is distinct and different from the philosophy of childhood education (pedagogy).[98] In contrast to secular education focusing primarily on learning knowledge, information and skills, relational Christian adult education must focus on "being" and "doing," individually and collectively including assumptions and beliefs that drive their perspectives (or worldviews) leading to a new

---

[97] Additional references on "transformative learning" and "transformative andragogy" are listed in Appendix 1.
[98] Mezirow, Jack and Associates. *Learning as Transformation: Critical Perspectives on a Theory in Progress.* 1 edition. San Francisco: Jossey-Bass, 2000, 3.

reality in Christ and new humanity in the Church.[99] This is in contrast to Mezirow's statement below:

> Central to [the process of helping adults enhance their understandings, skills, and dispositions] is helping learners to critically reflect on, appropriately validate, and effectively act on their (and others') beliefs, interpretations, values, feelings, and ways of thinking...Our human need to understand our experience, the necessity that we do so through critical discourse, and the optimal conditions enabling us to do so freely and fully provide a foundation of a philosophy of adult education. [100]

Mezirow's understanding of adult transformative learning is accomplished through "critical discourse." William N. Isaacs uses the term "dialog" similarly as saying:

> If people can be brought into a setting where they, at their choice, can become conscious of the very process by which they form tacit assumptions and solidify beliefs, and be rewarded by each other for doing so, then they can develop a common strength and capability for working and creating things together.[101]

Instead of "critical discourse" and within the framework of "relational realism," we emphasize "interactive learning" at personal level (including formal, non-formal and informal

---

[99] Stevens, David E. *Gods New Humanity: A Biblical Theology of Multiethnicity for the Church*. Eugene, Or: Wipf & Stock Pub, 2012; Stevens, David E., "God's new humanity in diaspora: a church of the nations and for the nations," in Pocock & Wan 2015:107—126.

[100] Mezirow, Jack and Associates. *Learning as Transformation*, 26.

[101] Isaacs, William N. "Taking Flight: Dialogue, Collective Thinking, and Organizational Learning." *Organizational Dynamics* 2 (1993), 25.

formats)[102] and within the learning community both vertically and horizontally. The paradigm of Christian transformative andragogy based on "relational realism" is integrative of elements listed below:

1. being + doing;
2. belief + behavior;
3. general understanding of "change" = cognition + volition + affection + action;
4. leads to transformative change:

    transformative change = divine aid + godly teacher's input + Christian learner's response

             (vertical)   (horizontal)

    i.e. adults (willing to grow and change) by entering a relational community can experience positive change through interactive learning vertically and horizontally.

The characteristics of Christian adult transformational learning

The characteristics of Christian adult transformational learning are as follows:

1. Ontological convergence of spheres in reality (interplay and overlapping) (divine & human as in Figure 1);
2. Pedagogical confluence in dynamic interaction (interactive throughout);

---

102 Rogers, Alan. *Non-Formal Education: Flexible Schooling or Participatory Education?* Hong Kong; New York: Comparative Education Research Centre, University of Hong Kong; Kluwer Academic, 2005.

3. Holistically inclusive of faith, love, hope cognitively, attitudinally, behaviorally;

4. Transformational change

The uniqueness of the relational paradigm

The relational paradigm (in contrast distinction to "conventional") is unique because it is:

1. Not individualistic; but **collective**: Trinity = both 3 and 1

2. Not personally private; but **transparent and community-based** and **interdependent**

    a) The Son's deference and dependence on the Father (e.g. Jn 4–8, 12);

    b) The Holy Spirit testifies to the Father and the Son (e.g. Jn 14:16–31; 15:26–27; 16:13–14; Acts 1:8);

    c) The Father sent the Son (Jn 17:6–8, 18, 21);

    d) The resurrection of the Son:

        •   The Father raised Him (Gal 1:1, Eph 1:17,20);

        •   The H.S. raised Him (Romans 8:11).

3. Dynamic: (see Figures 5 and 6)

    a) Multi-directional: ≠ unilineal in process of pedagogy (teacher → learner; growing together)

    b) Multi-dimensional: ≠ unidimensional in progress (not merely knowledge or behavior horizontally and humanistically only)

    c) TC = OC + PC

        transformational change = ontological convergence + pedagogical convergence

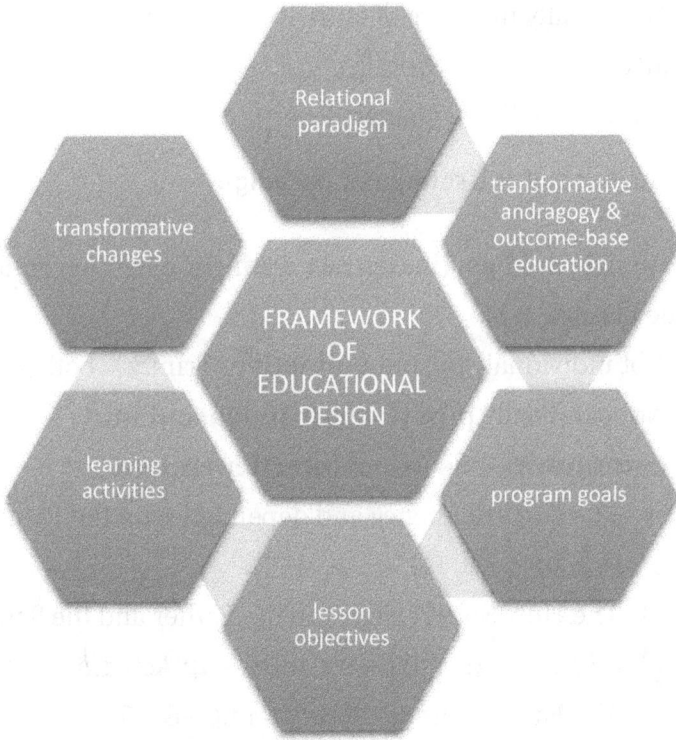

Figure 5: Cyclical Pattern of Transformative Process of Educational Design

Sequence of educational design (the core: Framework of educational design):

1. Theological and theoretical foundation: relational paradigm;

2. Educational philosophy: transformative andragogy and outcome-base education;[103]

3. Program Goals: cross-cultural missionary training;

---

[103] For a Christian perspective of OBE for transformative change, see Probe Ministries, "Transformational OBE," Probe Ministries, Plano, Texas. @ https://www.probe.org/about-us/ (accessed Oct. 1, 2016).

4. Lesson Objectives: developmentally specific to particular stage;

5. Learning Activities: multiple dimensions of cognition, volition, affection and action;

6. Program Outcomes: transformative change in belief and behavior;[104]

7. Cyclical: filtered through the theo-theoretical framework of "relational paradigm" and shaped by the educational philosophy of transformative andragogy and outcome-base

In case readers are interested in learning more about outcome-base education (OBE), items are listed in the footnote.[105]

---

[104] See Lewis, Jonathan, and Robert Ferris. Developing an Outcomes Profile." *In Establishing Ministry Training: A Model for Programme Developers.* Pasadena, CA: William Carey Library, 1995.

[105] Items are listed below for those who desire to learn more about OBE:

Brandt, Ron. "An Overview of Outcome-Based Education" ASCD, VA: Alexandria. @http://www.ascd.org/publications/curriculum_handbook/413/chapters/An_O verview_of_Outcome-Based_Education.aspx (accessed Oct. 1, 2016).

Probe Ministries, "Transformational OBE," Probe Ministries, Plano, Texas. @ https://www.probe.org/about-us/ (accessed Oct. 1, 2016).

Phyllis Schlafly What's Wrong With Outcome-Based Education? (May 1993) @ http://www.ourcivilisation.com/dumb/dumb3.htm (accessed Oct. 1, 2016).

William G. Spady, Outcome –based Education: Critical issues and Answers. AASA, 1994.

Schwarz, Gretchen and Cavener, Lee Ann, "Outcome-Based Education and Curriculum Change: Advocacy, Practice and Critique," *Journal of Curriculum and Supervision* 9, no. 4 (1994): 326-338.@http://webapp1.dlib.indiana.edu/virtual_disk_library/index.cgi/4273355/FID1736/journals/enc2371/2371.htm

Siyayinqoba, OBE- Outcomes Based Education (South African), Youtube 2009 @https://www.youtube.com/watch?v=G84uOMU2ofgeducation for cyclical adjustment and improvement.

Table 4: Relational Andragogy & Transformative Change in Spirituality: Three Dimensions[106]

Dimension	Transformative change		
	Faith	Love	Hope
Vertical	1. comprehension of the Gospel 2. gain understanding of major themes, genres, and teachings of the Bible	1. loyal to lordship of Christ as disciple 2. God-fearing, walk in obedience to God	1. the fruit of the Spirit & walk in the Spirit (Gal 4) 2. trusting God in obedient lifestyle
Horizontal	**Cognitive: Knowledge**	**Attitudinal: Attitudes**	**Practical: Skills**
	Recognize the importance of Christian community & mutuality: Understand the importance of the local church for learning and growth (church as body, reciprocity, "one and other")	Channeling the love of God to others, Practice the Great Commandment & fulfill the Great Commission	1. Successfully attend and participate in church and its ministries; Exercise spiritual gifts to serve other; Be an agent of transformative change

---

[106] For a good reference on adult learning in spirituality, see Tisdell, Elizabeth J. *Exploring Spirituality and Culture in Adult and Higher Education*. San Francisco: Jossey-Bass, 2003. http://public.eblib.com/choice/publicfullrecord.aspx?p=158016.

The table below shows the program outcomes in cross-cultural missionary training.

Table 5: Program Outcomes in Cross-cultural Missionary Training

Level	Knowledge	Attitude	Skills
Personal (individual)	Knowing: cultural differences, barriers and bridges	Free from self-centeredness & ethnocentrism[107]	Competence in communication and interaction
Group (institutional)	Appreciative understanding of one another	Mutuality with respect & reciprocity	Intercultural interaction, godly partnership and God-glorifying reciprocity

Goals, Objectives, and Activities at various stages with cyclical adjustment/improvement

In the training curriculum design process, an entry and exit profile (program outcomes in knowledge, attitudes and skills) are established, followed by specifying program goals, writing learning objectives, and designing learning activities. (See Appendix 3 for more on creating the climate for learning, and Appendix 4 on the content and sequence of cross-cultural training.) For each of the three dimensions of program outcomes of the two figures above, goals will be specified. In addition, sample learning objectives and activities will be suggested. The goals pertain to the entire program and its outcomes, whereas the

---

[107] Wan, Enoch. "Ethnocentrism." *Evangelical Dictionary of World Missions*. Grand Rapids, MI: Baker Book House, 2000, 324-325.

objectives and learning activities are narrower in focus and pertain directly to a particular lesson plan or unit that may be present within the overall curriculum.

Cross-cultural ministry readiness, faithfulness (vertical) and effectiveness (horizontal)

The specific program outcomes related to Christian formation have already been established in knowledge, skills, and abilities. However, it is also important to ask *why* "cross-cultural ministry readiness" is considered an integral part of the training program. What are the overarching goals or purposes of this curricular component?

First and foremost, the goal of "cross-cultural ministry readiness" is to introduce the person and message of Jesus Christ to the learners so that, through the work of the Holy Spirit, they might believe and receive him as Savior and Lord.

Secondarily, the goal of "cross-cultural ministry readiness" is to teach learners the basic relational and behavioral patterns of following Jesus. As can be seen in the program outcomes, these are: specific bases of *knowledge*, such as knowing basic Christian doctrine; *skills*, such as being able to use Bible study tools effectively; and *attitudes*, such as cultural adaptability for Christian mission.

These overarching goals work together with the program outcomes to form specific learning objectives and activities within a particular lesson or unit of each cycle. For example, at the beginning stage, each of these lessons would have its own learning objectives, often termed with language such as "learners will be able to..." The lesson ...., for example, might have the following learning objectives:

1. Learners will be able to identify the multiple factors of ...
2. Learners will be able to name three ways for cross-cultural communication...
3. Learners will be able to operate cross-culturally in a godly manner linking the learner to the Triune God, free from negative influence of satan, sin, self and corrupt aspects of the learner's socio-cultural background.

Discipleship and pastoral ministry within a "relational realism" framework

A "disciple" is "a person following Jesus Christ (being), being changed (becoming) to be more like Jesus and eager to bring others to Jesus with a Kingdom-orientation (belonging)" whereas "relational discipleship" is "the process of bringing others (people) to submit to the lordship (power and authority) of Jesus Christ primarily through vertical-relationship to the Triune God and secondarily through horizontal-relationship within the context of the Church/church in unity, mutuality and reciprocity."

Popular paradigms of Christian ministry (i.e. programmatic,[108] managerial and entrepreneur) in contemporary

---

[108]For the emphasis on relational approach in discipleship against programmatic way, Steve Hayner, "Discipleship: Now More Than Ever," Message delivered at the University Presbyterian Church 1984/10/01.
@ http://digitalcommons.spu.edu/av_events/2446/

context in the west are secularized and post-Christian. Evangelical Christians are not to conform to the worldly way; instead are to be transformed (Rom 12:1—4). These popular paradigms are to be re-examined from a "scriptural" (not merely "biblical")[109] and theological perspectives (see extensive critique elsewhere by Enoch Wan).[110] A simple comparison of popular approach with relational approach is shown diagrammatically in the table below:

Table 6: Comparing Paradigms: Popular and Relational

Element	Popular	Relational
What to be achieved?	Skills, knowledge, etc.	Spiritual maturity
Focus	Program and process	People
Strategy	Traditional	Interactive and andragogic
Success/evaluation	Measureable outcome	Not lineal, but holistic
What to be achieved	A proficient leader with followers; leaving a legacy.	An exemplary follower of Christ who inspires others
Focus	Making a leader according to prevailing cultural norms; success and authority	Cultivating a leader according to the Kingdom of God - one who shares God's love with others. Authority is based on humility (character) and mutuality (relationship).
Strategy	Leadership training material from various paradigms and various means: content based.	Teaching content in the context of relationships.
Success/evaluation	popular contest: gain votes	Faithfulness and fruitfulness

---

[109] Careful distinction between "scriptural" (not merely "biblical") is to be made, see Wan, Enoch, "Core values of mission organization in the cultural context of the 21st century." @ www.GlobalMissiology.org (January 2009) (access Oct. 1, 2016).

[110] For critique of popular paradigms (chapter 7) and proposal of "relational paradigm" (chapters 13-14), see Enoch Wan, *Diaspora Missiology: Theory, Methodology, and Practice*. (2nd ed.) IDS, 2015.

Below is a list of reflections on popular leadership which are often formulated on the basis of:

- functional efficiency (even "servant" leadership)
- within a competitive context (leading companies, military, etc.) so you need to "get out ahead"
- organizational skill (managerial)
- self-actualization (i.e. "be all you can be")
- evaluation that is performance-based (e.g. bonuses, leadership awards)

Relationship is foundational to discipleship, though it's missing or neglected from the popular approach. Leaders who disciple others cannot afford to exploit relationship as a means to the end (i.e. quantifiable outcomes of "success") in the training process.

> "From a biblical perspective, **relationships are fundamental** and part of what it means to lead is to have meaningful relationships and to love those that we lead. They are not optional... This goes beyond the ethos of our relationships with others that are proscribed in Timothy and Titus, where we are told not to be overbearing, quick tempered or quarrelsome and to be gentle. Our relationships as leaders are also not simply a means to an end, but are born out of a love for people and a desire to enable them also to serve and flourish."[111] (Emphasis added)

---

[111] Peckman, Jeremy. "Relational Leadership." *Evangelical Focus – Blogs – Forum of Christian Leaders*, n.d. file:///Volumes/NO%20NAME/Book_Missionary%20Training/Relational%20Leadership_process+diagram.htm. (access Oct. 1, 2016).

The popular approaches in ministry are programmatic, managerial; but not relational as shown in the table below with four aspects: focus, conceptualization, perspective and orientation.

Table 7: Approaches in Ministry: Programmatic, Managerial and Relational

Approach / Aspects	PROGRAMMATIC MINISTRY	MANAGERIAL/ ENTREPRENEUR	RELATIONAL (discipleship & pastoral)
#1 - FOCUS	-Program-oriented, Confident in program planning -Mindful of principle and details of program	-Market-oriented -Commodification of Christianity and consumerism thus "mercenary" instead of "ministry" -Recipient of Gospel as customers -Entrepreneurship: -Efficiency and outcome based; Profiting in relationship	-Relation-oriented: Focusing on both vertical and horizontal relationship with priority; Convergence of systems: Triune God, angel, human being
	- Emphasis: • Focusing on horizontal relationship with a low (or no) view of vertical • Subscribe to critical realism		-Emphasis: Focus on horizontal, even more on vertical -Subscribe to "Relational realism"
#2 - CONCEPTUALIZATION	• Effort-optimism: what counts is trying hard and long enough • Packaging: event and action	• Instrumentalism (functionalism): felt needs approach, receptor-oriented • Pragmatism: measurable success & outcome-base	• Multi-level • Multi-contextual • Multi-dimensional
#3 - PERSPECTIVE	- Performance-based; empirical; impersonal - "Babel Complex" (Gen. 10: man-centered)		- Relationally nurturing - Glorify God, first & foremost
#4 - ORIENTATION	- Management and entrepreneur studies		-Interdisciplinary approach
	- Extremely proactive - Concrete in planning: careful scheduling & detailed planning of event	-Emulating the secular business -management model -Humanistic and impersonal -Managerially statistical & strategic	-High touch, people-oriented, networking -Reciprocity and strategic - Kingdom partnership
	-Dichotomy: "the Great Commandment" vs "the Great Commission" saving soul vs serving human/social needs		-Holistic Christianity: integrating "the Great Commandment" & "the Great Commission"

We are to heed the warning against programmatic approach and should recover the relational way as warranted in the Scriptures:

The ideas behind Relational Leadership are a useful reminder to us as Christians of the importance of relationship in leadership. But as is so often the case, a Christian Worldview of leadership pre-empts many of the discoveries and developments in secular thinking, but also gives us a more balanced and rounded basis on which to lead. In the famous words of John Stott, "we need to listen to the world and to the word." In respect of leadership rather than preaching, we need to have the confidence that the Bible gives us a comprehensive and solid basis for leadership that avoids us latching onto the latest fads and fancies of the gurus and theorists.[112]

The table below shows various popular approaches at two levels integrated with the relational realism framework: individual (discipleship) and institutional (pastoral):

---

[112] Peckham, Jeremy, "Relational Leadership".

Table 8: Programmatic/Managerial/Entrepreneur and Relational Approaches in Discipleship (individual) & Pastoral (institutional) Levels

Level \ Approach		programmatic/ managerial/entrepreneur	relational discipleship & pastoral
(discipleship) Individual	goal	Knowledge & skills	Personal relationship
	focus	Program & procedure	Personal brings/Beings interacting
	strategy	Event, formulaic	Relationship: 1st vertical + 2nd horizontal
	preference	Quantitative success & measurable goal: bigger is better	Qualitative and relation-oriented
Institutional (pastoral)	goal	Effort-optimism: • Profit, benefit, fame • Win by all means & all cost	Network & nurturing relationships: **vertical + horizontal** • Building up the body • Growing in Christ
	focus	Popularity & fashionable	Triune God = foundation of being/doing & fount of blessings
	strategy	Careful planning, systematic, strategic, striving for success	-Networking & nurturing -relationships as track for the train to move & perform
	preference	Measurable outcomes as success; church "managers" evaluate pastors to renew contract; seeker-sensitive leads to consumerism of religion	• All submit to the Lordship of Christ; • Guided and empowered by the Holy Spirit who endows gifts; • Godly network of relationship that's edifying & God-glorifying

The vertical and horizontal dimensions of discipleship are intricately woven together; its priority is vertically Christo-centric (i.e. being, becoming and belonging); yet both vertical and horizontal are to be included:

"When we think about "Relational Leadership," viewed from God's perspective, we might consider that His concern ultimately is with the quality of both our <u>vertical and horizontal relationships</u>, rather than just the material outcomes of what we do as an organization..." (emphasis added)[113]

We are to be relation-oriented, rather than task-oriented: "Being more deeply relational may also require a shift of emphasis from the task-orientated nature of Western management practice to allow time and provide the context for developing relationships..."[114]

The table below is a comparison of popular approaches (i.e. Programmatic/managerial/ entrepreneur) in Christian ministry with relational approach (i.e. #1-discipleship and #2-pastoral).

---

[113] Ibid.
[114] Ibid.

Table 9: Popular Approaches vs. Relational Ministry
(#1-discipleship and #2-pastoral)

#	Aspects	Popular	Relational
#1 - Discipleship	Purpose	Knowledge, skills	Relationship, spiritual maturity, knowledge, skills
	Focus	program	People, process
	Strategy	Systematic transmission of knowledge	Relational modeling, Relational teaching
	Evaluation	Number of disciples	Quality of disciples' spiritual life
#2 - Pastoral	Purpose	Services for salary, job description	Relationship, spiritual modeling, knowledge
	Focus	program	People, process
	Strategy	Systematic transmission of services, such as counseling, preaching, teaching, etc.	Relational modeling, relational teaching, relational serving
	Evaluation	Numerical results, congregation's perception of pastor	Spiritual qualities Spiritual fruit of congregation

The dimensions of faith and practice (left column) of Christianity are to be flowing naturally from the relational reality (right column) at both individual and institutional levels (middle column) in the table below.

Table 10: Relational Theological Paradigm: Christian Faith and Practice[115]

Relationship dimension	Relational basis	Relational reality
Faith	-God's faithfulness & self-revealing -Christian trust/commitment to God	-doctrine from church history -systematic theology
Practice	-individual level	-regeneration, sanctification
	-converging (individual+institution)	-spiritual warfare -discipleship & evangelism
	Institutional level	-worship, fellowship

In the diagram below, "the outworking of the Triune God is presented as a progression of three phases (1, 2 and 3) to demonstrate his transformational mission through obedient disciples to make disciples."[116] "The reality of relational discipleship is evidenced by "Christ's followers, who are committed with loyalty, disciplined by God's truth and display a Christ-like lifestyle to glorify Him in individual walk and collective testimony"[117](see the right side in the figure below). Relational discipleship as shown in the figure below is offered as an alternative to popular approaches.

[115] Wan, Enoch. "Relational Theology and Relational Missiology," 4.
[116] Chittum, Matthew. "Unmasking Consumerism for the Practice of Relational Discipleship within the Contemporary American Cultural Context," Unpublished dissertation, Western Seminary, Portland, OR. 2014:83.
[117] Wan, Enoch. "Relational Theology and Relational Missiology," 1—8.

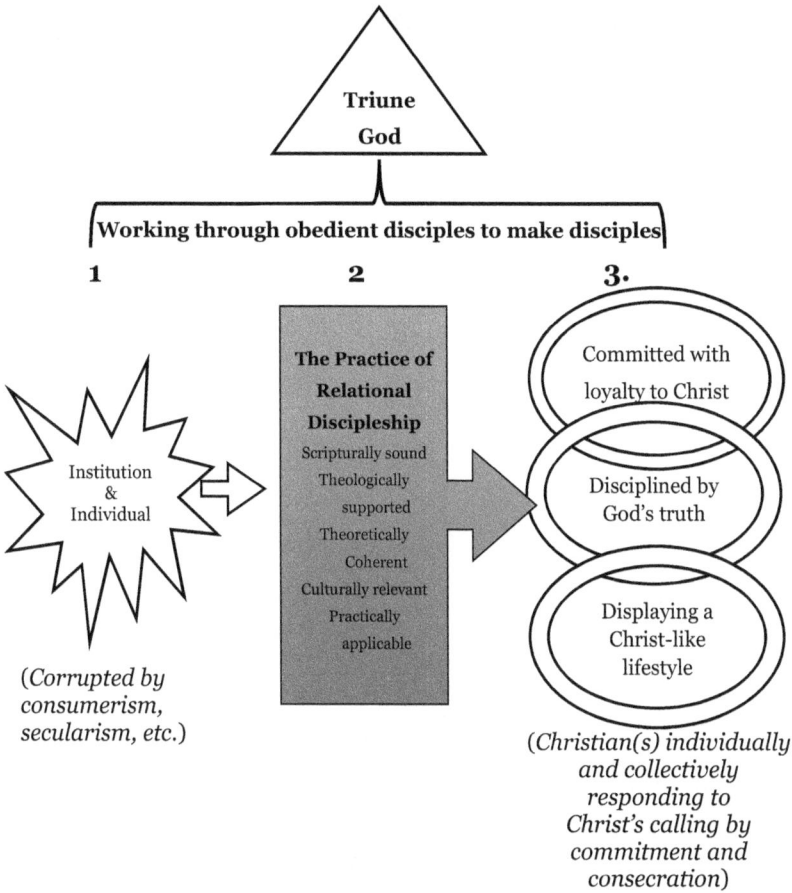

Figure 6: The Process of Transforming Change: From Corruption to Christ-Likeness[118]

As shown in figures 3, 4, 5, 6, 10, 15, there are two levels of discipleship: individual and institutional. At the personal level is what often called "discipleship" and at collective/institutional level it is called "pastoral ministry." The figure below shows the five-

---

[118] Chittum, "Unmasking Consumerism," 84.

step relational convergence between God and Christian community (i.e. local congregation).

Figure 7: Disciples: Five-step Relational Convergence between God & Christian Community[119]

For additional publications on "relational discipleship/leadership,"[120] readers are recommended to consult Appendix 1. In the table below, principle and process of relational ministry at two levels and two dimensions (vertical + horizontal)

---

[119] Chittum, "Unmasking Consumerism," 112.

[120] The items listed below are helpful in term of relational leadership/discipleship:

Joel Comiskey, *The Relational Disciple: How God Uses Community to Shape Followers of Jesus. CA:* CCS Publishing, 2010, 2016.

Mary Uhl-Bien, "Relational Leadership Theory: Exploring the socia process of leadership and organization," *The Leadership Quarterly* 17:6, December 2006.

Pearce, Conger and Locke, 2007 "Relational leadership as collective leadership: Mapping the territory," In Erica Gabrielle Foldy & Sonia Ospina, *Relational Leadership: New Developments in Theory and Practice Symposium.* rcrc.brandeis.edu/docs/relational-leadership-aom.docx

Michael Schluter and David John Lee, Lion Hudson, *The Relational Manager,* 2009. See more: http://evangelicalfocus.com/blogs/1527/Relational_Leadership.

are presented in diagrammatical format. The Triune God is the One who initiates and facilitates discipleship (left column), including the Father, the Son and the H.S. (a column each) as shown in the table below:

Table 11: Relational Initiation and Facilitation of Discipleship[121]

Activity	Father	Son	Holy Spirit	Disciples
Initiating of discipleship				
Drawing	Draws (John 6:44)	Sends disciples where to go (Luke 10:1, John 20:21)	Limits and guides (Acts 16:7–10)	Provides godly example (Matt 5:16); Goes to them (Luke 10)
Facilitating of discipleship				
Teaching and Preaching	Teaches (John 6:45)	Teaches what God has taught Him. (John 5:19, 8:28)	Teaches and reminds (Luke 12:11, John 14:26)	Preaches to those who have not heard (Rom 10:14–15)
Convicting and Illuminating	Chooses and predestines (Rom 8:29, Eph 1:4); Overcomes the world (John 16:33)	Opens eyes to scriptural truth (Luke 24:31); Intercedes (John 17:20, Heb 7:23–26); Sets free (John 8:36, 16:31–32)	Convicts of sin (John 16:8–11); Guides into truth (John 16:12–15)	Prays (Luke 18:1); Overcomes (John 16:33); Sanctifies by the truth (John 17:17)

From Romans 8, we can see the Gospel and grace from God downward are transformative in its outworking both vertically and horizontally as shown in the table below:

Table 12: Directional Understanding of Relationship[122]

Gospel & Grace	Relational Discipleship (Romans 8)		
	Dimension	Life according to the flesh	Born again by the Holy Spirit
Gospel & Grace	Spirit	Condemned (8:1)	Free in Christ Jesus (8:2)
	Soul	Hostile toward God (8:7)	Life and peace (8:6)
	Body	Dead because of sin (8:10)	Spirit will give life to mortal bodies (8:11)
Grace	A faithful follower of Christ in total submission to His Lordship as required by Christ (8:16—17)		

---

122 Ibid.103.

Table 13: Principle and Process of Relational Ministry at Two Levels and Two Dimensions (vertical + horizontal)

Level / Practice	Individual (discipleship)	Institutional (pastoral)
Principle	Being(character) - **primarily vertical** Root: being; fruit: doing (Eph1: 1-13; Rom 8:14-17; Jn 1:12-13; 15:15; Gal 2:20) ➤ Identity: Mk 1:9-13; 2Cor 1:21-22; Col 3:1—4 ➤ Intimacy: Is 41:8—10; 43:1—3; Acts 17:26—28 ➤ Character: Rom 5:3—4; Ps 51:6; Philip 2:12; 1Cor 15:33 ➤ Brokenness: Ps 32:3—5; 34:18; 51:17; Mt 5:3	Belonging (solidarity) – **vert. + horizontal** Body: called out & built up (Eph 4:4-6 ; Heb 10:24—25; 1Cor 12:7—30; Prov 27:17 ➤ Members of the body: Eph 4; 1Cor 12—14 ➤ *Koinonia* - Acts 2:42; Philip 1—2; 1Jn 1:3—7 ➤ Confession & healing: Is 53:5—6; Mt 10:1,8; 1Jn 1:9; Jas 5:14—16 ➤ Collective testimony: Jn 13:34—35; 1 Jn 2:7—6; Phil 2:15—16
Process	Knowing & doing – **vertical+ horizontal** Truth: unity of knowledge & action (Eph 4:7—11; Rom 12:2; Lk 10:26—28) ➤ Knowing: Lk 10:27; Phil 4:7 ➤ Growing: Eph 4:13; 5:18 ➤ Renewing: Rom 12:2; Phil 4:8 ➤ Authority: Lk 10:19; Mt 28:18 ➤ Testimony: Mt 5:14—16	Serving (loyalty) - **vert. + horizontal** Loyal to Christ (Head) & Kingdom expansion (Eph 4:12-13: 1Cor 5:18—20) ➤ mission: Is 52:7 ➤ evangelism: Mt 28:18—30; Rom 10:14—16 ➤ service: 2Cor 5:18—20 ➤ social justice: Prov 31:8—9; Mich 6:8; Mt 25:45

Lamenting the tragic fact of "Christianity in so many parts of the world is a mile wide and an inch deep because we think faith is best transmitted to people by preachers standing behind pulpits," J. Lee Grady proposed a "Five 'I's' of Discipleship" (i.e.

identify, invest, include, instruct, and intercede) that is relationally high touch.[123]

The description of how Jesus trained his disciples in the Gospel books is inspiring as Packham observed below:

> "Jesus was able to command others to follow him, but his approach to leading these followers was to build close relationships where he taught in small groups, challenged, mentored, and answered their questions...Our behaviour as a leader is prescribed by being "in Christ" and by <u>our being transformed daily</u> into His likeness, regardless of the outcomes. Viewed from this perspective our leadership approach is not optional. There is a way in which we are to lead and relate according to God's own heart and this then produces <u>an outcome that is glorifying to God</u>, whether or not the organisation meets with material success."[124] (emphasis added)

The way Jesus trained future leaders in Matthew's Gospel in terms of goal, focus, strategy and evaluations/success is listed in Table 14.

Table 14: Jesus Trains Future Leaders in Matthew's Gospel[125]

Element	Jesus' Relational Training
What to be achieved	Followers of the Leader who are willing to lay down their lives for HIS kingdom mission
Focus	Character formation with a heavy emphasis on humility and right relationships
Strategy	Invites people to follow, teaches didactically, occasionally and through example
Success /evaluation	Obedience (7:24–27), perseverance (10). Anti-success: miracle workers (7:21-23), "great ones" (20:25), contemporary religious leaders (23)

---

[123] Grady, J. Lee. "Why Relational Discipleship Has Become My Priority." *Charisma Magazine*, 2012. http://www.charismamag.com/blogs/fire-in-my-bones/15296-why-relational-discipleship-has-become-my-priority. (access October 1, 2016).

[124] Peckham, Jeremy, "Relational Leadership"

[125] Notes by Rob Penner from doctoral class DIS 715 at Western Seminary, Spring 2015.

Churches within the "Relational Discipleship Network" (RDN) use "the SCMD methodology" (i.e. Share, Connect, Minister, and Disciple) in a cyclical pattern for reproductive discipleship as shown in the figure below:[126]

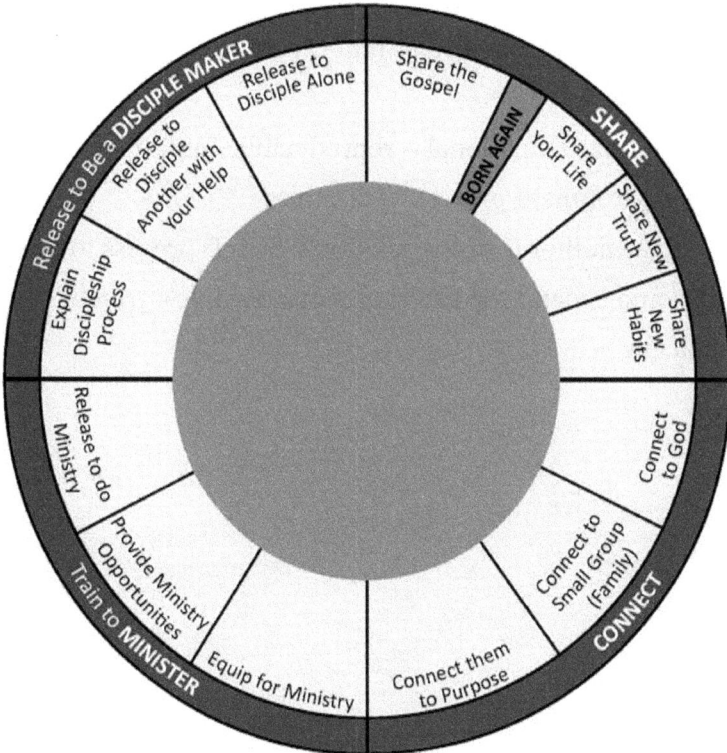

Figure 8: SCMD Methodology (Share, Connect, Minister, Disciple)

---

[126] Putman, Jim. Relational Discipleship Network (RDN) 2016 @ http://relationaldiscipleshipnetwork.com/looking-for-a-new-discipleship-method-maybe-we-should-return-to-something-old-the-way-jesus-made-disciples/ (accessed 10/1/2016).

Jim Putman in his paper entitled "Real Life Discipleship"[127] summarized three keys to the success of the discipleship of Jesus as follows:

1. Jesus was an intentional leader in every sense.
2. He did his disciple-making in a **relational environment.**
3. He followed a process that can be learned and repeated. In other words,

An intentional + relational + reproducible = infinite number
leader environment process of disciples

The author uses the relational SCMD process to further explain and expand the five stages of a disciple's growth graphically below:

---

[127] Putman, Jim. "Real Life Discipleship,"
2016. http://www.heartlandchurchnetwork.com/uploads/5/8/1/6/58163279/rea l_life_discipleship_1.pdf. (accessed Oct. 1, 2016).

Figure 9: Process of Discipleship: 5 Stages of A Disciple's Growth with a Reproductive Pattern[128]

In a book format, he proposed a five-step approach for implementing the discipleship ministry in a local church. [129]

---

[128] Ibid.

[129] Jim Putman, *DiscipleShift: Five Steps That Help Your Church to Make Disciples Who Make Disciples* (Exponential Series). HarperCollins Christian Pub. 2013.

Kleber D. Gonçalves tackled issues of urbanization, globalization and postmodernism in a paper entitled "Missional Models of a Church for Postmoderns in Urban Contexts"[130] then suggested "link model" - a highly relational approach of discipleship for missional church within the urban and post-modernist context.

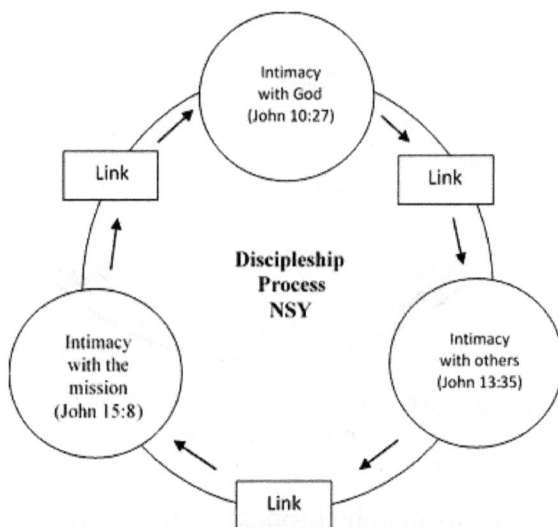

Figure 10: The Link Model Diagram[131]

There are various models of discipleship but the relational elements (vertical + horizontal) are key to them all. The following quotation is just a case in point.

A growing connection with God leads one to a deepening understanding of the relationship with him through the

---

[130] Goncalves, Kleber D. "Missional Models of a Church for Postmoderns in Urban Contexts." *Journal of Adventist Mission Studies*10, no. 95 (2014): 82–99 .http://digitalcommons.andrews.edu/cgi/viewcontent.cgi?article=1279&context =jams. (accessed Oct. 1, 2016).

[131] Ibid.

revelation of his Word; the resultant more selfless, growing connection with others as disciples who obey God's command to love others as themselves results in their ministering to the needs of those others. All the models that deal with discipling others involve disciples in one way or another equipping others through teaching, nurturing, or example to grow in spiritual maturity as they in turn begin to disciple still others.[132]

There are two levels of Christian discipleship (i.e. personal and community) with relationship at the core of the entire process of disciple-making as shown in the table below.

[132] Beagles, Kathleen. "Growing Disciples in Community: A Review of Scripture and Social Science." *Andrews University Seminary Studies:* 48, no. 1, Andrews University Press, (2010): 81–108.

Table 15: Growing Disciples in Community Model: Conceptual Framework[133]

PERSONAL PROCESSES OF CHRISTIAN DISCIPLESHIP   The processes through which an individual Christian grows in spiritual maturity and fruit-bearing (John 15:5-8).

UNDERSTANDING Learning the truth of God's relationship with humanity through Jesus Christ, the Word (John 8:31; Matt 4:4).	*MINISTERING* Participating in God's mission of revelation, reconciliation, and restoration (Matt 25:40; 28:19, 20).

CONNECTING   "Loving God completely, ourselves correctly, and others compassionately" (Boa, 25ff.; Matt 22:37-38; John 13:35).
"All Christians are disciples and are called to participate in the discipleship process,   ⇓⇑   both by receiving instruction and living out their faith for others to see and imitate" (Samra, 234).
EQUIPPING   Intentionally walking "alongside other disciples in order to encourage, equip, and challenge one another in love to grow toward maturity in Christ" (Ogden, 129; Deut 6:4-9; Eph 4:15-16).
COMMUNITY PROCESS OF CHRISTIAN DISCIPLING   The "discipleship living" within the "body of Christ" (local church, Christian home, Christian friends, Christian teachers) that impacts others' attitudes toward and engagement in the individual processes of maturing as a disciple.

As evangelical Christians, we have a high view of Scripture which is to be the guide and ground of our belief and behavior. Its importance in the process of discipleship (i.e. changing our

---

133 Ibid.

cognition, volition and affection) is clearly shown in the figure below.

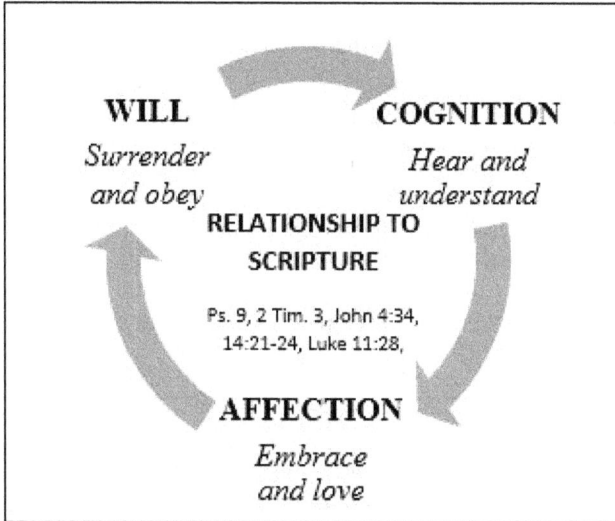

WILL — Surrender and obey

COGNITION — Hear and understand

RELATIONSHIP TO SCRIPTURE

Ps. 9, 2 Tim. 3, John 4:34, 14:21-24, Luke 11:28,

AFFECTION — Embrace and love

Figure 11: Multi-dynamic Relationship to Scripture[134]

Steve Addison, author of *Movements that Change the World*, has stated well regarding the change of head, heart and hands in the process of discipleship:

> Jesus' teaching was obedience oriented. His model of training assumed that the disciples did not know something until they had learned to obey it. He trained the head, the heart, and the hands of His disciples and expected them to pass on what they learned to others.[135]

---

[134] Chittum, "Unmasking Consumerism," 105.
[135] Addison, Steve. *Movements That Change the World: Five Keys to Spreading the Gospel.* Downers Grove, IL: IVP Books, 2011, 95.

Jim Putman's [136] emphasis on discipleship is also closely tied in with head, heart, and hands as shown in the two tables below.

Table 16: Relational Discipleship Reflects Holistic Transformation[137]

NATURE	The indication of spiritual transformation	The expectation for kings (Deut. 17:14-20)	The High Priestly prayer (John 17)	The early church practices (Acts 2:42-47)
HEART	*Committed with loyalty to Christ* (Matt. 22:37, 1 John 3:23)	Heart not lifted up above his brothers, fear of the Lord	I ask . . . for those who will believe in me	Praised God, prayed, broke bread, devotion
HEAD	*Disciplined by God's Truth* (John 8:31–32, 1 John 3:24)	Write out the law, keep it with him, read it all the days of his life	That they also may be sanctified in truth	Devoted to the apostles' teaching
HANDS	*Displaying a Christ-like lifestyle* (1 John 2:17, 3:23)	Keeping all the words of this law and these statutes, and doing them	That they may become perfectly one	Devoted to each other, glad and sincere hearts
Rejection of consumerism and materialism	Do not collect many horses, wives, or excess silver and gold	Unifying love for God and others instead of the world	Sold possessions and distributed the proceeds to those in need

---

[136] Jim Putman, "Real Life Discipleship."
[137] Chittum, "Unmasking Consumerism," 118.

Table 17: Expectation for a King's Multi-Dynamic Relationship to Scripture[138]

Nature	Relationship to Scripture	Expectations for kings
Head	Hear and understand	He shall write for himself in a book a copy of this law (Deut. 17:18)
Heart	Embrace and love	It shall be with him, and he shall read in it all the days of his life (Deut. 17:19)
Hands	Surrender and obey	That he may learn to fear the LORD his God by keeping all the words of this law and these statutes, and doing them (Deut. 17:20)

Changes in the process of discipleship are not just personal and internal; there are objective, observable, and impactful social consequences as shown in the figure below.

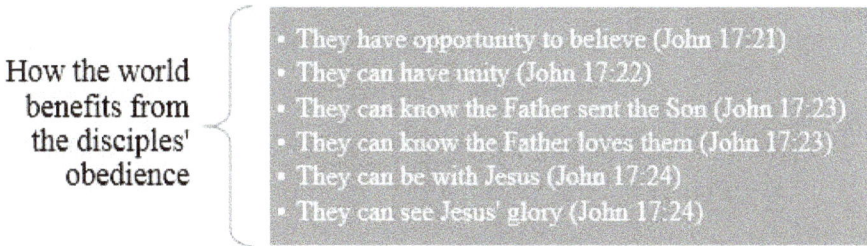

How the world benefits from the disciples' obedience

- They have opportunity to believe (John 17:21)
- They can have unity (John 17:22)
- They can know the Father sent the Son (John 17:23)
- They can know the Father loves them (John 17:23)
- They can be with Jesus (John 17:24)
- They can see Jesus' glory (John 17:24)

Figure 12: How the World Benefits from the Disciples' Obedience[139]

In this last part of chapter four, we have demonstrated the importance and advantages of integrating relational realism paradigm with discipleship both at the individual and institutional levels. These ideas have been presented in detail due to their special relevance to relational realism within the context of Christian ministry.

---

138 Ibid., 119.
139 Ibid., 122.

Summary

Educational theory and practice is clearly an important topic to consider as part of the concept of mission training. This chapter has attempted to identify the educational theory that best fits the content area in which we are interested. In other words, what kind of training best prepares adult learners from one culture to enter gospel work in another culture? In this chapter, we have found that such training should include certain key elements:

We are training adults and so adult education methods are essential.

We are training for a task that is both cognitive and practical, and so methods need to give practical, experience-based accomplishment, not simply cognitive understanding. Tools such as experience-based teaching, mentoring and coaching can be powerful in providing training that is at once cognitive, practical, and relational.

We are training for work in a highly relational task, and so training needs to include both skill/knowledge acquisition AND relational interaction.

Equally important, training for mission by nature requires that one reconsider the cultural beliefs and values of Christianity as practiced in the homeland. Some of those values and beliefs will be validated; some may well be corrected through biblical interaction with other cultures. Christian workers need to be shaped through deliberate application of transformative education that challenges the cultural expression of Christianity as practiced in the home culture, giving room for scripturally valid Christian expression in the new cultural context. This transformative education of the worker, to be better prepared to enter unreached parts of the world, is at once a horizontal and vertical task. It is at once the role of the gifted individuals within the church and the witness of the Christian community as a whole.

Chapter Five
Specialized Educational Forms

Introduction

A variety of specialized forms of education are relevant to the task of preparing missionaries. In this chapter, we will look at current trends in theological education, comparative education, explicitly Christian education, intercultural education, and specific approaches at training people for intercultural Christian ministry.

Theological Education

Edward Farley traced the development of theological education in the United States through three stages.[140] The first of these is what he called the "pre-seminary" days from A.D. 1700 – 1800. The subsequent stage, which developed around A.D. 1800, paralleled the university system and its increasing specialization. During that period seminary training developed around a fourfold model that included specialized training in Scripture, Dogma, Church History, and Practical Theology. That last area of

---

140 Farley, Edward. *Theologia: The Fragmentation and Unity of Theological Education.* Philadelphia: Fortress Pr, 1983. 6, 7, 78, 89.

specialization (practical theology) became the focal point of pastoral preparation which, in Farley's third stage of theological education, tended toward an attitude of professionalism within the seminary environment.

While Farley did not specifically mention the implications of this developmental sequence in terms of missionary preparation, there are points in common between missionary and pastoral preparation in that "practical theology" branch of the seminary. Missionary training, to the extent that it happens in seminary settings, is often seen as a form of "practical theology" rather than as a natural outgrowth of the very nature of God and his revelation. The historic separation of disciplines within the seminary has led to the criticism that God's activities are presented as distinct from his person.[141]

Fortunately, new voices are suggesting more unified approaches to theological education, to avoid the false dichotomy between that which is "theology" and that which is "practical." In terms of theological preparation for missionary service, the work of John Piper has been particularly important in tying the mission of the church tightly to biblical and theological studies.[142] Another recent author who ties together theology and ministry is Ray Anderson in his volume, *The Shape of Practical Theology*.[143]

---

[141] I am indebted to D. James O'Neill for this phrase, one that he has used in many classroom and missionary training activities.

[142] Piper, John. *Let the Nations Be Glad!: The Supremacy of God in Missions*. Grand Rapids, MI: Baker Pub Group, 1993.

[143] Anderson, Ray S. *The Shape of Practical Theology: Empowering Ministry with Theological Praxis*. 1/16/01 edition. Downers Grove, IL: IVP Academic, 2001.

Another author who has called for a new approach to theological education is Robert Banks. He has called for "a new form of ministry formation that preserves all that is valuable in our present model yet also goes beyond it."[144] He outlined six areas that could be improved in theological training (and, by extension, in missionary training).

1. Theological education must occur within the larger community of believers, not simply focusing on the academic training of an elite core.

2. Theological training must include in-service ministry activities where intellectual, spiritual and practical concerns "form a seamless whole."[145]

3. Training should include a season of time devoted to a living and working partnership with a person experienced in ministry.

4. A clear break from previous occupational and living arrangements is necessary for the theological student, in order to mirror the common scriptural pattern of leaving the familiar so as to follow God and his plan.

5. Strong connections between the seminary and the local church need to be cultivated.

6. Mentoring in one-on-one or small group environments follows the model of Paul's ministry.

---

144 Banks, Robert. *Re-Envisioning Theological Education: Exploring a Missional Alternative to Current Models.* Grand Rapids, MI: William B Eerdmans Publishing Co, 2000, 262.
145 Ibid. 127.

As Robert Banks and others have written and reflected on beneficial revisions to the theory and practice of theological education, other authors have suggested entirely new patterns and structures. The work of Jeff Reed of BILD International is illustrative. The "Paradigm Papers" published on that organization's web site speak of theological education which is church-based rather than focused on academic theological institutions. The BILD organization seeks to promote a new level of church-based mission outreach.[146] The "Paradigm Papers" offer critique of the current status of theological education and mission practice, followed by the outline of a new approach by which churches network together to promote and facilitate international mission outreach.

One final source that is relevant to the concept of theological education as it pertains to missionary training is in the area of curriculum design. Working from "learning outcomes focus," Leroy Ford's work in curriculum design gave a detailed model for the development of curricula in theology, including the academic side of missionary preparation. This work is tied to institutional models of education, and shows the logical sequence of thought beginning with an institution's overall focus and moving toward the precise wording of goals and objectives,

---

[146] Jeff Reed, "Church-Based Missions: Creating a New Paradigm" (1992) and "Church-Based Theological Education: Creating a New Paradigm" (1992). <www.BILD.org.>, accessed Dec 6, 2015.

teaching methods, learning activities, testing and evaluation, and course descriptions.[147]

Comparative Education

Since the mid-1950s, education as it is practiced in diverse cultures of the world has been the subject of the field of comparative education. Societies display various approaches to such activities as the framing of educational goals, the development of educational methods, and the process of educational evaluation.[148] Even the concept of knowledge differs among the peoples of the world, and so it is to be expected that different cultures would approach the transmission of knowledge in different manners.[149]

Preferences in terms of what is considered an ideal environment for teaching and learning also vary among peoples. The primary categories of learning modes have been identified as "formal, informal and nonformal."[150] Those three terms were coined by Philip Coombs and Manzoor Ahmed in A.D. 1974. As they define these modes of learning, informal refers to a "lifelong process by which every person acquires and accumulates

---

146 Ford, Leroy. *A Curriculum Design Manual for Theological Education: A Learning Outcomes Focus*. Nashville, TN: Baptist Sunday School Board, 1991.
148 One example of helpful literature in this discipline is Thomas, R. Murray, ed. *International Comparative Education: Practices, Issues, & Prospects*. 1st edition. Oxford England, New York: Pergamon, 1990.
149 William K. Cummings, "Evaluation and Examinations. Why and How are Educational Outcomes Assessed," In *International Comparative Education: Practices, Issues, & Prospects*. 1st edition. Oxford England ; New York: Pergamon, 1990: 87–106.

knowledge, skills, attitudes, and insights from daily experience and exposure to the environment."[151] Formal learning is that which is marked by a "highly institutionalized, chronologically graded and hierarchally structured education system."[152] Nonformal learning occurs in the context of, "organized, systematic, educational activity carried on outside the framework of the formal system."[153]

The training of missionaries needs to intentionally incorporate the implications of comparative educational studies. As R. Murray Thomas pointed out, Christian mission helped to develop educational systems around the world, yet those systems were "to a great extent modeled after European and North American school systems."[154] Lois McKinney made the same point when she wrote,

> Most of us who have taught across cultures are at least vaguely aware that learners in other contexts have needs, thinking styles and pedagogical expectations which are different from our own. We wonder how to contextualize our instruction in the light of those differences."[155]

---

[149] Thomas J. LaBelle and Judy J. Sylvester, "Delivery Systems – Formal, nonformal and informal." in *International Comparative Education: Practices, Issues, & Prospects*. 1st edition. Oxford England, New York: Pergamon, 1990:141–160.
[151] Coombs, Professor Philip H., ed. *Attacking Rural Poverty: How Nonformal Education Can Help*. Baltimore: The Johns Hopkins University Press, 1974, 8.
[152] Coombs and Ahmed, 8.
[153] Ibid., 8.
[154] R. Murray Thomas, in *International Comparative Education*, 4.
[155] McKinney, Lois. "Contextualizing Instruction: Contributions to Missiology from the Field of Education." *Missiology, An International Review* 12, no. 3 (July 1984). 311.

McKinney's article outlined three specific foci in which contextualization of educational styles should occur:

1. Instruction needs to be contextualized to the needs of the learners.

2. Instruction needs to be contextualized to the needs of the communities.

3. Instruction needs to be contextualized to the ways people think and learn.

She went on to point out that such contextualization takes place using appropriate educational methods and appropriate media.[156]

Howard[157] reached similar conclusions, calling the international educator to consider six factors in the establishment of methods and materials:

1. The nature of the learning objectives;

2. The available technology for a given cultural context;

3. The sociopolitical conditions in which the instruction takes place, by which an available technology might or might not be an appropriate technology;

4. Accommodation to individual differences among learners;

5. The teacher's skills, knowledge and preferred instructional style;

---

[156] Ibid., 311.
[157] Jiaying Zhuang Howard, "Instructional Methods and Materials" in *International Comparative Education: Practices, Issues, & Prospects.* 1st edition. Oxford England, New York: Pergamon, 1990, 59–84.

6. The location of the teacher and the location of the learner. There are times when distance learning is an appropriate option.

Among these issues of contextualization is one which bears emphasizing, and that is the realm of cognitive styles. McKinney mentioned this as one of the three areas of study which are particularly important for mission[158] and also as one point in which contextualization is essential.[159]Another author, Peter Chang, not only developed the concept more deeply, but illustrated the differences in epistemological preferences between Eastern and Western cultures.[160] These authors have argued that from one culture to another people differ in their preferred patterns of thought. Thus, for instance, Western thought patterns are typically linear, presenting a fairly direct series of arguments that lead to a given conclusion. Many other cultures take a more highly contextualized approach to thinking. In those "contextualized" thought patterns, reasoning occurs as people think about not only a given problem, but all of the attendant circumstances which are associated with that problem.

A recent publication at the popular level illustrates the power of this comparative approach. *The Geography of Thought: How Asians and Westerners Think Differently, and Why* points to both the intercultural dynamic that marks the 21st century, and

---

[158] McKinney-Douglas, "Learning Theories," 569.
[159] McKinney, "Contextualizing Instruction," 315.
[160] Chang, Peter. "Steak, Potato, Peas and Chopsuey. Linear and Non-Linear Thinking in Theological Education." *Evangelical Review of Theology* 5, no. 2 (1981).

also to the importance of understanding and appreciating the different ways that human thinking can occur.[161]

The paramount challenge of comparative education provides a final useful element which arises from the discipline. This field exists, according to Wolfgang Mitter, in order to consider both the universal state of human teaching/learning and also the particular principles of education within a given cultural group.[162] The wording used by Mitter is suggestive of the Trinitarian literature which speaks of the simultaneous importance of both the universal and the particular – of overarching human themes and the specific cultural preferences of a particular people group.

Explicitly Christian Philosophy of Education

The wide spectrum of approaches to education that has been presented in this chapter is consistent with the plethora of approaches which are used and promoted in our contemporary educational context. Missionaries are today being prepared for service under paradigms of training touched by general pedagogical principles and by principles specific to the adult learner. Missionary preparation also includes elements that are

---

161 Nisbett, Richard E. *The Geography of Thought: How Asians and Westerners Think Differently...and Why.* Reprint edition. New York: Free Press, 2004.
162 Wolfgang Mitter, "Challenges to Comparative Education – between Retrospect and Expectation," in *Tradition, Modernity, and Post-Modernity in Comparative Education.* Dordrecht Netherlands, Boston: Kluwer Academic Publishers published in cooperation with UNESCO Institute for Education, Hamburg, 1997, 407.

specifically focused on theological education and cross-cultural education, and which are informed by an understanding of the role that culture plays in setting preferences of learning styles. One final area of interest in this review of trends in education has to do with the development of educational philosophies and methods that are uniquely and explicitly Christian.

The Christian school movement, with its roots in the middle of the 20th century, developed a genre of literature and a way of thinking about education which takes its genesis from the Bible. Authors such as Frank Gaebelein pointed out that the educational theory of the secular classroom grows from assumptions which are contrary to scriptural revelation, and that it is therefore important to integrate Christian educational philosophical foundations with all of the activities and methodologies of a Christian educational system.[163] In his review of Gaebelein's ministry, William Falkner pointed out that Gaebelein was "convinced that much of Christian education falls short of living up" to the proper integration of Christian faith and academic excellence.[164]

Christian educators have identified at least three reasons for the development of expressly Christian philosophy of education. Ruth Armstrong understood that a Christian view of learning will differ from a secular view in terms of "the nature of

---

[163] Gaebelein, Frank E. Christian *Education in a Democracy*. New York: Oxford Univ. Press, 1951, 284.
[164] Falkner, William F, "Gaebelein, Frank" in *Evangelical Dictionary of Christian Education*. Grand Rapids, MI: Baker Academic, 2001, 308.

the learner and the learning process."[165] Cornelius Van Til added a more universal reason why Christian education must be approached differently than secular education when he wrote that Christian schools serve,

> the one Triune, self-sufficient, sovereign God of the Bible, and if they claim to teach that the Bible is the absolute authority for life and learning, then it clearly follows that the Christian philosophy of education . . .must be in complete antithesis to non-Christian educational philosophy, for non-Christians do not claim to serve God, nor do they claim to live or educate by Biblical authority.[166]

The conclusion reached by many Christian educators is that educational paradigms by and for Christians should take a different approach than the approaches seen outside of the Christian community. Robert Pazmiño framed the call for a Christian philosophy of education in the language of contextualization when he wrote,

> All Christian educators, even those most enamored with practice itself, have philosophies or theories with which they operate. Without attention to philosophical foundations, Christian educators have wandered in the deserts of cultural accommodation or cultural irrelevance and have failed to provide that vision necessary to guide their generation and those to come in relating God's truth,

---

[165] Ruth M. Armstrong, "A Christian Approach to Learning Theory" in Norman De Jung, ed. *Christian Approaches to Learning Theory: A Symposium*. Lanham, MD; [Palos Heights, Ill.: University Press of America; Trinity Christian College, 1984]. 3.

[166] Cornelius Van Til, quoted in Gregory J. Maffet, "A Scriptural Model of the Learner – A Van Tillian Perspective" in Norman De Jong, ed, *Christian Approaches to Learning Theory: Vol. 2; the Nature of the Learner*. Lanham: University Press of America, 1985. 27. Original quote from Van Til, Cornelius. *Essays on Christian Education*. Nutley, N.J.: Presbyterian and Reformed Pub. Co., 1974, 79–82.

in its beauty and wholeness, to the task of Christian education. It is no longer possible to affirm this irresponsible approach and claim to be faithful.[167]

In terms of the importance of a consistently Christian philosophy of education, Pazmiño offered a definition of Christian education as, "the process of sharing or gaining distinctive of the Christian story and truth (information) and fostering the change of persons, communities, societies, and structures (transformation) by the power of the Holy Spirit to a fuller expression of God's reign in Jesus Christ."[168] Pazmiño noted how this definition differs significantly from other authors in that there are three focal points for the Christian educator: content, persons, and context (in which he includes the local community, the general culture, and the immediate educational setting). This definition allows for the dynamic interplay of information, spiritual and moral formation, and transformation.[169]

Another distinctive element in Pazmino's definition of Christian education is seen in the title of his book, *God our Teacher*. The explicit assumption that God the Holy Spirit is actively involved in teaching/learning relationships is a significant and crucial point for relational paradigm training.

Robert Pazmiño's insightful work not only called attention to the unique nature of Christian education, but he also offered a

---

[167] Pazmiño, Robert W. *Foundational Issues in Christian Education: An Introduction in Evangelical Perspective*. Grand Rapids, MI: Baker Books, 1997, 122.
[168] Ibid., 44.
[169] Pazmiño, Robert W. *Principles and Practices of Christian Education: An Evangelical Perspective*. Grand Rapids, MI: Baker Book House, 1992, 44.

model of Christian education which fit the definition he provided. Of particular interest is the fact that Pazmiño's volume titled *God Our Teacher – Theological Basics in Christian Education* is a deliberate attempt at forming Christian education upon a Trinitarian theological foundation.[170] He based his model of Christian education upon what he called three "forms" of education and three "principles" of education.

In terms of "forms," Pazmiño used that word to describe three basic sets of relationships key to the Christian educator. The first of these is a simultaneous consideration of persons, context, and content. That is to say, Pazmiño called educators to simultaneously consider all of the people who are involved in a given educational setting, the context in which the education takes place, and the content that must be imparted in the educational setting.

The second "form" that Pazmiño highlighted refers to what he called the five tasks of Christian education. The church exists, in Pazmiño's understanding, for worship, proclamation, community, service, and advocacy. Christian educators must approach their ministry with a view toward the simultaneous development of students in each of these five tasks.

Finally, specifically in view of classical Trinitarian theological formulations, Pazmiño wrote that Christian educators need to see life in terms of unity, differentiation, and order.

---

[170] Pazmiño, Robert W. *God Our Teacher: Theological Basics in Christian Education*. Grand Rapids, MI: Baker Academic, 2001.

Humanity is joined in unity, and yet there are distinguishing characteristics particularly between the believing and the non-believing worlds. In that context of unity and diversity, there is a divine order that defines the preeminence of our relationship with God over and against (when necessary) our unity with other humans.

Pazmiño's model of education also focused on three "principles" that he said must be part of the Christian experience. The first of these "principles" is the centrality of transformation as the goal of Christian education. The second "principle" is that of connectedness, in that human beings are all interconnected and so community is part of the reality of Christian education. The third "principle," again drawn from explicitly Trinitarian considerations, is what the author called the "Galilean principle." This principle calls educators to involve learners in both "huddling" with other Christians for edification and worship, and in "mixing" with the world in witness and service. The factors of the unity of all humanity and the differentiation of believers as distinct from non-believers gave rise to that "huddle and mix" formulation.[171]

Pazmiño offered one other useful and innovative concept in his consideration of Christian education. He took to task the assumption that education must be either learner-centered, society-centered, or content-centered. Pazmiño, in this discussion,

---

[171] Ibid., 12.

referred to the work of educator Hollis L. Caswell[172] who wrote in 1935. Caswell described three possible foci for education: education can center on the content, on the student, or on the society in general. These three options in fact have become key dividing lines between various philosophies of education; so that, for instance, liberal arts education is said to be content (or curriculum) centered, behavioral educators favor student-centered approaches, and John Dewey or Paulo Freire seek the good of society as the central organizing principle of their models.

Pazmiño[173] rejected the assumption that a Christian educator is limited to only one of those three options. He developed what he called a "God-centered" approach. The benefit of reeognizing God in the center of educational schemes is that His presence allows a simultaneous consideration of the real needs of learners, curriculum (or content) questions, and social good. Thus with one eye on the fact of God's centrality in the issues of life – including the issues of education – one can see content, learner, and society in their correct relationship to one another. To use Trinitarian language, by seeing God at the center of educational theory and practice, it is possible to develop a both/and conceptual relationship between God, content, persons, and society at large.

---

[172] Caswell, Hollis L, and Doak S Campbell. Curriculum Development. New York; Cincinnati: American Book Co., 1935, 141 – 189, cited in Pazmiño, *Principles and Practices*, 17.
[173] Pazmiño, *Principles and Practices*, 17.

Two other authors have made foundational contributions to the discipline of Christian education. The first of these two authors is D. Bruce Lockerbie. Lockerbie summarized his philosophy of education by using the Greek word *paideia*. As Lockerbie defined and described this word, it was used by ancient Greeks to discuss the outcomes desired in their educational activities – outcomes that sought to instill in the learner all of the knowledge and ability needed to be a profitable member of his society. Lockerbie tied this term into the concept of Christian education when he wrote,

> For the educated man of the New Testament age, the word that applies [to education] is *paideia*, meaning the full exposure of the human being to culture, knowledge of literature, the arts, athletics, ethics and religious duty. This was the curriculum of Greek education, taught by *paideutes*, assisted by a *paidagogos*, from which we have our English word pedagogy. St. Paul knew and used these words, urging his readers to bring up our children in the *paideia* of the Lord, reminding his readers that all Scripture is useful for teaching and *paideia* in righteousness.[174]

What this has to do with Christian education in the 21st century is explained when Lockerbie wrote that a Christian *paideia* is "this process of training the whole person to think and act like a Christian."[175] Others have used the term "holistic" to describe the same idea, an approach to education that is not

---

[174] Lockerbie, D. Bruce. *Thinking and Acting like a Christian*. Portland, Or.: Multnomah, 1989, 68.
[175] Ibid., 68.

simply academic, nor even limited to the cognitive, affective, and psychomotor domains made famous by Benjamin Bloom.[176] For the Christian educator, the concept of a *paideia* education – one that brings the learner into increasing understanding and skill of all of the issues involved in a Christian approach to life – is a welcome and useful tool.

The final Christian educator that has made recent contributions helpful to the development of missionaries is C. Doug Bryan. He developed an approach to education that focused on what he called "relationship learning."[177] Bryan's perspective was summarized around a call for Christian education to aim for restoration and growth in four key relationships: to God, to self, to others, and to the created order. Bryan's work drew largely upon Deuteronomy 6 to build a model of education that ties knowledge, attitudes, performance, and understanding in all subject matter with the result being growth in those four key relationships. Other authors, notably George Knight, also have focused on relationships as the key focal point of Christian education. When describing the purposes of education, Knight described redemption and reconciliation as the central purposes, seeking the restoration of a relationship with God and the restoration of the likeness of God in

---

176 Bloom, Benjamin. *Taxonomy of Educational Objectives, Book 1 Cognitive Domain.* New York: Longman, Inc., 1956, 6–7.
177 Bryan, C. Doug. *Relationship Learning: A Primer in Christian Education.* Nashville, TN: Broadman Press, 1990.

the hearts of fallen humanity.[178] The significance of this phrase for a relational paradigm training program is hard to miss.

Intercultural Training

In light of the globalization of the late 20th and early 21st centuries, yet another theoretical sub-discipline has important implications for the training of missionaries. The study of and training for intercultural life and work has become an important issue in business, academic, military, and political spheres besides its obvious importance for those seeking to minister in intercultural contexts.

L. Robert Kohls, together with his colleague Herbert Brussow, has written and taught extensively on this issue. He wrote that seven issues are of primary importance for the training of workers for cross-cultural work:[179]

1. Different approaches to training are appropriate for different cultures.
2. We need to be aware of the hidden; but obtrusive cultural assumptions that underlie all of our statements and actions.
3. Training for the cross-cultural sojourner needs to include both awareness of general principles of cross-cultural life

---

178 Knight, 194.
179 Kohls, L. Robert, and Brussow, Herbert L. *Training Know-How for Cross Cultural and Diversity Trainers*. Duncanville, TX: Adult Learning Systems, 1995, 46–50.

and work and also content about the specific cultural traits of the receiving culture.

4. Content is important for the cross-cultural worker, and so is the process by which that content is learned. Kohls suggested that the trainer's role is best understood as a facilitator, a coach, rather than as an authoritative teacher.

5. Cross-cultural training should be approached from the perspective of behavioral objectives.

6. There are two primary obstacles to the training of effective cross-cultural workers. The first obstacle is an attitude which seeks a simple list of appropriate behaviors for the receiving culture, as opposed to an attitude of wanting to learn how to learn. The second counterproductive attitude is to oversimplify the commonalities between cultures, arriving at the reductionist conclusion that all people are alike. This simplistic generalization allows the cross-cultural sojourner to feel justified at learning only the superficial differences between home culture and host culture.

7. Finally, training materials need to be developed.

Kohls and his colleagues explained cross-cultural training to be a sort of adult education.[180] They approached their topic from a perspective of behavioral objectives. They understood the student to be self-directed, participating in the learning process, and motivated by a desire to solve problems that are personally

---

[180] Ibid., 63–65.

relevant. The trainer's role, according to Kohls, is to facilitate and coach as the learner looks for solutions to his or her own problem areas. Two tools that Kohls described for cross-cultural training are games and role-playing situations. As learners evaluate their performance in these illustrative situations, they become increasingly aware of their need to develop better strategies for facing cross-cultural tensions.[181]

In the years since Kohls wrote, insights into intercultural training have become increasingly sophisticated. One of the recent approaches to the identification and sending of skillful intercultural workers is the seen in the body of work on intercultural competency. Though varying authors and schools of thought include different elements to the idea of intercultural competency, yet there are identifiable components.[182] Working from a grounded theory model, Darla Deardorff identified five important categories for intercultural competence:

1. Attitudes: respect, openness, curiosity, and discovery.
2. Knowledge: cultural self-awareness, culture specific knowledge, deep culture knowledge including other worldviews, and sociolinguistic awareness.
3. Skills: observation, listening, evaluating, analyzing, interpreting, and relating.

---

181 Kohls, L. Robert, and John M Knight. *Developing Intercultural Awareness: A Cross-Cultural Training Handbook*. Yarmouth, ME, USA: Intercultural Press, 1994.
181 Deardorff, Darla K. "Theory Reflections: Intercultural Competence Framework/Model," n.d.https://www.nafsa.org/_/File/_/theory_connections_intercultural_competence.pdf. (Accessed October 30,2016).

4. Internal Outcomes within the sojourner: flexibility, adaptability, ethno-relative position, perspective, and empathy.

5. External Outcomes: the ability to behave and communicate effectively and appropriately in the new culture.

Researchers and intercultural consultants Ursula Brinkmann and Oscar van Weerdenburg looked at those lists of intercultural competencies, with a desire to simplify the topics by identifying which of those categories are predictive of others. In other words, their research sought to narrow the focus of intercultural competency training by putting primary attention on those competency areas which will most successfully open people to growth in other areas. Their helpful analysis led to four predictive categories, each with two subcategories:[183]

1. Intercultural Sensitivity
   a. Cultural awareness
   b. Attention to signals
2. Intercultural communication
   a. Active listening
   b. Adapting communication style
3. Building commitment
   a. Building relationships
   b. Reconciling stakeholder needs
4. Managing uncertainty

---

[183] Brinkmann, Ursula, and Oscar van Weerdenburg. *Intercultural Readiness: Four Competences for Working across Cultures*, 2014, 36.

a. Openness to cultural diversity

b. Exploring new approaches

Looking at recent work in intercultural competence, an important pattern has emerged which relates to the relational paradigm. Some authors such as Darla Deardorff ,[184] Janet M. Bennet, and Allison Abbe et al.[185] approach the topic using Benjamin Bloom's classic "cognitive, affective, and psychomotor" [186] categories of learning.

Ting-Toomey looked at intercultural competence from a different perspective, and included the ability to do "face work" as an identifiable part of cultural competence.[187] This "face" element brings relationship issues clearly into the intercultural competence discussion.

Ruth Wall of All Nations Christian College in the UK added another relational element to the discussion. First, she recognized that Bloom's learning realms grew from a particular cultural background. "Importantly, Bloom's taxonomy was developed in the context of Western academic institutions," she wrote, adding

---

[184] Deardorff, Darla K. "Identification and Assessment of Intercultural Competence as a Student Outcome of Internationalization." *J of Studies in International Education* 10, no. 241 (2006).

[185] Abbe, Allison, Lisa M. V Gulick, Jeffrey L Herman, U.S. Army Research Institute for the Behavioral and Social Sciences, and Leader Development Research Unit. Cross-Cultural Competence in Army Leaders: A Conceptual and Empirical Foundation. Arlington, VA: U.S. Army Research Institute for the Behavioral and Social Sciences, Leader Development Research Unit, 2007. http://www.hqda.army.mil/ari/pdf//SR_2008-01.pdf.2.

[186] Bloom, Benjamin. *Taxonomy of Educational Objectives, Book 1 Cognitive Domain*. New York: Longman, Inc., 1956.

[187] Stella Ting-Toomey and Kurogi, 1998. "Facework-based model of Intercultural Competence". Quoted in Deardorff, Darla K. *The Sage Handbook of Intercultural Competence*. Los Angeles, CA: Sage, 2009. 12

the marginal comment that "today we better understand ways in which Bloom's three domains are culturally shaped."[188]

Wall's reflections continued by pointing out that "all learning is both situated (cannot take place in a vacuum) and a social process."[189] To rephrase, learning happens in a context and within social relationships. In fact, her conceptualization of learning, and particularly mission learning, operate along two axes which she attributed to K. Illeris[190]: an acquisition axis that shapes thinking and feelings, and an interactive axis that focuses on skills including social skills.

How, then, does one go about training others for intercultural ministry? The intercultural competency school of thought will answer by saying that the starting point is to look for certain key personality traits, and then teach concepts, attitudes, and skills. Into that mix, some will say that relational skills are important. The continued refining of intercultural competence thought can be expected for some time, including continued expansion into yet other related fields of study.[191] One interesting

---

[188] Wall, Ruth. "Equipping the Whole Person." *Bulletin of the International Mission Training Network*, January, 2015 http://www.missionarytraining.org/mt/index.php/forum/bulletin-no-1-equipping-the-whole-person/3-equipping-the-whole-person. (Accessed October 30, 2016).

[189] Wall, 2.

[190] Illeris, Knud. *The Three Dimensions of Learning: Contemporary Learning Theory in the Tension Field between the Cognitive, the Emotional and the Social.* Copenhagen: Roskilde University Press, 2004, 227.

[191] Of special note, the July 2013 edition of the *Journal of Cross-Cultural Psychology* was devoted entirely to research on the identification and measurement of intercultural competence. Some of the topics discussed included: the role and assessment of metacognition in intercultural competence; an evaluation of multiple assessment tools that seek to assess intercultural competence; the role of

area of recent research expands the idea of intercultural competence from individuals to organizations.[192]

There is another area of recent research that is related to and yet distinct from the intercultural competence area. This is the area of cognition across cultures. Beginning with Robert Kaplan's "doodles"[193] that described thought patterns of various cultures, rhetoric studies and discourse analysis have identified different approaches to thinking and communicating. As brain research has accompanied these studies, there are now parallels seen between brain function and culture. [194] This area of research is very young, and there will be much more published on this topic in days to come. Whereas the intercultural competence school of thought seeks to find the intersection between the person and cultural skills, the new "intercultural mind"[195] looks for the connection between one's cultural background and the intuitive responses that arise within the mind of that person.

There is one strand in the intercultural school of thought that has significant relational paradigm implications. Authors

---

personality as determinant of intercultural competence; and metaknowledge of culture as one promoter of intercultural competence.

[192] Adair, Wendi L, Ivona Hideg and Jeffrey R Spence, "The Culturally Intelligent Team: the Impact of Team Cultural Intelligence and Cultural Heterogeneity on Team Shared Values," *Journal of Cross-Cultural Psychology* 2013 44:941; Also, Driel, Marinus van, and William K. Jr. Gabrenya. "Organizational Cross-Cultural Competence: Approaches to Measurement." *Journal of Cross-Cultural Psychology* 44, no. 874, 2013.

[193] Kaplan, Robert. "Cultural Thought Patterns in Intercultural Education." *Language Learning* 16, 1966.

[194] Nisbett, Richard E. *The Geography of Thought: How Asians and Westerners Think Differently...and Why.* Reprint edition. (New York: Free Press, 2004. Also Shaules, Joseph. *The Intercultural Mind: Connecting Culture, Cognition, and Global Living,* 2015).

[195] Shaules, 194.

Scollon, Scollon and Jones'[196] text on intercultural communication has a section titled, "The problem with culture." They describe the problem as being that the concept of culture is so broad that "no one seems to know exactly what it means."[197] They rightly see culture as a heuristic – a tool for thinking. It is a useful tool; but at the same time it is a tool that few can easily define. Most people find themselves using metaphors to make whatever point they wish about culture - for instance, culture is likened to an iceberg or an onion.

Seeking to avoid the metaphors, Scollon, Scollon and Jones look to discourse communities as the main place where "culture" takes place. Using the phrase, "culture is a verb," which was originally coined by anthropologist Brian Street,[198] the authors came to the conclusion that the work of culture takes place through discourse, and the work of discourse takes place in discourse communities. One implication of this flow of thought is that all people are really members of many "cultures" or, better said, many discourse communities. We all know the feeling of having one set of words and actions that we use when we are with family, words and actions that are different from our professional conversations, and different again from the words and actions seen in our place of worship. Where it might feel like it was

---

[196] Scollon, Ronald, Scollon, Suzanne B. K., and Jones, Rodney H. *Intercultural Communication: A Discourse Approach.* Chichester: John Wiley & Sons, 2012.
[197] Ibid., 3.
[198] Street, Brian V. "Culture Is a Verb." In David Graddol, Linda Thompson, and Mike Byran, eds., *Language and Culture, Papers from the Annual Meeting of the British Studies in Applied Linguistics.*, Vol. 7. Towanda, NY: British Assoc of Applied Linguistics in association with Multilingual Matters, Ltd., 1993, 23–43.

stretching the point to call each of those a distinct "culture," it is not at all a stretch to recognize that each is a unique discourse community. The rules of discourse vary between the family, the work place, and the worship center. We are all adept at shifting from one discourse community to another, and to following the appropriate and familiar forms within that particular community.

From a relational paradigm perspective, this discourse community concept is exactly right. The issue for mission work is not to learn the generalized perspectives of a wide national "culture." Neither is the important thing to identify the cultural attributes of a given ethno-linguistic group (though both of those sets of information may, in fact, give approximate help). The real point that helps an intercultural gospel messenger is to get to know a given new neighbor within the communities where that person lives, works, and worships. By narrowing the view from "ethnic group" or "national culture" to a person and his/her networks of friends, kin, neighbors, or co-workers, we in fact are now talking about a level where relationships can indeed be personal and significant.

This point was well made by J.H. Bavinck in words that are dated in terms of vocabulary but relevant in terms of concept:

> "In practice I am never concerned with Buddhism, Yet with a living person and his Buddhism. I am never in contact with Islam Yet with a Moslem and his Mohammedanism. If I seek to take a man by storm with general rules and norms derived from books, it is possible that I many miss the mark, and what I say may go over his head, because what he himself finds in his own religion, and the way in which he lives it, is something entirely different from what I had

originally thought. . ... It is not enough for me to know what a man teaches. I must also know how he experiences it."[199]

From the perspective of a relational paradigm, the focus on involvement with a specific person within the communities in which he/she interacts is exactly the point. The national and ethno-linguistic insights are of value; yet it is the local network of real people who relate to each other within communities that is the focal point for mission in the relational paradigm.

Intercultural communication is also a field which is germane to the training of missionaries. Recent developments about the nature of language are of value to the discussion on relational realism.

Traditional understanding of language would suggest that human speech or writing carries cognitive and affective content. Missionary training, in fact, has focused on the concept of language as the vehicle or the carrier of concepts.

In a world where good translations are available, then, why should an intercultural sojourner learn the language? Isn't it possible to get an idea across with a good translation program or personal interpreter? If that which is shared through language is just cognitive or emotional, that would seem to be a reasonable approach.

---

[199] Bavinck, J. H. *An Introduction to the Science of Missions.* Philadelphia: Presbyterian and Reformed Pub. Co., 1960, 2:240, 242. Quoted in Smith, Donald K. *Creating Understanding: A Handbook for Christian Communication Across Cultural Landscapes.* Grand Rapids, MI: Zondervan, 1992, 122.

Joseph Shaules in his book, *The Intercultural Mind*, asks that same question.[200] His conclusion is that the "information-centric" view of language is at best a superficial evaluation of what happens when people share a language. The deeper, and truer, view of language is that it carries experiences. As people share language, they share experiences both at a personal and at a community level. The youth group that shares its newest slang is really creating an experience. When an adult tries to use that language it comes across as amusing or embarrassing precisely because the adult is not part of that shared experience. Likewise, when a newcomer into a community tries to learn language without sharing experiences it is not accepted. When the experiences are truly shared, though, the language carries a sense of commonality not just at the level of meaning but of experience.

It would be incorrect to say that language does not carry information or emotion. Clearly both of those are involved. Yet the concept of shared experience is key to understanding communication, and has a particularly important role to play in intercultural communication from a relational perspective. Relationship is the basic reality of life; primarily, relationship with the Trinity and secondarily, the horizontal relationships between humans. A relational paradigm will encourage learning languages because that creates interactive, relational, shared experiences[201].

---

[200] Shaules, Joseph. *The intercultural Mind*. 187–188.

[201] Jim Harries and the organization, Vulnerable Mission are particularly good examples of practitioners of this "shared experience" perspective. Their encouragement is the use of local language because of their shared worldview and experiences that may

Alongside the growth in intercultural competence and insights into culture at the ethnic, national, or community level, we are also experiencing growing awareness that there are cultural preferences for learning and teaching. David Kolb provided early analysis of learning styles across cultures. His foundational work distinguished four areas within a cycle of learning: concrete experience to reflective observation, on to abstract conceptualization, and then active experimentation.[202]

Other cultural elements have also been identified as important to teaching/learning; for instance, the relational aspects of culturally appropriate teacher/student interactions can be seen in Hofstede's work.[203] Hofstede's Power Distance data, for example, helps explain the variety of teacher/student relational patterns that exist across cultures. In some places, active questioning of a teacher's statements is applauded in the name of free-thinking; in other cultures, such questions are understood to show such lack of respect for the teacher that they are met with violent discipline.

While it is hard to refute that different cultures have developed varying approaches to teaching and learning, it is also

---

not, in fact, be translatable into regional or trade languages. http://www.vulnerablemission.org/ (Accessed October 30, 2016).

[202] Kolb, David A. *Experimental Learning: Experience as the Source of Learning and Development*. Englewood Cliffs, London: Prentice-Hall, 1984. Also Kolb, David, and Simy Joy. "Are There Cultural Differences in Learning Styles?" Weatherhead School of Management, Case Western Reserve University, Dept of Organizational Research. n.d..

[203] Hofstede, Gert Jan, Geert H Hofstede, and Michael Minkov. *Cultures and Organizations: Software of the Mind: Intercultural Cooperation and Its Importance for Survival*. New York: McGraw-Hill, 2010, 70.

easy to misunderstand and misapply the practical importance of those differences. Some mission trainers would suggest, for instance, that the student's cultural perspective must be identified before training begins, and that all teaching should conform to what has been identified as the cultural norm of the learner. Other educators take a more flexible perspective. Ronald Hyman and Barbara Rosoff in particular make a very good point in their article, "The Jug and What's In It."[204] Based on Argyis and Schön's seminal 1974 presentation of "Two Models,"[205] Hyman and Rosoff gave a more practical and flexible approach to matching teaching and learning styles. Instead of slavishly seeking to adapt to learners' preferences, Hyman and Rosoff suggest that a variety of strategies be developed over the course of years of practice, leading the teacher to flex as he/she interacts with specific students in specific contexts to work in specific content areas. The relational paradigm implications of Hyman and Rosoff's approach are made abundantly clear when they write,

> "The task of teachers is complex and diverse. What the student learns from a teacher goes far beyond our present ability to measure. The student learns humanness as he/she blends the knowledge, skills and values taught by teachers, explicitly or implicitly. What the student learns does not remain separated into neat cubbyholes; but becomes an integrated whole. The student learns as he/she experiences, reflects individually and with the aid of

[204] Hyman, Ronald, and Barbara Rosoff. "Matching Learning and Teaching Styles: The Jug and What's In It." In *Theory into Practice*. San Francisco: Jossey-Bass, 1984, 35–43.
[205] Argyis, C, and Schön, D.A. "Increasing Professional Effectiveness." In *Theory into Practice*. San Francisco: Jossey-Bass, 1974.

teachers, and reconstructs experience, so it is impossible to identify one bit of learning from the other. This broader concept of learning is not presently (will it ever be?) compatible with precise measurement. Yet teachers – and the learning psychologist – are in peril if they neglect this broader concept in favor of a restricted cognitive concept of learning which can be quantified."[206]

Specific Training for Missionaries

As we consider the preparation of missionaries, we have looked at forms of training that can serve mission but are wider than that: they focus on training for a wide range of users. There is another educational setting that we still need to consider: training centers that are specifically focused on training for missionary service. Growth in this area has accelerated greatly since 1989 when the World Evangelical Fellowship held its Manila consultation, specifically considering a growing network of missionary training centers.[207] The book *Internationalising Missionary Training*[208] was published as a compilation of the papers presented at that consultation. A rapid increase in the number of missionaries being sent by churches of the Global South and the establishment of missionary training societies and fellowships like the International Missionary Training Network

---

[206] Hyman and Rosoff, 40.
[207] Ferris, Robert W. "Standards of Excellence in Missionary Training Centers." First published in *Training for Cross Cultural Ministries*. 2000, no. 1 (January 2000).http://www.wearesources.org.
[208] Taylor, William David, World Evangelical Fellowship, and Missions Commission, *Internationalizing Missionary Training: A Global Perspective*. Exeter, U.K.; Grand Rapids, MI: U.S.A.: Paternoster Press; Baker Book House, 1991.

(formerly "Fellowship")[209] have also contributed to this growing body of literature.[210] Regional mission organizations such as the *Cooperación Misionera Iberoamericana* (COMIBAM) in Latin America and the Iberian Peninsula have developed both structures and approaches to mission training. COMIBAM is organized around four key tasks necessary for mission sending; training is one of those four.

COMIBAM's training vision is seen in its website description:[211] "Training: oriented towards training centers and mission professors, support for the preparation of trainers, help in curriculum design, continuing education for the missionary, and missiological reflection."[212]

Beyond this example of COMIBAM, there are many other African, Latin American, and Asian groups which are actively involved with training their own intercultural ministry teams.

As these diverse groups look at missionary training, they have opened dialog about training that fits into the context, cultural norms, and resource availability of the sending nations. A 2015 series of webinars led by Dr. Omar Gava, training coordinator of COMIBAM at that time, illustrates this trend.

---

[209] Hoke, Steve. "International Missionary Training Network (formerly 'Fellowship') Gains Ownership Through Participation," October–December 2003. www.globalmission.org. Accessed Sept 12, 2005.

[210] Harley, C. David. *Preparing to Serve: Training for Cross-Cultural Mission*. Pasadena, CA: William Carey Library, 1995.

[211] "Capacitacion: Orientado a Centros de Capacitacion Y Profesores de Misiones, Apoyo a La Preparación de Capacitadores, Asesoría En Desarrollo de Currículo, Capacitacion Continua Del Misionero, Y La Reflexión Misionolgica." *COMIBAM*, n.d. comibam.org. Translation from original Spanish to the English text by M Hedinger

[212] <comibam.org> accessed December 6, 2015.

Titled, "Rethinking our missionary training" the webinars opened discussion among Latin American mission trainers about how to meet the twin challenges of providing high quality training that is also economically sustainable in the Latin American context.[213]

A very practical reason for the proliferation of literature on missionary training arises from statistical studies on missionary retention and attrition. Margaretha Ardiwardana, for instance, reported that inappropriate training of missionaries is considered by some to be a significant reason for attrition of missionaries.[214] Looking at missionaries who were sent out between A.D. 1981 – 2000, Detlef Bloecher reported a significant correlation between missionary training and the retention of missionaries on the field. Bloecher concluded,

> "In summary, ReMAP II [the study of missionaries who were sent out between 1981 – 2000] confirms the close correlation between missionary retention and mission training. High retaining agencies and enduring missionaries require good pre-field training, especially in Missiology. . . . Best practice agencies give their missionaries opportunity for continuous training and development of new gifts and encourage their missionaries to actively work towards the continuous improvement of their ministries."[215]

---

[213] Personal communication; Omar Gava, COMIBAM training coordinator and Director of Recursos Estrategicos Globales.

[214] Ardiwardana, Margaretha. "Formal and Non-Formal Pre-Field Training, Perspective of the New Sending Countries." In *Too Valuable to Lose.* Pasadena, CA: William Carey Library, 1997, 207.

[215] Bloecher, Detlef. "Missionary Training Makes Missionaries Resilient – Lessons from ReMAP II," October 18, 2003. http://www.wearesources.org.

Bloecher later pointed out how training for missionaries is important due to the diversity of roles that a missionary may play over his or her career. Since one may expect to serve in various ways over the years (for instance, evangelist, then church planter, then trainer of other church planters, etc.), it is easy to see the importance of on-going training if an agency is going to retain personnel.[216] This correlation between personnel retention and training gives a strong incentive for agencies to provide missionary training.

That training ought to be provided for missionaries is rarely debated. Harley began his volume by asking about the necessity of training; but then answered his own question by describing how the theological education he had received would not have prepared him sufficiently for the challenges of serving cross-culturally.[217] He also commented about the negative consequences of ill-prepared missionaries: consequences to the missionary, his family, and to the ministry as a whole.[218] When the question is raised about the necessity of missionary training, it is often answered to the affirmative by statistical, anecdotal, and inferential evidence.

The more difficult questions arise when the focus shifts from whether training should be provided to more specific questions such as what kind of training, provided by whom, undertaken in which venue, and toward what end. David Harley

---

[216] Ibid., 4.
[217] Harley, *Preparing to Serve*, 7.
[218] Ibid., 9.

organized his volume on missionary training [219] around six questions. Those questions are: who is to be trained, what kind of training should they receive, how long should the training last, should the training be residential, who should do the training, and what curriculum elements should be included in the training? To Harley's six questions, two others will be added in this chapter: what institution should oversee the training, and what outcomes should be sought as a result of the training?

Each of these questions can easily become complicated. As Dave Broucek pointed out in his consideration of the best practices of missionary training, the world of missions and mission training is not a simple world.[220] In the first place, mission work is highly diverse. It is not possible to train for one simple task given the fact that activities which are rightly called mission are as varied as they are. The second complicating factor is that there are large numbers of missionaries, sending agencies, schools, and churches, and each of these entities often has its own internal definitions of what a good missionary is and does. If there are differing definitions of what a good missionary is and does, it stands to reason that there are also differences in how best to train for mission. A third complication that Broucek mentioned is that defining missionary effectiveness is decidedly difficult. Since missionary activity is varied and quality missionary work may or

---

[219] Ibid., iii.
[220] Broucek, Dave. "Best Practice Standards for Missionary Training." presented at the IFMA/EFMA Personnel Conference, International Mission Board of the Southern Baptist Church, Rockville, VA, December 2003, 3–5.

may not have visible results, it becomes all the more difficult to know how best to train missionaries.

The concept of "best practices for mission training" is a valid and active question. Steve Hoke [221] summarized the question by listing the following seven practices that will be seen in a best practice training program:

1. it will identify the learning and performance needs of trainees;
2. the program will be well aligned with the vision, mission, and values of the parent organization;
3. it will intentionally promote spiritual formation, dependence on God, and Christian community;
4. it employs adult learning theory and practice;
5. it makes careful use of spiritual, human, and financial resources;
6. it evaluates on the basis of a clear, measurable, and feasible plan;
7. it is accountable to stakeholders and peers.

With those caveats in mind, then, this review will attempt to examine missionary training from the perspective of the following questions.

Training Provided for Whom?

Various forms of missionary training have differing targets in terms of who will enter the program. Harley suggested that

---

[221] Hoke, Steve. *Connections*, 2007. worldevangelicals.org. Accessed December 6, 2015, 2.

early on in the process of program development, one must ask if the program is intended for career missionaries, for Christian professionals who will serve in tent-making ministry, or for short-term missionaries.[222]

Ferris also considered the characteristics necessary for the person who is accepted into a mission training program. He cited three key questions relating to a potential candidate for missionary training: does the person give evidence of a personal calling and commitment to cross-cultural ministry? Does the prospective candidate have the physical and emotional stability necessary for cross-cultural ministry? And does the candidate show evidence of moral purity and spiritual maturity necessary for ministry leadership?[223]

It is noteworthy that, with a few exceptions, there are no right answers to these questions raised about the characteristics of the candidate for missionary training. There can be a wide range of acceptable candidates. The important thing is that a given training program should be designed with an idea of who will be entering it. While many possible answers are acceptable, the best programs will be geared to a clear profile of incoming trainees.

What Kind of Training Should be Provided?

Harley's answer to this question dealt with the realms of biblical education on the one hand compared to vocational

---

[222] Harley, *Preparing to Serve*, 28.
[223] Ferris, *Establishing Ministry Training,* 4–5.

training that is uniquely designed for the cross-cultural laborer on the other hand.[224] Harley assumed that missionary trainees enter their programs with an adequate knowledge of Bible and doctrine. He stated his preference to focus training on areas of character, spiritual life, interpersonal relationship, and cross-cultural communication.

Ferris largely concurred with that assessment, although he suggested that there are times when even Bible and doctrine can profitably be included as part of a missionary training program. His rationale was that, assuming a living community in which the training occurs, the time that one spends in that environment provides good informal and nonformal training, making the study of basic Bible and doctrinal themes a profitable way to be trained in missionary skills and attitudes.[225]

How Long Should the Training Last?

Given the breadth of the possible answers to the previous two questions, it is no wonder that varying answers have also been suggested for the question of how long a training period should last. On the one hand, Harley pointed out that two weeks of training is better than no training at all.[226] On the other hand, there are programs that last for up to three years.[227]

------

[224] Harley, *Preparing to Serve*, 29-30.
[225] Ferris, *Establishing Ministry Training*, 2–4.
[226] Harley, *Preparing to Serve*, 31.
[227] Ibid., 31.

Ferris suggested that the duration of a program should be determined by its scope and the preparedness of the candidates who enter the program. Since training is increasingly understood to involve development of relational skills and formation in spiritual and character realms, it would be expected that longer periods of time would be necessary.[228] Without trying to overly simplify the multitude of issues related to program duration, Harley suggested that a holistic program would require a minimum of six to ten months.[229]

Should Training be Residential?

Some programs develop around a concept of in-service training or even distance learning. Other programs, though, develop a residential site where training takes place in the context of daily life. Harley[230] analyzed both the advantages and disadvantages of residential programs. In favor of a residential program are the opportunities to study intensively, away from the normal pressures of everyday life. Students also can give encouragement to one another, and the living conditions simulate to some degree the pressures of cross-cultural living. In residential programs, the staff has opportunities to get to know program participants more deeply than is possible in daytime programs. Finally, and perhaps most importantly, a residential program gives opportunity for the whole person to develop as academic, spiritual,

[228] Ferris, *Establishing Ministry Training*, 6.
[229] Harley, *Preparing to Serve*. 31.
[230] Ibid., 31–35.

relational, skill, and attitude issues intertwine in everyday life situations.

On the other hand, residential programs carry the disadvantages of higher costs and a tendency to remove students from their native environment (with the implied danger of making the training appear to be disconnected from normal life). Another potential problem with residential programs is the danger of creating dependency on specialized tools or resources which are available at the training center, but are not available in subsequent ministry locations. Another potential disadvantage that Harley mentioned is that residential situations can bring about unhealthy relational situations which ultimately prove damaging to the spiritual or social life of the participants. Finally, Harley also recognized that a residential program has space limitations which are more pronounced than those faced by day programs.

Having reviewed the advantages and disadvantages of residential programs, though, it is important to note that in response to a questionnaire about best training practices, a group of experienced mission trainers offered ten suggestions to those who are beginning new programs. Among the recommendations is found, "If circumstances allow, set up a residential rather than a non-residential programme. Insist from the start that staff and students live together, and stress the value of cross-cultural community living."[231]

---

[231] Ibid., 124.

Internet Distance Mission Training

In light of increasing internet availability in vast portions of the world, and in light of increasing use of the internet for educational purposes, it is important to mention issues which connect mission training and the internet.

The first of these issues is the simple reality that reduced costs and large-scale involvement of the internet in education across many disciplines are having a profound impact on mission training. It is now routine to include internet-based training in nearly any program. In some instances, internet interaction augments what is done in some other training venue. So, for instance, content and skills developed in a residential setting are later practiced with mentoring/coaching from a distance. In other cases, trainers from various regions and national backgrounds can interact via internet to develop new ideas and new levels of partnership. Commercial applications of culture-general training now often use short internet or DVD based content sections (as short as 10 – 15 minutes long) to present concepts which are then discussed in private sessions via internet.

D.R. Garrison of the University of Calgary provided a helpful review of the important educational issues that arise from the use of technology. [232] He concluded that "balancing socio-emotional interaction, building group cohesion and facilitating

---

[232] Garrison, D.R. "Online Community of Inquiry Review: Social, Cognitive, and Teaching Presence Issues." *Journal of Asynchronous Learning Networks* 11, no. 1 (April 2007): 61–72.

and modeling respectful critical discourse is essential for productive inquiry."[233] An overview of his work reveals that on-line education must find ways to stimulate both relationship and content. It is not enough to simply give information by internet: a relationship between teacher and student, and a real interaction between learners are also needed if learning is to occur.

Yet, there are others who would suggest that internet is by nature incongruent with relational learning. Enoch Wan vividly makes this point in his blog entitled, "A Warm Yet Empty Voice. Reflections on Face-to-Face Interactions."[234] His conclusion is that "real personal relationship is a distinctive of Christian faith and practice."[235] In a follow-up to that blog, he defines genuine relationship as, "authentic, spontaneous, sincere, and heart-and-soul bonding of persons together in unity."[236]

Taking these two warnings seriously, the question arises how, if at all, technology can be used for relational paradigm training. It is important to note that in neither of the two articles mentioned (Wan or Garrison) is there a suggestion that internet simply cannot be used for relational education. The point is that internet can never replace personal face-to-face relationships.

---

[233] Ibid., 69.
[234] Wan, Enoch. "A Warm Yet Empty Voice? Reflections on Face-to-Face Interaction." *Evangel-Vision, Billy Graham Center at Wheaton College*, December 2, 2013. http://www.gospel-life.net/a-warm-Yet-empty-voice-reflections-on-face-to-face-interactions/. (Accessed October 30, 2016).
[235] Ibid.
[236] Wan, Enoch. "Relationship in the 21st Century: Theory and Practice." *Evangel-Vision, Billy Graham Center at Wheaton College*, March 7, 2014. http://www.gospel-life.net/relationship-in-the-21st-century-theory-and-practice/. (Accessed October 30, 2016).

Internet can be used to build existing personal relationships, much as telephone was able to do for previous generations. And yet, even recognizing that information, attitudes, and life stories can indeed be communicated via internet it remains a valid point that mission training and any other training that seeks to bring Christian growth cannot be reduced to simple knowledge transfer. Personal interaction is required.

Who Should do the Training?

As important as the issues of curriculum, duration, and residential environments might be, Ferris made an important comment when he wrote, "Perhaps the most critical decisions in the establishment and administration of an effective missionary training center relate to the selection of the training staff. No training institution can rise above the level of its staff."[237]

Ferris listed several characteristics that must be true of the successful missionary trainer. Such trainers are not recent graduates of academic programs, but have extensive cross-cultural experience. They will be marked by spiritual maturity, highly developed interpersonal skills, a good reputation and a healthy family life. They will be gifted in teaching and mentoring adults, and will have developed competencies in one or more of the curriculum components central to their particular training center.[238]

---

[237] Ferris, *Establishing Ministry Training*, 1.
[238] Ibid., 2.

Harley included another important observation about characteristics of trainers: mission trainers must be active in ministry in their own right besides functioning as trainers. This is important, according to Harley, "so that students see that their mentors are not only theorist but also practitioners." [239] Harley also noted the importance of trainers working together in teams. The members of this training team should represent diverse backgrounds and life situations so that any given trainee can see cross-cultural ministry modeled by people who come from backgrounds similar to his or hers.[240]

What Curriculum Elements Should be Included?

Of all the issues relevant to missionary training, this question has received the most extensive coverage in the literature. The following paragraphs will highlight curriculum issues as considered from two perspectives. First, there are numerous authors who have written from the perspective of what topics ought to be included in a curriculum. Secondly, other authors (far fewer) write from the perspective of how cultural preferences should be incorporated into curriculum design.

Topics to Include in Curriculum Design

This question can be approached from various directions. William Taylor issued a call for Bible students and mission

---

[239] Harley, *Preparing to Serve*, 54.
[240] Ibid., 56–57.

trainers to "return to Scriptures to tease out not only the examples of cross-cultural equipping, but the broad principles that can be contextualized in every training programme and centre."[241]

Taylor proposed six elements to include in an integrated whole in order for training to be effective. The curriculum elements that he suggested are personal disciplines, local church, biblical and theological studies, cross-cultural studies, pre-field equipping by the agency and on-field career training.[242]

Steve Hoke and Bill Taylor published a grid that outlines training components at various stages of a missionary's life-cycle. Hoke and Taylor's work highlighted growth in character, ministry skills, and knowledge. Within each of these domains, they discussed numerous subcategories.[243]

Yet another guide for curriculum development in mission training comes from Paul Savage. He created a taxonomy of issues to include in theological education which has relevance to missionary training. In his taxonomy, he included as curricular elements the missionary as a man of God, the use and understanding of the Bible, effective communication, the

---

[241] Taylor, William David. "Introduction: Setting the Stage." In *Internationalizing Missionary Training*. Grand Rapids, MI: Baker Book House, 1991. 2.
[242] Taylor, 3.
[243] Hoke, Stephen, William David Taylor, and World Evangelical Fellowship. *Send Me!: Your Journey to the Nations*. Wheaton, IL; Pasadena, CA: World Evangelical Fellowship Missions Commission; William Carey Library, 1999. 26–27.

establishment and shepherding of a local church, and understanding of culture.[244]

Jonathan Lewis took a different approach to the question of missionary training curriculum. His desire was to see a practical element in missionary training. As he phrased it,

> Research has repeatedly demonstrated that practical issues related to language learning, cultural adaptation, interpersonal skills, coping with family needs, job satisfaction and a host of other practical issues bring missionaries home prematurely and relegate others to ineffectiveness.[245]

Lewis continued to suggest that training in practical skills should be semantically identified by training components with titles such as "how to learn a language," "how to handle conflict," and "how to contextualize ministry."[246]

The question of which specific curriculum topics to include in a program was also considered in David Harley's work. He suggested that missionary training should include Bible, doctrine, and pastoral studies (including family and singleness issues). His largest area of concern was related to mission, and in that regard he suggested training in the biblical basis of mission, world religions, history of mission, cultural anthropology, evangelism

---

[244] Paul Savage, unpublished paper. Quoted in Smallman, William H. *Able to Teach Others Also: Nationalizing Global Ministry Training*. Pasadena, CA: Mandate Press, 2001, 195–204.

[245] Lewis, Jonathan. "International Missionary Training Fellowship. What the Army Needs." *Journal of the WEA Missions Commission*, February, 2003, 47. www.globalmission.org. Accessed September 12, 2005.

[246] Lewis, "International Missionary Training," 47.

and church planting, linguistics and language learning techniques, research methods, cross-cultural life and work, contemporary world Christianity, and case studies on these various issues.[247]

Ferris took a wider approach to the question of curriculum. His idea of topics to include in missionary training reflected a holistic approach to character and skills, living in community, and the deliberate use of informal and nonformal training. Significant field experience was also stressed as part of his model, as was a treatment of specifically missionary themes such as theology of mission, history of mission, cultural studies, evangelism and church planning. He pointed out that the actual listing of topics needs to be tailor-made for each training situation.[248]

Also considering the curricular elements important for missionary preparation, Lois McKinney made the observation that training for cross-cultural gospel ministry should include spiritual, psychological, theological, historical, cultural, and missiological concepts. She further suggested that training should augment relational skills, should include entire families, and should prepare missionaries for the performance of ministry skills in new cultural contexts. McKinney also astutely pointed out the reality of suffering in most of the world's experience, and called for missionary training that prepares the missionary to suffer and to minister to those who suffer. She pointed out that vocational skills are an important element in some sorts of cross-cultural ministry.

---

[247] Harley, *Preparing to Serve*, 69–77.
[248] Ferris, *Establishing Ministry Training*, 2–4.

She concluded that the effective teacher of cross- cultural workers will emphasize learning in community, interactive learning, and direct, purposeful field experience.[249]

One final work deserves mention with reference to the design of missionary training curriculum, namely Robert Ferris' guide for establishing ministry training.[250] As Ferris and his colleagues worked through the specific issues involved in developing a ministry training program, they produced a helpful review of curriculum design issues. Of special significance to missionary training curricula are the ten commitments, found in the quote below, which they suggested as foundational values:

1. Training objectives should be determined by the understandings, skills, and qualities required for effective service.

2. Training is "church related"; learning occurs best in the context of community.

3. Training structures and relationships must be consistent with training goals.

4. Training strategies should be appropriate to the learner's ways of thinking and learning.

5. Training strategies should incorporate and build upon the learner's experience.

6. Theory should be validated by Scripture and by general revelation.

---

[249] McKinney, Lois. "New Directions in Missionary Education." In *Internationalizing Missionary Training*. Grand Rapids, MI: Baker Book House, 1991.
[250] Ferris, *Establishing Ministry Training,* 145.

7. Information should be appropriated and obeyed.

8. Skills-learning should include instruction, demonstration, and guided practice.

9. Character qualities and values are effectively communicated only when teaching includes modeling and reflection.

10. Training equips the learner for effective ministry and continuing growth.[251]

Cultural Issues and Curriculum Design in Missionary Training

Three recent authors have focused on curriculum design from a cultural perspective rather than from a topical perspective. James A. Plueddemann considered the interaction between education and cultural traits. Using the concept of "high context cultures" and "low context cultures," he developed a useful model of teaching in cross-cultural situations. "High context cultures" are those which grasp meaning in relation to content as well as the subtler issues of place, time of day, clothing styles, relational patterns, etc. "Low context cultures" are content to focus on simple factual presentation, and do not see wider environmental and contextual issues as inherently related to meaning.[252]

Plueddemann's conclusion is that both a high degree of content orientation (preferred in low context cultures) and a high degree of practical application in socially appropriate interaction

---

[251] Ibid., 145.
[252] See Edward T. Hall, *Beyond Culture*. IL.: Anchor Books, 1997, 105–116 for foundational thoughts on high and low context.

(preferred learning style of high context learners) are necessary skills for the worker in cross-cultural ministry. As he phrased this integrative concept,

> Good missionary preparation in any culture will challenge students to bring together practice and theory. High-context students may prefer to learn practical "how-to-do-it" techniques. If high-context students merely learn a "bag of tricks" for ministry they will not be able to solve complicated problems. Low-context students may prefer to study theoretical knowledge. If low-context students learn only theoretical "book knowledge" about missions they will have difficulty knowing how to put their knowledge into practice. Teaching methods need to stimulate integration.[253]

He concluded that "Training that integrates theory and practice will increase the effectiveness of missionaries from any culture."[254]

Another author who has specifically considered the relationship between cross-cultural training and Christian ministry is Donald K. Smith. Approaching his topic from the perspective of communication science, much of what he wrote is germane to the question of how best to prepare Christian workers for cross-cultural ministry. His 23 propositions provide tools for the cross-cultural worker to understand the communication processes of the host culture. These tools of communication are

---

[253] Plueddemann, James E. "Culture, Learning and Missionary Training." In *Internationalizing Missionary Training*. Grand Rapids, MI: Baker Book House, 1991, 228.
[254] Ibid., 229.

part of the content of culture-general training and give tools to a missionary who wants to gain skill in how to learn the specifics of ministry in his or her new cultural context.[255] In other words, conscious incorporation of Smith's propositions both as topics to be taught and as guidelines for ministry methods will give trainees an appreciation of how to adjust their ministries to the cultural and worldview perspectives of the people to whom they minister.

One final author who wrote about curriculum design from a cultural perspective is Michael David Sills. His premise was that teaching needs to be approached in culturally appropriate forms. In particular, he called on trainers to develop skill in communicating to oral, preliterate peoples. Rather than train missionaries under the rubrics of literate thought patterns with written texts as a foundation, Sills called on trainers to learn how to teach those who share knowledge through narratives. His approach tied together chronological Bible teaching with teaching methods appropriate for high-oral learners.[256] Like Plueddemann and Smith, Sills called on curriculum designers to approach their work with sensitivity to the cultures in which the missionary will later work. Appendix 3 and 4 give further resources into the issues of curriculum design.

---

[255] Smith, Donald K. *Creating Understanding: A Handbook of Christian Communication across Cultural Landscapes.* Grand Rapids, MI: Zondervan, 1992.

[256] Sills, Michael David. "Training Leaders for the Majority World Church in the 21st Century." *Global Missiology*, April 2004. www.globalmissiology.net. (Accessed October 23, 2016).

What Institution Should Provide the Training?

To answer this question, various authors consider the relative strengths and weaknesses of four different institutions as being part of the training of new missionaries. Those institutions are schools, training centers, churches, and mission agencies.

Larry Sharp's comments to the Evangelical Missiological Society meetings in March 1999 pointed out the changing nature of relationships between training entities. He wrote,

> It is no secret that mission agencies have ceased to count on most Bible Colleges for a complete preparation of students for intercultural ministries. No longer do missiological concerns drive the curriculum of the Bible college movement. Though there are clear exceptions, it seems that the reality is that for most, the curriculum is market-driven with the colleges responding to the demands of the parents, students, church and employment markets.[257]

Granting Sharp's point that academic institutions are no longer at the vanguard of missionary training (while also agreeing with him that exceptions do exist), local churches, specialized training centers and mission agencies are all, in various ways, trying to fill the need. George Shultz of the Center for Intercultural Training studied mission agencies' preferences related to the use of in-house and outsourced training. Schultz found three broad

---

[257] Sharp, Larry. "A Mission Agency Director's Perspective on the Changing Relationship between UFM, The Church, Training Institutions and the Mobilizers of Mission." Unpublished paper presented at the Evangelical Missiological Society, Lancaster, PA: March 20, 1999.

categories in terms of mission agency training: agencies that provide their own training, agencies that outsource their training, and agencies which partner with other agencies or institutions to provide training. His study concluded that "research indicates that none of these models is better in and of itself. It is the model as it relates to the particular need or situation that makes it better or worse."[258] The important questions that direct an agency toward one of those three models include the agency's values, the available resources, the size of the organization, and the level of commitment that it has to training.[259]

Rob Brynjolfson took a more holistic approach to the question of whether it is best that training be done by the church, the school, or the agency. His perspective is that the task of missionary training is "too grand for one entity, organism or institution alone to achieve."[260] He suggested that over the course of a lifetime, all three of those institutions have key roles to play in the progressive development and life-long learning of a missionary. His holistic model is summarized when he wrote,

> "We need cross-cultural training to be intentionally delivered over the entire ministry life cycle of the worker. Upon adopting a ministry life cycle approach to training we can encourage schools to excel in developing understanding and building theoretical foundations. Furthermore, we can encourage training centres and

---

[258] Schultz, George. "The BEST Missionary Training Model?" *Evangelical Missions Quarterly*, January, 2003, 91.
[259] Ibid., 90.
[260] Brynjolfson, Rob. "Effective Equipping of the Cross-Cultural Worker." *The Journal of the WEA Mission Commission*, April, 2004, 72. www.globalmission.org.

agencies to work in conjunction towards the development of needed cross-cultural skills. Finally, and most significantly, we can begin to develop training programs in churches, agencies and missionary training centres that intentionally use communities to foster growth in needed character qualities and adjust attitudes for field effectiveness."[261]

What Outcomes are the Desired Result of the Training?

Three approaches are found concerning the desired results of a training program. Hoke and Taylor pursued that question from the perspective of student-centered educational theory. They wrote,

"The best way to develop a sound missionary training curriculum is to determine the desired outcomes – what a missionary needs to *be,* and be able to *know* and *do,* (emphasis in the original), and then build backward to develop all the resources needed to reach those goals."[262]

For Hoke and Taylor, the outcomes desired from a training program are seen in the attitudes, abilities, and knowledge of the graduates.

Rob Brynjolfson[263] took a different approach to the question of desired outcomes to see from a training program. His view of training is shaped around the term "the right kind of training." The outcomes proposed by Brynjolfson to grow out of "the right kind of training" are: increased world-wide work force of

---

[261] Brynjolfson "Effective Equipping of the Cross-Cultural Worker," 79.
[262] Hoke and Taylor, *Send Me!*, 23–24.
[263] Brynjolfson "Effective Equipping of the Cross-Cultural Worker," 75.

gospel messengers, increased effectiveness of individual messengers, and an increased effectiveness of entire groups of missionaries (including missionary organizations and missionary teams).

One final literature source deserves mention as an important piece of the literature on missionary training. David Harley's helpful volume ends with a list of ten pieces of advice that experienced mission trainers offer newcomers to the field:[264]

1. Study missionary training centers that already operate in your geographical area.
2. If possible, seek to develop cooperative programs with other organizations.
3. Start small and allow the program to grow.
4. Seek dedicated teachers and administrators.
5. Choose the location of the program carefully, considering cost, accessibility, resources, and future ministry of the students. In particular locate the program in a place where staff can be involved in direct ministry.
6. Set up residential rather than day programs.
7. Whether residential or non-residential, develop a holistic approach.
8. Prepare whole families for service.
9. Continually focus on the servant attitude of the Lord Jesus Christ, keeping Him as the model to be copied.
10. Build the program on a foundation of prayer.

---

[264] Harley, *Preparing to Serve*, 123–124.

Summary

There are many facets to ministry, and even more when we consider ministry that crosses cultural barriers. Chapter Five has presented some specialized educational approaches which answer the needs of those diverse facets of ministry. In this chapter we have described training and education which is specialized for theological and mission service, philosophies of education that grow from explicitly Christian sources, and the growing field of intercultural study, including both comparisons of education across cultures, and preparation created for people who intend to live and work in intercultural situations. In the next chapter, we will look for practical ways that these diverse training approaches can be used to prepare Christian workers for cross cultural service.

Summary and Conclusions of the Theoretical section.

Missionary training does not take place in a vacuum. It is influenced by the educational perspectives of the culture around it. For that reason, we have looked at current trends in education. This review has included general and adult teaching and learning, and also sought insight from the work of theological education, intercultural education, and specialized mission training.

For all that we have looked at in this chapter, perhaps the best summary comes from Samuel Escobar:

> "Observing training situations in Latin American and reflecting about discipleship processes in churches and para-churches, I have come to the conclusion that forming

people for mission is an activity that should take place within the frame of a "person to person" relationship, which is as fundamental as the environment for the educational process. No amount of academic excellence or doctrinal orthodoxy can substitute for this personalized dimension of the training for mission."[265]

The work of mission is relational in every sense: a relational God seeking the love and trust of His creation. Missionaries who know God seek to make Him known to others. The relational nature of mission work calls us to minister in relational ways, and that calls us to train in relational ways. The overview of educational approaches has demonstrated some forms of education that are highly relational, and other forms of education that are not at all relational. As one considers the relational realism paradigm, the preference is to choose teaching and learning approaches that are relationally strong.

---

[265] Escobar, Samuel. "The Training for Missiologists for a Latin American Context" Chapter Ten in Pierson, Paul Everett, John Dudley Woodberry, Charles Edward van Engen, and Edgar J Elliston. *Missiological Education for the Twenty-First Century: The Book, the Circle, and the Sandals: Essays in Honor of Paul E. Pierson.* Maryknoll, N.Y.: Orbis Books, 1996, 105.

Part Three: Practical Application

Introduction to Section Three: Four Practical Implications of a
Relational Realism Paradigm

The premise of this book is not particularly complicated.
We maintain that relationship is the key reality of human life. We
define relationship as "the interactive connection between
personal beings/Beings." We understand that reality is primarily
based on the vertical relationship between God and the created
order, and secondarily on the horizontal relationships within
created order.[266]

From those simple statements, how can we best approach
the task of preparing people for intercultural ministry?

We have looked at that question from several points of
reference: we've considered the theological and scriptural
foundations of a paradigm of relational realism, and we've
considered educational issues that go into training. We have also
considered specific issues relevant to missionary training.

---

[266] Wan, Enoch." The Paradigm of Relational Realism."

In this final section, we shift attention from foundational theology and theory to a consideration of practical application of a paradigm for relational realism missionary training. We begin with four implications that grow from our study. These four implications are introduced here because they are foundational to our ability to practically apply the relational realism paradigm.

1. Implication of the word "Paradigm"

Within the realm of practical consideration, we begin with the concept of "paradigm." By that we mean a way of looking at life. It is meant to be a framework for thinking. Our intention is to promote a way of understanding life and ministry that begins with deliberate attention to the nature of one's relationship with God and with man.

The problem we face is that Western thought patterns revolve around finding the right program, technique, or method. Yet the Paradigm of Relational Realism is not a method. It is a reminder that the primary focus for life and ministry has to do with our walk with God and our walk with one another.

Technique –focused ministry leads to a factory mindset; as if to say, just bring in the right raw materials and apply the right methods in the right sequence and you should expect the right outcomes.

A relational paradigm approach is not against recognized results: it just does not expect those results to arise mechanically.

A relational paradigm is not satisfied knowing about God. A relational paradigm wants nothing less than to know God. In the same way, a relational paradigm is not satisfied with knowing about people; it seeks to really know those people. Ministry training can treat people like abstractions; and especially when intercultural issues arise. It is easy to classify as "high power distance" and "low on the I/C scale" and completely miss the reality of the person and his/her family, work, neighborhood. The relational paradigm is thankful for the concepts that can be learned through intercultural studies; but the focus of the relational paradigm is the people, not the abstract concept that might describe the people.

Why would we promote such a relational paradigm? As Wan phrased it, everyone has parents. In other words, relationship is inherent to human life. Desired outcomes of training or particular discussions about cultural dynamics can be helpful but will always be a step removed from the reality of people. The reality that is core to relational realism is in the first place a real relationship with the living, Triune God. In the second place, relational paradigm seeks to know the flesh and blood people within their natural network of human relationships.

We have all seen situations where real people were treated as projects or a simple means to an end. When one knows about people yet does not know them, manipulation or abuse are the frequent results. Marketing rightly done puts real people into contact with products or services that will serve them well. Marketing done poorly leads experts to learn a lot about a group of people so as to "sell" them. It is manipulation, using knowledge of a people for the good of the marketing company, not necessarily for the good of the audience. Manipulation, abuse, and "project" mentality is the result.

Christian ministry can make the same error, and training for Christian ministry can make the same error. Trainees can become projects. Students or training partners can become customers whose main purpose is to provide cash flow. We can unwittingly extend stereotypes of cultures by lumping all people of a given nation into the cultural descriptions written by an expert. Christian ministry that loses the relationship perspective can easily become focused on providing fodder for donor appeals instead of serving the King by serving His people. For these reasons we want to develop a way of looking at life, that is to say, a paradigm, of relational realism.

2. Implications of Relational Realism for analysis and problem solving

Some years ago, a doctoral class in intercultural education brought me (Mark) to one of the "aha" moments that form the background of this book. A group of graduate students were analyzing a case that highlighted a dysfunctional educational system. The assignment given to the group was to first analyze and then suggest solutions to help a largely North American group of mission educators to see better results in their interaction with a Latin American school that had been founded by North American missionaries.

The analysis began with a Western approach: identification of the problems, discussion of native thinking/educational methods of the students in the school (based largely on etic analysis), discussion of limiting factors again from an etic perspective, etc.

One of the graduate students asked if he could present the situation in a different way. This particular student was a native of an East Asian nation, and had served for years within another East Asian nation. His agency, though, was largely North American and so he had become familiar with Western approaches to problem solving.

He asked if he could analyze the situation from the perspective of his Asian thought patterns. Taking his turn at the white board, he drew a circle and began identifying all of the people or groups that were part of the situation: the mission leadership, the teachers (some national, some expat), the financial supporters, the students, parents of the students, church leaders who had sent the students, local government officials who had levels of responsibility over any schooling situation, denominational leaders in the host country. The graduate student looked at the circle and quietly suggested that instead of seeing a problem to solve, it would be better to look at education that would best serve each of the relationships expressed on that white board. We started looking at each relationship pair (dyad) on the white board, and soon an entirely new perspective on the situation began to arise.

That grid of "look at the relationships" led us to better solutions to the case than any previous group had found. That grid of "look at the relationships" has become a thinking pattern that I have used in numerous situations since then. That grid of "look at the relationships" is, in fact, the direction of this book.

3. Implications of Relational Realism on outcomes

When we look at a relational realism paradigm, relationship becomes both the organizing principle for analysis and the organizing principle for outcomes. A mechanistic, behavioral approach can identify student-learning outcomes that a given course of study wishes to facilitate. The problem, though, is that ministry is about relationship – first with God, and secondarily with people. The outcomes that really matter may not be visible in lists of books read, papers written, or other objective outcomes achieved. The outcomes that matter are whether one is growing in the grace and knowledge of the Lord Jesus, and interacting with other people in sincere relationships that bring them, too, into a growing relationship with the Triune God.

Again, we are not against the idea of identifying outcomes and working deliberately to achieve them. If the outcomes come from mechanistic conceptual perspectives, they will only be of limited value to the actual relationships involved. The desired outcomes, in fact, need to come out of a relational paradigm as well.

4. Implications of Relational Realism regarding flexibility

Yet another important practical outcome of this study is to realize that by focusing on sincere relationships between the people involved in a mission training ministry, we are in fact closing the door to a pre-programmed course of study. The introduction of a relational paradigm means that a given training network must be flexible enough to shift according to the realities of the learning community with which it works. Flexibility in using any number of learning/teaching strategies as the need may arise is one hallmark of a relational paradigm. A program is cut and dried; it is mass produced and ready to use with any audience at any time. A relationship will bend and flex to fit the contours of the individual people involved. Mission training from a relational paradigm perspective will have many core thoughts, skills, and concepts but will look for ways to apply those core thoughts, skills and concepts within the realities of the people involved.

In this third section of our book, we will look at some possible ways to develop a relational paradigm ministry of mission training. This is far from suggesting a program: it is meant to spark thought and discussion about what a relational paradigm mission training approach could look like, depending on the people involved and other factors. Above all, a relational paradigm is a way of thinking, not a blue print that details the specifics of a project. Over the next three chapters, we will present some ways of thinking that may help us to keep our eyes on the relationships; first of all with Triune God and secondarily with other created beings.

Chapter Six
Seven Missionary Relationships within a Relational Paradigm of Intercultural Ministry Training

Introduction

How shall we consider the practical application of the paradigm of relational realism? The practical nature of the topic leads us to look for an equally practical presentation. This chapter is organized around the very practical idea of dyad analysis: looking one at a time at the possible relationships that could be involved in a missionary endeavor. Figure 2 (see chapter two) graphically describes the multiple relationships that take place where there is Christian ministry underway. The seven relationships that are seen in that Figure 2 will be the framework for this chapter.

Relationship One: Relationships within the Trinity

"The Trinity is not so much a mystery to be grasped as a model to be emulated" is a paraphrase of an insight by Justo

Gonzalez.[267] What elements of relationships within the Trinity can and should be modeled within human ministry training?

Perichorisis, the mutual indwelling of the members of the Trinity, may seem like it has no horizontal counterpart. Indeed, the closest parallel of this relational trait would be seen in the indwelling of the spirit in the lives of Christians.

There is, though, one horizontal human relationship that Scripture says is parallel to the mutual indwelling within the Trinity. In the creation account, Triune God created humanity, male and female, in his likeness. "So God created mankind in his own image, in the image of God he created them; male and female he created them." (Gen 1:27). That image of God later led to the forming of woman out of Adam's rib, with the statement that "she shall be called 'woman,' for she was taken out of man." That is why a man leaves his father and mother and is united to his wife, and they become one flesh." The relationship between husband and wife is based on the unity and diversity of the Trinity. The significance of this truth is multiplied in light of Ephesians 5:32 that says the relationship between husband and wife is meant to help us better understand the relationship between Jesus and the church.

Ministry of all kinds needs to respect the deep lessons that God has woven into the marriage relationship. Ministry training and ministry practice – both within one's own culture, and in

---

[267] González, Justo L. *Mañana: Christian Theology from a Hispanic Perspective*. Nashville: Abingdon Press, 1990. Chapter Seven, "The One who lives as Three." 101–115.

intercultural situations – must include healthy, growing relationship between married partners. Training, coaching, theological insight and high standards of marriage within sending organizations are required.

This practical application calls for human marriage to seek to fulfill the inter-animation that is seen in the Trinity. The beauty of intercultural understanding is to recognize, though, that the unity and diversity of marriage can be accurately portrayed through a variety of cultural forms. For example, the romantic sense behind Western ideas of marriage is not something that must be transplanted into non-Western cultures. The values of biblical marriage include traits like a married couple's distinction from the parents, faithfulness, love and honor. Those traits can be incorporated in a romantic cultural milieu through "Love Languages" or "Date nights." Yet the biblical values can just as well be incorporated into cultural milieus where romanticism is not the key. The marriage vows of a couple who are wed through a matchmaker can equally demonstrate biblical values.

The practical outworking of this trait is that those being sent for ministry to an unfamiliar language and culture need to understand and live the deep values of marriage, and be able to demonstrate those values in a variety of cultural contexts.

Polyphony is another trait that is shared between the members of the Trinity. This trait reminds us that any situation or Scripture that draws attention to One member of the Trinity in no way diminishes the importance of other Members.

This trait is also important for ministry training. Anyone who has been long in ministry will have experienced moments when the spotlight is on one person and others are at least tempted to feel marginalized. Some Western cultures have recently encouraged expectations that in any sporting or academic contest, ALL participants will be named as winners. In part, this could be seen as aversion to polyphony.

Mission training needs to learn the lesson of polyphony, and more strongly develop the Philippians 2 principle that we put aside our own interests, and instead serve one another. This may be more difficult when the minister comes from competitive cultures, because in those contexts it can become so easy to consider that giving credit to one person is somehow minimizing another. The Trinity gives us a better way – highlighting what One member has done does not minimize the Others. Incorporating that concept into training will help to develop healthy relationships.

Taxis is the Divine counterpart to human status/role discussions. Within the Trinity, there are eternally ordered areas of responsibility, including an ordered structure of authority and submission. Training for ministry needs to include this concept in practical and academic ways.

Human cultural patterns show a major distinction between what Geert Hofstede[268] calls "high power distance" and "low power

---

[268] Hofstede, Geert et al, *Cultures and Organizations*, 2010.

distance" cultures; roughly equivalent to hierarchical cultures on one end of the continuum, and egalitarian cultures on the other.

The more hierarchical cultures can better understand and apply the concept of submission and authority. Egalitarian cultures, though, perceive inherent injustice in situations where one person or Person is authority over others. Mission training must include the twin topics of authority and submission. Mission and church leadership structures should likewise mix together appropriate levels of submission and authority. The evangelical church of the West, with its context of individualism and egalitarianism, has a particular difficulty in serving under the leadership of any structure or person.

There is a second element to taxis that is just as important. While it is true that authority/submission are relational patterns that are seen in the Trinity and should inform human ministry relationships, yet the love and honor that is shown by each member of the Trinity to the Others is just as essential. The simple truth is that humans abuse authority. Within the Trinity, though, there is no abuse of authority. The Son, though submissive to the Father, still honors the Father. And the Father mixes together authority with praise and honor for the Son. Likewise, the Spirit is at once submissive and a loved, respected member of the Triune God.

Human relationships are never going to be perfect in this world, and perhaps the Triune perfection of healthy, respectful, loving relationships that also includes levels of authority and submission is a challenge that is almost beyond human imagination. In a relational paradigm, though, the mixing together of humility/authority with loving and honoring relationship is an area for church and mission to deliberately include when training takes place.

Finally, the Triune God demonstrates love, joy, peace and a long list of similar relational traits as the members interact with one another. Human relationships within mission teams and across ministry teams need to progress and grow in these same attributes. Training for this point can include areas like conflict management, team health, and the development of worshipful patterns within work settings.

The relational paradigm that we are discussing is not in contradistinction to program, yet neither is it satisfied with simple activity. Training programs can and should include discussion about easily measured things like goals, budgets, and numbers of trainees. Yet from human management we know that what we measure regularly becomes the driving force for our activities. Though it is admittedly difficult to measure the fruit of the Spirit, yet in our honest assessments we know if those traits are with us. 2 Peter chapter one tells us that if we have a series of relational markers that are "present and increasing" then we will be fruitful in our ministry. The practical application is that ministry training needs to include markers of healthy relationship through such traits as the Fruit of the Spirit and the characteristics listed in 2 Peter chapter one. Ministry training needs to set a high standard for paying attention to the relational health of the church and ministry team as seen in those traits.

Relationship Two: God and the Messenger

Relational paradigm ministry training does not start with the techniques and methods that a given missionary will use to make the Word known to a new audience. Questions of method and technique have their place, but the first priority is the relationship between God and the messenger.

John 15:4 summarizes this concept: "Remain in me, as I also remain in you. No branch can bear fruit by itself; it must remain in the vine. Neither can you bear fruit unless you remain in me."

How do we train for that kind of abiding life in Christ? One mission trainer from Latin America answered that question by simply patting his knees. Learning to abide, learning to pray, learning to hear the voice of the Lord as he directs through his Word, through prayer and through his people. Many times these are insights that come more from time together with others in ministry than from a developed curriculum. Whatever the form, though, trainers and trainees need to spend time together in the presence of the Lord as part of learning to abide. In liturgical settings, prayer, meditation, the practice of spiritual disciplines, journaling to keep record of God's involvement in one's life: the methods are nearly endless and the significance is impossible to overstate.

Relationship Three: God and the Audience

In one of the most glorious of all mysteries, God does his work using at one and the same time his Presence and his human agents. As we saw in the example from Acts 16:14, God was at work in Lydia's heart to open his truth to her even though it was Paul who opened the Word.

Mission training needs to prepare mission candidates to see God at work. We have to expect him to be active, and we have to develop sensitivity so that we recognize his fingerprints when we see them.

One good suggestion for this kind of sensitivity is through the use of mission biographies and through mission history. Knowing what God has done in the past makes us aware that he is active in our own days as well. He rarely seems to repeat what he did – ministry is not a simple matter of learning the template and then repeating it. On the other hand, seeing how God opened nations to his Word in the past, and seeing how he led in the lives of his messengers in the past, gives us the kind of imagination that lets us see him at work in our day as well.

Relationship Four: Messenger and Audience

Missionary training needs to include ideas about technique and method. We need to know what to do to grow close to an audience, and how to adapt and adjust so that our lifestyle does not create unnecessary barriers with the people to whom we were sent.

Some specific areas of training for intercultural impact
include the common themes of intercultural training programs.
The four competences and eight sub-points in Brinkmann and van
Weerdenburg's work[269] are a good illustration:

1. Intercultural Sensitivity
   a. Cultural awareness
   b. Attention to signals
2. Intercultural communication
   a. Active listening
   b. Adapting communication style
3. Building commitment
   a. Building relationships
   b. Reconciling stakeholder needs
4. Managing uncertainty
   a. Openness to cultural diversity
   b. Exploring new approaches

These main concepts of intercultural life and work,
important as they are, are not sufficient for the kind of
transformational impact that Gospel work seeks. For that reason,
we would add to the above, including training in cultural analysis
to identify worldview issues like core values, core beliefs, and
expected emotional reactions of the new people. Transformation
will occur when those culturally-based assumptions about how life
works are challenged and ultimately shaped or replaced by
scriptural assumptions about the core things in life.

---

[269] Brinkmann, Ursula, and Oscar van Weerdenburg. *Intercultural Readiness*

Mission training needs to include growing skill at adaptation to live within the norms of the people. Mission training needs to include skill development so that the intercultural sojourner knows how to live within governmental and societal expectations. All of these levels of training are important.

Issues of training for language acquisition and training for intercultural competence are themes that a relational paradigm must likewise include. How will you develop a sincere relationship with people from another culture if you never speak any common language and never adjust to live within their cultural norms?

That being said, though, it is the contention of this study that those elements by themselves will not lead to intercultural ministry impact. Communication is a tool for bringing people into a vibrant relationship with the Triune God and with other people. Training in intercultural competence may be exciting and interesting, but all by itself it will not result in disciples who are learning all that Christ taught. The techniques and methods of intercultural sciences and even of ministry development are skills to include but always in their proper place as a tool to relationship.

Relationship Five: the Messenger and His/her culture

One of the most important relationships to include in a training program will lead to understanding of one's own culture. Paul, when he went to Macedonia, was still Paul. He knew his own people and His own cultural expectations. Some of those cultural traits he willingly maintained. Others he voluntarily set aside.

Mission training similarly needs to give tools for people to understand why they do what they do. We would probably all be surprised (the authors of this study included) by how much of what we consider to be basic Christianity is in fact our culture's application of Christian truth. When we are within our own culture, that application may be just fine (depending on how accurately scriptural values have been "dressed" in our cultural clothing). However, once we set out to carry the Gospel into new cultures we need to be sure that we are carrying the Word of God and not saddling a new culture with expressions that feel normal to us and foreign to them.[270]

Cultural training that focuses on worldview issues in fact can help with both the messenger/audience relationship and also with the messenger's relationship to his/her own culture. Worldview training will give insight into the values, beliefs, and feelings that are at the invisible core of a culture. Worldview training will also allow mission trainers to look to the Word and understand what the driving values, beliefs, and feelings are within the Kingdom of God. In that way, trainees can compare their human cultures with the kingdom. At times this is not a pleasant exercise, because so often the familiar and comfortable way that we have grown in Christ will be challenged. However, it is in the long run a glorious challenge!

---

[270] For more discussion, see O'Brien, Brandon J, and E. Randolph Richards. *Misreading Scripture with Western Eyes.* Downers Grove, IL: IVP Books, 2012. Also, Wan, Enoch. "Sailing in the Western Wind." *Chinese Around the World*, March 21, 1999.

Romans 12:1—2 call us to not be conformed to this world, but to be transformed. The call is to recognize the places where our home culture does not align with the kingdom, and then make the deliberate decision to reject "the world" as it appears within our own culture. God's Kingdom becomes the point of reference.

One of the blessings of intercultural Christian ministry is exactly on that point. By seeing other cultures, we begin to see our own. And as we see our own culture, the point of comparison is not between human cultures as if we were trying to decide which is better. Rather, the point of comparison is the kingdom with its values, beliefs, and feelings. Mission training needs to give tools and insights for cultural analysis, and then point participants to analyze their own cultural tendencies in the light of the Bible.

Relationship Six: The Audience in Culture

We never speak to an audience without also speaking to the culture of that audience. As we saw in the discussion of Relationship Five, the Messenger in Culture, mission training must prepare people to identify the worldview issues that are at the root of a culture. As those observation and analysis tools are mastered, a messenger can better form healthy relationships within the new culture.

The issue of appropriate, healthy relationships is at once part of the goal and part of the process. By entering into relationship with the people of a given culture, we form relationships through which we can share all of our lives, including the Gospel. Those same relationships become the key way to become learners of the culture, as one both interacts and reflects on the ways of life of his/her new neighbors.

One of the common metaphors for culture is an onion, with the point being that the deep core issues at the heart of the onion (or culture) are in fact united with and form the foundations for the layers that are outside of that core. Considering that analogy, what is the purpose of missionary work? In too many situations, missionary work has been content with seeing changes on the "outside" of the onion. Changes that go no deeper than how a business is run or how school classes are taught run the risk of being misguided. The call of ministry is to bring people into a deepening relationship with God. Simple changes to the outside of the culture will fall short of the goal.

One of the participants in our training program, looking at the model of culture as an onion, used a phrase that has become famous within our training: the hill to die on is the core – it is the worldview. We have heard missionaries who want to bring change to the government or nutrition level or business practices alone. That is so very underachieving. The call of the missionary is to understand the audience in culture, and to seek ways to bring God's values to the very core of the people. Doing that, there will be change all through the "onion:" schools, government, economic assumptions, health care change. Yet for missionary work to be true to its calling, those changes will grow from a transformed core, not from a superficial change in habits.

As we consider this cultural interaction, we also return to the concept of discourse community. While there is value in understanding the values that unite large groups of people, our interest is not in culture at the national or even people-group level. We are interested in seeing a given group of interacting people shift from following the gods of their fathers and instead develop a relationship with the Triune God. The focus of mission work is the local community – perhaps a family or a village or a network of people within a city. It is at that level that real relationship takes place, and it is at that level that culture is ultimately expressed.

Relationship Seven: Involvement of evil beings

There is one additional relationship that grew from our analysis of the relationships found in mission: the presence and relationship with evil. Christians of all times and places, and intercultural Christian missions especially, must recognize the presence of the evil one and realize that the goal of Satan and demons is to disrupt any relationship that seeks to glorify God and bring his truth into new lives.

Mission training must include what is commonly called Spiritual Warfare. Bible knowledge of the wiles of our enemy is an essential first step. Mission stories, biographies, and history tell stories of evil and how God responded to it are important for mission training. Understanding and practicing scriptural teachings about resistance to the devil and his demons is key. Paul and Timothy model this element of mission training (for instance,

Acts 16:16-18), and for current mission trainees from any land, wisdom about recognizing and dealing with spiritual opposition is an important part of a relational paradigm.

It is important to repeat again that relationships are not always healthy. There are some interactions between beings that clearly do not honor God; this fact is not contrary to the relational paradigm. The relational paradigm helps us to see life and ministry as a series of relationships. Within those relationships, as Christians we want to deal appropriately with those (like demons) that would have us diminish our relationship with God and man. We want to recognize that we are in a relationship with a liar, a murderer, and a thief (John 10:10). In the context of that relationship we reject what we hear from him, we refute his lies, and we flee from his presence. We deliberately choose healthy relationships with God and man over against the sinful and destructive relationship with evil.

Summary

A practical application of the Paradigm of Relational Realism has been presented through the method of dyad analysis. The seven key relationships that one finds in mission work allow us to clarify our thinking and develop specific ideas and skills for working within any one of those relational groupings.

Table 18 will summarize the ideas presented in Chapter
Six:

Table 18 : Practical Ministry Training Elements

Aspect	Description	Training Implications
#1 Within the Trinity	"Interanimation" Polyphony Taxi Characteristic relational markers	-Training for healthy marriage based on scriptural values -Delight to see others advance -Training to serve others within authority and submission relationships. -Train and evaluate based on markers like Fruit of Spirit and 2 Peter 1.
#2 God/messenger	Abide	Personal walk with God through personal and corporate meditation, prayer, disciplines, worship, journaling, etc.
#3 God/audience	Recognition of God's presence	Expectation of seeing God active. Prayer as a key part in mission work. Mission history and biographies of what he has done in the past.
#4 Messenger/audience	Intercultural competence Language acquisition Methods & techniques	By all means continue to include these skills and insights but always within the larger contexts of relationship and transformation.
#5 Messenger in his/her culture	Do not be conformed to this world	Identify kingdom values, and recognize home culture assumptions that differ from the kingdom.
#6 Audience in his/her culture	"The hill to die on"	Train for cultural observation and cultural analysis, with intention to understand worldview of the people within ethnic, national and especially local community levels. Transformation is when that worldview becomes subject to the values, beliefs, and feelings of the kingdom.
#7 Evil	Know the wiles of the evil one, flee	Mission training includes insight into spiritual warfare.

Chapter Seven
Training Methods and Relational Paradigm

Introduction

In the last chapter, we considered the nature of relationships in mission work. The seven basic relationships gave us a way to identify relational, as well as cognitive and affective, elements that are important to mission work.

In the first part of chapter seven, we look at how relationships and educational methods interact. In the second part of the chapter, we will look again at the seven key mission relationships to illustrate methods that would appropriately train mission candidates for healthy relationships within each of the seven model missionary relationships.

Human relationships in the training context

There is a straightforward, commonsense principle that we can suggest to begin this chapter. If the goal is that people go about missionary work in a relational way, it makes sense that the training of those workers should be relational. As we have defined the relational paradigm, this means that training will take place in the context of interactive connections between the trainer, the trainee, and other beings and Beings who are part of the picture.

Though this principle seems self-evident, there is a strong appeal to use methods that grow from philosophical backgrounds and techniques that are far from relational. Whether relying solely on written materials, video recordings, or one-way lectures, many parts of the world have long history of equating teaching/training with uni-directional information transfers. In our review of educational theory, we noted how any given educational philosophy tends to be student-based, society-based, or content-based. A relational paradigm will deliberately and consciously look at the range of relationships between beings/Beings as the preferred option upon which to build teaching methods.

The current popularity of MOOCs (Massive Open Online Classes) is an example of this information-sharing tendency. Information is certainly changing hands: the lecturer is sharing valuable insight with mass audiences who join the internet class. Some of those lecturers are able to interact to some degree through personal stories that create a certain emotional affinity. Feedback to the professor is limited to course evaluation tools, unless perhaps the unusual happens and a personal note is sent, received, and recognized.

These comments about MOOCs are not meant to be negative. The professors and institutions are not offering some kind of relational interaction; they are offering people information via a virtually 100 percent uni-directional method. MOOCs are exactly what they claim to be, and there is value in what they offer.

However, MOOCs represent something far different than a relational paradigm. The relational paradigm calls for interaction on a personal level. If mission work is to be done on the level of personal interactive relationships, then the training process must both model and encourage that same sort of relationship.

Far from Freire's "banking model" of teaching[271] (which is exemplified by MOOCs), Relational Paradigm will instead actively seek methods that augment personal interaction.

As we consider the methods, then, that are consistent with the relational realism paradigm, a first consideration has to do with the size of training groups. Any given person is only capable of a certain number of real, sincere interactive relationships. Social network analysis has identified what is called the Dunbar number[272] which represents that maximum number of relationships possible for a given person. This number is estimated to be approximately 150 people. The point is that for humans, there is a limitation to the number and intensity of our relationships. The Triune God is infinite; the Spirit is quite capable of being in significant relationship with every created being. We humans, though, are not infinite. We can only have interactive relationships with a finite number of other humans.

One way to overcome that limitation is to realize that the number of participants at a given training event can in fact be limited, so as to encourage significant interpersonal interaction

[271] Freire, Paulo, and Bergman-Ramos, Myra. *Pedagogy of the Oppressed.*
[272] Dunbar, Robin, 2015. socialsciencespace.com/2013/11/robin-dunbar-on-dunbar-numbers. (Accessed October 30, 2016).

between trainers and trainees. The ability of trainers to cap the size of a training event is one means of assuring the possibility of real relationship between trainers and trainees.

Another approach to this problem can come in the form of collaboration. In the internet world, this is an especially important concept. Perhaps one key trainer shares through either synchronous or asynchronous internet connections. This trainer, it would seem, will be hard pressed to develop rapport with the trainees. If that trainer, though, is part of a network or team that has local members and the interactive elements of the training include significant involvement by the local team members, then a relational approach can develop even though the "main" trainer might be far away.

A variation of this picture is to require that at least some portions of mission training be done in community. When trainers, trainees, and other staff are all literally living with one another for some portion of the training, there are open doors for interaction that cannot take place if everyone leaves the training event in the evening. Going back to the best practices standard that called for training to happen in a residential center if at all possible,[273] the idea of community training that puts trainers and trainees into a common living and dining facility will create opportunities for interaction.

Another way to consider this problem is by seeing a given training event as part of a more long-term series of interactive

---

[273] Harley, *Preparing to Serve*, 124.

encounters. Perhaps the lead trainer is geographically distant from the trainees for an event in October and his/her interaction is via internet connection. That same trainer, though, might be physically present and interactively involved in an event with the same people held in January. In other words, interaction can be seen through a long term perspective.

Donald Smith used a phrase that captures the essence of this principle: Communication is involvement.[274] The trainer or training program that tries to deliver "information" as an abstract and distant commodity will not, in fact, represent a relational paradigm. That information transfer will give at least the impression that mission work and disciple-making can happen via similarly impersonal means. The trainer who models involvement will be modeling the life-on-life complexity of real world disciple making.

Another element in relational paradigm is to recall that the concept of relationship is culturally conditioned. Whereas some cultures understand "relationship" to be a synonym for friendship, others will see relationship as the appropriate social interaction between people, each maintaining a personal rapport while also fulfilling culturally appropriate roles.

In other words, the distinction between teacher and student (or administrator/teacher, for that matter) should not be lost in the process of mission training. If that distinction is lost, it is very possible that those being sent out from Western nations

---

[274] Smith, Donald K., *Creating Understanding*, 23.

will naively assume that the egalitarian training relationships they are used to will be present in the host culture. In fact, relational paradigm calls for interactive connections that create human relationships in culturally appropriate ways.

One last comment about the methods which foster relational missionary training returns to the transformative education discussion in chapter four. The goal of mission training is not simply to exchange information, nor simply to develop skills or attitudes. The very process of gospel work in unfamiliar cultural backgrounds creates the "disorienting dilemma" that, in the best of cases, leads to evaluation of life assumptions. As Christians, we know that many of those assumptions will be validated because they grow from Scripture. Yet we also know that all Christians need to continually grow in their understanding and application of scriptural truth. The deliberate application of transformative education from a Christian perspective is a key to the training process.

A few principles can be drawn to summarize the last few pages.

1. Relational Paradigm teaching/training methods will be relationally interactive. Significant involvement of the people involved is a necessary element in training methods.

2. Relational paradigm teaching/training methods may extend across years and across geographical divisions.

3. Relational paradigm teaching/training can be pursued in community living/learning environments.

4. Relational paradigm teaching/training methods are not necessarily contrary to internet technology. The wise use of teaching teams can effectively bridge the gap between distance technology and true interaction. Similarly, a training schedule that includes some on-site interaction interspersed with distance learning methods can also bridge the gap between distance and interaction.

5. Relational paradigm training is aware of and responsive to cultural definitions of what is a healthy relationship. Hierarchical cultures see the relational paradigm as building healthy sincere relationships within the framework of appropriate roles. Similarly, egalitarian cultures will build relationships with fewer elements of hierarchy. Training relationships, methods, and content must help participants know how to adjust and adapt to the expectations of any host culture.

6. Relational paradigm training is by nature transformative. As such, transformative education principles are key to the training program and the training content. This includes both a willingness to evaluate Christian practices that may be more cultural than scriptural (some level of syncretism can be seen in every Christian community on earth!), and a recognition that transformation takes place through the interaction of vertical and horizontal relationships. Once again we suggest that readers consider Appendices 1 – 4 for more detailed information about a variety of teaching methods.

Human Relationships and Learning Styles

Another important question for development of methods has to do with the learning and teaching preferences of the people involved.

People learn and teach in part according to the expectations of their cultural groups. Training for missionaries needs to include insight into the diversity of learning and teaching styles across cultures.

The complexity, though, does not stop there. The missionary who is being trained will be going to a place that has its own culturally-conditioned learning and teaching preferences. So simply adapting all styles to the students' preference may in fact be a disservice. What the mission candidate needs to know is not only how to teach and learn in his/her home culture, yet in the culture to which they are going as well.

The best way to model and encourage a relational paradigm methodology that is interculturally transferable is for trainers to take two steps:

1. Use a wide variety of methods, with special focus on the more interactive forms of teaching: case study, role play, small group interaction, real-world observation, apprenticeship –style "MAWL" methods (where the trainer works through a progression of Model, Assist, Watch, and Leave). As was noted in the "Jug and

What's In It"[275] article, familiarity with a wide number of teaching strategies will help to develop a wide variety of methods.

There are also methods that are by nature less interactive: reading, written projects, library or internet research, lecture-style presentations, and asynchronous internet presentations. These methods may be necessary and helpful, yet in each case should be crafted for maximum interpersonal interaction; for instance, reports presented to interactive student groups, written projects which receive response from the trainers, or video presentations followed by interactive discussion with local training staff.

2. Trainers should transparently adapt their teaching forms to the students' preferences, pointing out that they, as teacher/trainer are serving the learners by adjusting to the learners' preferences, with the stated expectation that the learners will likewise adapt to the needs of their own learners in days to come. A transparent and visible recognition of that teaching flexibility may help to foster similar flexibility in the learners.

Human Development and Training Styles

Our review of Trinitarian theology included the observation that human beings grow and develop. This helps explain what every educator understands: there are times when a lesson is appropriate, and times when it is not. The concept of

---

[275] Hyman and Rosoff, "Matching Learning and Teaching Styles".

"learning readiness" is one practical outworking of the developmental nature of human life.

This idea is a strong support for the relational realism paradigm. Training that is mass-produced will likely be built on a theoretical, assumed level of participant development. The steps of training, and in fact the assumed starting place at which learners enter a program, will often be of some ideal "model" student. The Relational Paradigm offers two alternatives:

1. By working within the realm of real relationships, tailor-made training is very possible. That is to say, though there might be an overarching assumption about the level of preparation of a participant, in fact the trainers and participants can work together to design training that takes into account the actual level of preparation of a given participant.

2. The wise use of distance education in conjunction with relational realism paradigm lets a trainer provide appropriate pre-field training before a candidate leaves his/her homeland and then follow that pre-field training with internet-based coaching/mentoring after arrival in the host culture. This is not a small point. It permits trainers to form a face-to-face relationship in the homeland, but not have to use that relationship to teach concepts that could easily be premature. The formation of the relationship can combine with distance training at the right time to create a teaching/training situation impossible before the internet.

As a training program is developed, we would recommend that trainers consider the following time periods to help track with the developmental nature of mission training:

Pre-field: the things that a candidate needs to know in order to successfully arrive in the host culture and begin their life/ministry.

Continuing Education: the on-field topics that would be premature to present in pre-field training, yet that can be effectively taught through internet or other distance-education methods. The relationships with the training staff are still important, though now they are less face-to-face and more internet-based.

Post-field: the question of what is needed to effectively return to one's homeland? This includes two areas: ability to understand and communicate what happened during one's sojourn overseas, and what areas of adaptation and adjustment are necessary upon return to one's homeland.

Cyclic development: all missionaries to some extent, and especially those who spend multiple years in their host country, find themselves developing in two ways: there is the intercultural development that happens as one becomes increasingly effective in the host culture, and there is the lifecycle that is common to all people. Those lifecycles, though, may be complicated by an overseas life and ministry. Areas such as raising children, sending grown children back to their homeland for university, or dealing with aging parents are common to all people: cyclic development recognizes that those topics are at once common to all people, and yet complicated for those who serve in intercultural ministry.[276]

Illustrations of Methods for the Seven Key Mission Relationships.

If a training program is to develop relational-paradigm practitioners, the training itself needs to model that kind of relational strength. With that in mind, Table 19 suggests some possible ways to train for the seven relationships with methods that are themselves relational:

Table 19 Training Methods for Relational Paradigm:

Relationship	Description	Examples of possible training method choices
#1 Within the Trinity	Though humans do not enter directly into the Trinity's inner-relatedness, we are called to understand and model what we see in Scripture. Trainers should help trainees to better understand the relationships that occur between the members of the Trinity.	Bible studies that see the activity of the different members of the Trinity. Bible studies that see how the members of the Trinity interact. Discussion about how the Members of the Trinity might be involved in a given life situation.

---

[276] Wan proposed a "10 stages in counseling" with a cyclical pattern in a recent publication - Enoch Wan. *En-qing Theology: Interdisciplinary Studies and Practice.* (in Chinese) Hong Kong: TienDao Publisher. 2016: chapter 8. www.toelibrary.com

Relationship	Description	Examples of possible training method choices
#2 Between Trinity and Gospel messenger	The gospel messenger in a significant relationship with Triune God: God sends, protects, provides, enables, empowers, gives wisdom. The trainee needs to see in both Bible and personal experience how God is active in his/her life.	Bible readings that show God at work in the life of other gospel messengers. Biographies that show God at work in the life of other gospel messengers. Bible studies that demonstrate the rich relationship between Triune God and those he sends. Group discussions about how God acts as a means of encouraging one another. Internet coaching on the field which includes times of recognizing where God was active. Journaling to recall God's previous activity in the messenger's life.
#3 Between Trinity and audience	God has given to humans the responsibility to share the Gospel. Yet God himself opens the heart of the hearer. Messenger is called to act boldly and wisely and at the same time in dependence on God.	Methods include active sharing of testimonies of salvation to recognize that God is at work in audiences. Prayer for receptive hearts by the audience, and for wise proclamation by the messengers. Bible study to recognize God's role in salvation and discipleship. Use of debrief after ministry events to recognize how God responded in that event.

Relationship	Description	Examples of possible training method choices
#4 Between messenger and audience	God expects his people to actively enter new cultures with the Gospel.	Methods could include: apprenticeship so that new personnel work with experienced missionaries to learn how they do their work. Internet sessions to hear practitioners from various places sharing methods of ministry they use, and what results they have experienced. Readings in methods from various places including group discussions. Intercultural training on key topics, presented in light of learning-readiness of the participant.
#5 Between messenger and home culture	The gospel messenger has been formed with a worldview from a particular place, time, and people. Knowing one's own background leads to better possibility of adjustment and adaptation.	Review of worldview issues, with opportunity for self-reflection on how those issues are seen in the missionary's home culture. Group discussion about effects of home culture. Written review of cultural heritage that highlights strengths and weaknesses in light of Scriptural values and beliefs. The written document to be reviewed during service on the field. On-field coaching that includes questions of adjustment and adaptation to the new culture with particular sensitivity to the heritage received from the missionary's home culture.

Relationship	Description	Examples of possible training method choices
#6 Between audience and culture	The audience does not respond to messenger alone, Yet as part of a social/cultural group. Good intercultural communication requires that the Gospel messenger has culture-general knowledge of major cultural dynamics and has skill in learning culture-specific adaptation.	Teacher-led interactive discussion about major cultural distinctions, including discussion of student experiences. Observation and interview experiences that help gospel messengers to learn the culture of another people. Interactive discussions with practitioners in similar cultures to hear what methods have been effective with the cultures in view.
#7 Between evil powers and messengers	The appropriate relationship between a Christian and evil powers is to recognize, resist, and flee.	Reading of books related to animistic worldviews, with discussion and analysis of how the evil spirits worked and how Gospel workers respond. Discussion with experienced practitioners who discuss recognition and responses in spiritual warfare issues. Reading of direct books/articles on the topic. Reading of scriptural passages related to spiritual warfare.

Training Environment and Relational Paradigm

In this practical application section, we have looked at the methods for a training program that is relational. This last section continues that same practical application, now asking what environment will best foster a relational approach to mission training.

Phrasing this question another way, we could ask what kind of environment best fosters relationship, and best fosters the development of skills for mission.

The best environment will align with the cultural preferences of learners.

Kolb's quadrants[277] come in especially helpful for this question. There are cultures whose teaching/learning preferences include hands-on, practical work. Other cultures prefer conceptual, theoretical work. Knowing the relative preferences of how learning and teaching take place will help to set the right environment. Some environments will favor lecture-style classrooms. Other learner preferences will seek interactive environments.

The best environment will prepare people for the kind of work that they will be doing.

This sounds like a truism, but it is not. In practice, mission training tends to settle everyone into the same location. And so those who will be working in a jungle village and those who will be serving in an urban center go to the same mission training programs. Similarly, mission training tends to settle all learners into a generic culture training program while in practice some folks will work in education, some in medicine, some in business, some in traditional church work.

Recognizing that there are factors like financial expense and availability of personnel that will mitigate this point, still a

---

[277] Kolb, David A. *Experiential Learning.*

relational paradigm will help people to learn to live in the environment where they will be working. The missionary trained in a forest camp may find it hard to create relationships with neighbors in an apartment complex later on. Likewise, the missionary who learns to understand the economic and banking industry in preparation for a business as mission ministry will do better than the one who is only exposed to generic cultural patterns without reference to their social functions.

The best environment will foster interactive relationship between students and teachers.

This can include a mixture of digital and face-to-face training. From personal experience, I know that warm and real human relationships can be formed and maintained by internet connection. Even as I say that, I also admit that it requires a deliberate effort to create and sustain those electronic connections.

In some cases, internet connections actually promote relational paradigm ministry even more than face to face might. Think, for instance, of a mission candidate who has recently arrived on location in the nation where he/she will serve. In the absence of internet connection, there may be one or two visits a year from the home office. There is in fact very little relationship possible because of the need to travel.

On the other hand, the candidate who arrives on site and then begins weekly meetings by audio and/or visual telecommunication is in fact building a relationship with his/her mentor.

Summary

This chapter has focused on methods and environments that are helpful for relational paradigm training. The conclusion is that a relational paradigm needs to be presented by methods which themselves are relational. We looked at interpersonal relationships in teaching methods and across timelines, and we talked about the interaction between human relationships and preferred learning and teaching styles. Finally, we looked at the seven key missionary relationships to suggest possible illustrations of how methods could be developed that use relational methods to achieve relational ends. Methods are closely related to environment, and the environment for training is determined by factors such as learning style preferences, likely field assignment, and how a relationship can best be formed and sustained.

Chapter Eight
Training Content and Relational Paradigm

Introduction

In the experience of the authors of this study, this chapter is perhaps the topic with the widest range of practical possibilities. If one is going to "the ends of the earth" or to a people whose language and culture differs from his/her own, what areas of preparation are necessary? For the purposes of this study, we will define that question even more tightly: what are the topics that a relational paradigm training program must take into consideration to prepare relational intercultural gospel workers? What scope of study should a relationally-based training program include?

Basic Framework: what Paul taught Timothy

A starting place for this question is in the things that Timothy learned from Paul. Please note that the following discussions may or may not be within the scope of the training program itself. In other words, there are many areas of training that could be "pre-requisites" to a mission training program. Still, those pre-requisites are essential for the overall success of the trainee and the program.

This chapter will be organized around the 12 topics that Paul taught to Timothy (see list in Chapter Three).

Before we consider these topics, there are three vocabulary issues that will help us to place Paul's training concepts into our 21st century:

Etic/emic

When people from two cultures meet, human nature is practically universal in pointing each person involved towards evaluation of the "other" based on the criteria, norms, and familiar habits of his/her own culture. In short, we are all ethnocentric.

In missionary training, that stance of understanding the other culture in comparison to one's own familiar norms leads missionaries to take on the posture of "outsider." This "outsider" role is one who, uninvited and possibly unwelcome, brings a critical eye to the host culture and in essence begins to say what must change. The changes that are prescribed will typically push towards closer alignment of the host culture with Christianity <u>as it is practiced in the missionary's land</u>.

One tool to help avoid this unintentional but frequent mixing of culture with Christianity is to learn the distinction between an etic perspective and an emic perspective.

The two terms, developed by Kenneth Pike of the Summer Institute of Linguistics, are common terms in cultural research. Etic refers to a perspective that grows from an outsider. This posture will create categories and questions that are important to the outsider, and then describe the culture in those terms.

Emic approaches, on the other hand, seek to understand from an insider's perspective. The emic perspective encourages recognition of how the people of a given culture understand life. In terms of gospel work, the emic approach will encourage people to first understand a host culture and then make gospel truths available within the categories and question that are important to the insider.

Adapt/adjust

When cultures and languages come in contact, any given person in that milieu will have two sets of changes to consider: interculturalists today use the words adjust and adapt to refer to these two sorts of changes.

Adjust refers to the internal attitudes and perspectives of the person who is working in an intercultural setting. The "well-adjusted person" is able to feel relatively self-confident and comfortable even as he/she is learning a new way of living. Adjustment areas include the mental and emotional shifts needed for successful transition to life in a new culture. Adjustment includes learning to be internally at peace with the host culture and yet still maintain healthy relationships with the home culture. The "go native" scenario is usually understood to be a poor adjustment – the person has become critical of his/her home culture and uncritically accepting of the host culture. On the other hand, maintaining a long term hostility or judgmental attitude against the host culture is likewise evidence of a lack of adjustment.

Adaptation, in contrast, does not speak to the internal state of the intercultural sojourner. Rather, "adapt" speaks to the behavioral changes that a person makes in order to fit into the normal ways of life, communication, and thought of the people to whom he/she is sent.

We could imagine a person from the majority culture of the United States who moves to Mexico. He or she has the opportunity to make changes in two ways: attitude changes that are largely unseen and behavioral changes that will shift his/her normal patterns to more closely align with the people among whom she is now living. These two issues are both important, and in fact may occur independently of one another. It is very possible for one to learn to eat tortillas and *salsa picante* (that is, learn to adapt) and still yearn for catsup and even have a bitter attitude (lack of adjustment). Similarly, one can be successful at developing a healthy attitude, and yet not learn to shift actions and speech so as to adapt to the culture.

Researcher and trainer Milton Bennett developed a six-stage model to describe the developmental process leading to adjustment to a new culture.[278] This model can be helpful for missionary training. The model, presented in the following paragraphs, describes a developmental process that ranges from least adjusted to most adjusted, noting accompanying adaptation to a new way of life in the higher levels of development.

---

[278] Bennett, Milton J. "Becoming Interculturally Competent." In Wurzel, Jaime S. *Toward Multiculturalism: A Reader in Multicultural Education*. Newton, MA: Intercultural Resource Corporation, 2004, 62–77.

Stage one: denial. The intercultural sojourner denies that there are differences between cultures. "We are all human; we are all the same" is this person's attitude.

Stage two: defense. This is a polarized posture in which some recognition of other ways of life is acknowledged. Yet those "others" are seen as somehow wrong; not merely different, but inferior and erroneous.

Stage three: minimization. The person recognizes some differences and acts on the belief that his/her cultural patterns are simply the right choice. People in the minimization stage would expect that once they tell the host culture that there is another option, the new culture will flock to it. This stage believes that "The way 'we' do things is obviously better."

Between stage three and the next stage (four) there is an internal shift from ethnocentric to ethnorelative posture. Stage four begins to admit that life can be understood appropriately from the emic perspective.

Stage four is acceptance. In this stage, one's own culture is seen as one of many viable options. The differences between people are seen as legitimate variations on how to handle the issues that all people face.

Stage five is adaptation. Bennett's model considers that adaptation is the point where perception and behavior begin to shift deliberately to become more aligned with the host norms. The sojourner does not, in this view, reject his/her homeland, yet expands to see multiple ways to deal with the human condition.

Stage six in Bennett's construct is integration. In this level, the person can shift from one culture to another and act appropriately in both of them. This person has mastered the ability of "when in Rome, do as the Romans" without losing the ability to likewise understand and live according to the norms of homeland.

Intercultural/multicultural

While there is some variation in use of terms, there is also a growing recognition that intercultural and multicultural speak to different dynamics. Intercultural speaks to a situation where people from two different cultural backgrounds interact. Multicultural refers to situations where there are people from three or more cultural backgrounds all in some kind of interactive situation.

In Acts 20:16, Paul is seen as working with a group with representatives from Berea, Thessalonica, Derbe, and Asia. The multicultural background would mean that each person would have to develop skills in working with each of the other people and each of the other cultural backgrounds. In comparison, when Paul wrote to Titus he gave specific instructions on how to live and work effectively with one group of people – those from Crete. Learning to live and work in an intercultural relationship is actually quite a different skill set, though based on similar knowledge base, as the ability to live and work in a multicultural setting.

With these background concepts in mind, we now want to look at the content of relational paradigm mission training. Our primary organizing concept for this discussion will be the inductive study of what Paul taught to Timothy in the course of the years that they served together.

What Timothy Heard from Paul in the Presence of Many Witnesses

Paul/Timothy Topic #1 Cultural Sensitivity (Acts 16:1)

When we think of the content of mission training, the issue of culture or discourse community comes to the fore quickly. Mission training in a relational paradigm will seek to give practical skill as well as theoretical insight into the ways that people from one culture relate to those from another.

The intercultural competence literature is filled with specific skill and knowledge areas that have been shown helpful in preparing people to serve outside of their own culture and language. Fred Lewis has adapted information from several other sources (most notably from Darla Deardorff) to prepare the following list.[279] These topics would be part of the cultural preparation of a new Gospel worker.

Attitudes and Motivation to Enable Adaptation:

1. Curiosity
2. Willingness to temporarily withhold judgment

---

[279] Lewis, Fred. "Towards Intercultural Effectiveness: Attitudes, Knowledge and Skills to Enable Competence in Intercultural Ministry." unpublished, 2014. Adapted from Deardorff, Darla K. "Identification and Assessment of Intercultural Competence as a Student Outcome of Internationalization." *Journal of Studies in International Education* 10, no. 254 (2006). http://jsi.sagepub.com.

3. Desire to learn and adapt
4. Willingness to learn from mistakes and successes
5. Tolerance for ambiguity
6. Respect for the ways of life of another people, based on the fact that the good in them and their culture have their source in God.
7. Perseverance
8. Desire to follow the example of Christ (Phil 2:6–8)

Knowledge to Enable Adaptation

9. Awareness of the influence of home culture values, beliefs, worldview, and expected emotional responses on oneself.
10. Sociolinguistic awareness
11. Deep culture-general understanding
12. Deep culture-specific understanding
13. Awareness that there may be many possible explanations for a single event.

Skills to enable adaptation

14. To deliberately shift social/cultural/communicational frames of reference in order to adopt different perspectives towards another person, situation, etc. (cognitive empathy)
15. To regulate and modulate one's own emotional reactions and expressions to fit different cultural contexts
16. To observe and analyze another culture to understand it and people on their own terms.

17. To evaluate cultural practices, beliefs, and values from biblical and historical perspectives
18. Emotional empathy

Ministry and Life Adaptation

19. Behaving and relating appropriately in different cultures, and in different settings within a culture
20. Changing communication style and content to fit the people, social setting, etc.
21. Modifying ministry forms and styles to suit local sensibility.
22. Adding to or deleting ministry activities based on felt and real needs of local people.

That list of competence areas can work well in situations that permit extended time for training activities. Brinkmann and van Weerdenburg's list of four competencies offers an approach that is helpful when the available time is short. Brinkmann and van Weerdenburg looked for the intercultural competency areas of intercultural skill that associate with successful adaptation and adjustment. A training program that includes these four areas (each with two sub-points) will likely be good foundation for effective intercultural ministry, especially when the time available for training is limited.

1. Intercultural Sensitivity
   a. Cultural awareness
   b. Attention to signals
2. Intercultural communication

a. Active listening

b. Adapting communication style

3. Building commitment

a. Building relationships

b. Reconciling stakeholder needs

4. Managing uncertainty

a. Openness to cultural diversity

b. Exploring new approaches

Paul/Timothy Topic #2: Multiple ethnicities in the church as Jews and Gentiles came together (Acts 16:5)

As Paul and Timothy saw the church grow, they also found it necessary to manage differences across cultural lines. The Jewish/Gentile divide in the First Century church was just as real as the cultural barriers that we find in communities and churches today. Content areas helpful for the multi-cultural mission team or the members of a new multicultural Christian community would include:

1. Intercultural conflict management

2. Intercultural negotiation (not limited to business contexts, but to the wider perspective of negotiating on every point of life where more than one opinion needs to be resolved.)

3. Interpersonal skills areas

Paul/Timothy Topic #3: Church growth (Acts 16:5)

Anyone wanting to be involved in mission also needs to have experience in church. I do not necessarily mean that mission should focus on church planting or church growth; too often that phrasing turns into a transplanting of methods and structures that work in the church of one part of the world, regardless of what church ought to look like in the place where the missionary is working. The issues of church planting and church growth easily become the methods and techniques, quite different from a relational paradigm.

Saying that, though, there are healthy relationships that one expects to see between members of a Christian community. The missionary-in-training needs to know the joys and the tears of church work. He or she needs to understand by personal experience what are healthy relationships and what are the symptoms of a sickly or toxic church.

Relational paradigm church will focus on seeing growth and development of the people who are part of a local congregation. Far from focus on programs that take on a life of their own, the relational paradigm church will seek healthy and culturally appropriate interactions between the members and leaders of the church.

Paul/Timothy topic #4: The Spirit's involvement in directing missionary outreach (Acts 16:6)

The relational paradigm understands that each Member of the Trinity is involved in seeing the Gospel arrive to the unreached. The content area of recognizing Spiritual activity in the work of mission and church is fundamental for the relational paradigm. The "closed system" of human management systems[280] does not admit room for an active God. And yet, mission work is based on the promise made by the Lord, "I am with you always." (Matt 28:20). The sent one from any group of churches needs to develop a relationship with the Lord that shows confidence, obedience, love, and expectation. The sent one from any national background needs to expect God's Spirit to do the work that only he can do.

This content area can be best taught through apprenticeship or internship methods. The actual prayer and watching with expectation to see God open hearts, borders, and provisions is part of the training of missionaries that needs to begin well before any given training program, and needs to extend well past the conclusion of that program.

Paul/Timothy Topic #5: Evangelism and Baptism (Acts 16:15)

Paul and Timothy co-labored in many ways, including in the sharing of Gospel with communities, and in the baptism of new believers. These same areas need to be part of mission training.

Müller's series, *The Messenger, The Message, and The Community*[281] is an important part of the training in how to share the Gospel and how to encourage towards baptism. Any given

---

[280] Wan, Enoch. *Diaspora Missiology.*
[281] Müller, Roland. *The Messenger, the Message & the Community: Three Critical Issues for the Cross-Cultural Church Planter.* Osler, Sask.: CanBooks, 2010.

community will have certain core beliefs that need to be addressed by the Gospel. Over the centuries, though, we see that often the missionary presents to a new people the Gospel as it was most powerful in their home culture. A well-trained missionary will recognize the worldview issues of the community they are trying to reach and will give an accurate and scriptural explanation of the Gospel that interacts with the worldview assumptions of the people.

As an illustration, Western civilization has a strong cultural inclination towards universal law. All people at all times are expected to obey the law. Thus, when one explains the Gospel in these Western contexts it makes sense to put the emphasis on the idea that we are all guilty, we have all broken God's law, and all of us deserve His just penalty. That forensic explanation is certainly a clear and very accurate Gospel presentation.

Guilt/Innocence is not the only accurate way to present the Gospel, though. The Gospel can just as accurately be described as taking away our shame and replacing it with the honor of being adopted into God's household. Do we deserve this honor? Not at all. We deserve to be cast out and shamed because of our rejection of God. Yet God, rich in love, has covered our shame and replaced it with honor.

Fear/power and even clean/unclean [282] are other common responses to the separation of humanity from God. This level of

---

[282] Jabbūr, Nabîl. *The Crescent through the Eyes of the Cross: Insights from an Arab Christian.* Colorado Springs, CO: NAV Press, 2008.

evangelistic contextualization maintains the integrity of Scriptures and yet makes the connection of God's grace with the heart of the person. Such ability in evangelism and baptism is part of the relational paradigm as it seeks to make a relational connection between a person (whatever his worldview) and the Lord and his Word.

Paul/Timothy Topic #6: Recognition of and reaction to demonic activity (Acts 16:16)

The seven key missionary relationships that have served as outline for much of this book gives attention to the reality of evil in this world. There are evil beings, and those evil beings are active in the affairs of mankind. With that in mind, the gospel messenger must be relationally astute to see evil where it exists, and to respond to it appropriately. Remember that when we speak of relational paradigm we do not mean that people should pursue every relationship that they are offered. The relational paradigm looks for appropriate scriptural interactions between Beings/beings. In the case of interaction with evil, the Christian will in fact be tempted and tried. We will have interactions with evil. Even though we ask our Father to deliver us from evil, we will be tempted by the evil one.

Christian workers need to recognize the wiles of our enemy. That can happen by pre-training internships or by sections of mission training that focus on spiritual warfare. Interaction with experienced missionaries who both model and coach can serve as an effective, relational approach to teaching about the evil one. Through whatever means, the appropriately trained missionary will have a frame of reference by which to understand evil beings, and by which to gauge the most appropriate way to deal with him.

Paul/Timothy Topic # 7: Persecution, jail, beating and suffering for the gospel (Acts 16:22)

A very real part of Gospel ministry relates to the possibility and even likelihood of suffering. Timothy learned from firsthand experience that suffering for the Gospel is a normal part of Christian life.

This is a significant issue for relational paradigm.

The Western church with its worldview of comfort and its rejection of pain and suffering[283] often equates comfort with God's blessing. By the same token, the assumption of Western missionaries is that suffering, persecution, and death are evidences that one is being punished by God. The relational paradigm sees God and man interactions that are not always pleasant or comfortable, yet which nevertheless create deep, healthy relationships. Job's companions tried hard to vilify Job, seeing his suffering as evidence that his relationship with God was somehow faulty. In the same way, Western Christianity sees suffering as evidence of some disruption with one's relationship with God. In truth, though, suffering is not evidence *per se* of

---

[283] duBois, Cora. "The Dominant Value Profile of American Culture." *American Anthropologist* 57, no. 6 (December 1955): 1236.

God's displeasure. In fact, Jesus himself suffered for our sake, not because his relationship with the Father was somehow faulty.

Through Bible study, through interaction with believers from high-persecution lands, and through reflection this issue of suffering is a critical part to relational paradigm mission training.

Paul/Timothy Topic #8: Strategy of who goes to new towns and who stays to disciple new believers (Acts 17:14, 15)

Training for mission work includes growing in the ability to make decisions about how best to reach a given group of people. Is the best strategy for all of the team to go? Or for some to wait in one town while others travel? Should a business be opened? Or is traditional preaching a better approach?

These and a host of similar strategic questions lead to one of the key realities of relational paradigm: the both/and perspective that God is active and guides us, and yet that we also need to think and plan as best we know how. That kind of strategic planning, weighing the pros and cons of various possible actions, is part of what Paul taught to Timothy. It is likewise part of healthy mission training today.

There are implications to the usefulness of strategic planning that are worth mentioning. First, the mission teams in the Book of Acts had visible leadership, and the entire team was respectful of that leadership. Paul, for instance, was not sure what to do in Acts 16. Should the team go to Asia? Or to Bythinia? Paul had his perspective but the Lord stepped in and changed those plans. For some days that I personally think may have been quite uncomfortable for the entire team, they were not sure where they should go. God then gave the Macedonia call so that, in author Luke's words, "when Paul had seen the vision, we sought to go into Macedonia, concluding that God had called us to preach the Gospel to them."

The leadership issues in those few verses of Acts 16 are remarkable, and are important for understanding relational paradigm. Luke's words reflect a deep understanding that the whole team relied on the relationship between Paul and God. They did not ALL receive the Macedonia call; the vision only came to Paul. Yet that one vision was accepted as a call to the whole team. The relationship between God and Paul proved to be the guiding relationship for the entire team.

Interestingly, though, later on Paul made decisions that do not give reference to divine guidance. In the both/and of relational paradigm thinking, we believe that at times God makes his will explicitly visible. At other times, he lets what appears to be human wisdom make the decision. In either case, though, the relationship between leader and God, between leader and team are both vitally important for the proper fulfilling of God's direction.

In the egalitarian nations of the West, such a trust of the leader is counter cultural and not a little bit uncomfortable. Mission training needs to deal with areas of relationship between the leader and God, the team and God and the team and the leaders so that appropriate relationships are maintained. God works through those appropriate interactions.

Paul/Timothy Topic #9: Preaching in difficult circumstances (Acts 18:5)

"In season and out of season" is when a gospel messenger should give testimony of his/her relationship with God, and of how that relationship is likewise available to others. Yet how does one learn to preach the good news, and especially how does one learn to do that in times of persecution or war or disaster? Paul and Silas preached while imprisoned. In other moments, public outcry against the Gospel and its messengers led to trials. How does one learn to preach under distressing situations?

This, as in the case of suffering, is a topic that mission training needs to include. Western missions typically look for ways to avoid suffering and persecution. There are times, though, when accepting the presence of the difficulties and reacting appropriately might mean preaching during wartimes. Biographies of people like as Gladys Aylward [284] can give missionary candidates a new perspective on how to take advantage of the circumstances so as to preach, "in season and out."

Paul/Timothy Topic #10: Missionary finances (Acts 18:5)

Mission training needs to be practical about finances. Jesus' followers had those who kept the purse. Paul communicated with ministry friends about financial involvement (for instance,

---

[284]Aylward, Gladys, and Christine Hunter. *Gladys Aylward, the Little Woman, as Told to Christine Hunter*. Chicago: Moody Press, 1970.

Rom 15:24). There is a need for money, and mission training needs to be transparent about that reality.

There are two aspects of mission finance that are especially important from a relational paradigm. First, the money is never seen in Scripture as the key issue. God-honoring relationships are the key issue. The money is an expression of concern, a gracious gift that helps to move the Gospel forward. It is not sought *per se*, yet it is an expression of relationship.

This point is vital for understanding relational paradigm ministry. In the West, money is seen as an objective item. People seek it for its own sake, and in fact, many in ministry act and speak as if money were a goal in and of itself.

The relational paradigm, though, will see finances as Paul did – not a right, and not a matter limited to money. Rather, Paul saw funds as expressions of concern and collaboration. Giving a gift to a ministry is a relational, not merely a financial, transaction.

A second point worth considering in the content area of ministry finance is that at times the funding of ministry comes from gifts and donations. At other times, the gospel worker receives a salary for the work that he/she does. Paul made tents on occasion. In other occasions, he lived on the gifts that were given for his work (for example, Acts 18:1–5). Both options are viable, and both in fact have relational significance.

When he was making tents, Paul worked with Aquila and Priscilla. Reading a bit into the text, it seems that the hours of working in the trade of tent-making also provided hours for interaction and discipleship in gospel-related topics. A trade is not just a path to a paycheck; it is a role that permits interaction with others. Trades and professions provide relational roles through which the Great Commission can be fulfilled.

The traditional missionary with the goal of "full time Christian service" has some clear advantages in terms of being able to focus solely on Christian ministry. Yet the "full time Christian service" model also has liabilities; most importantly, the gospel worker who is involved in community economic life will have natural bridges of relationship. Whether selling and buying or eating lunch at the market, the Christian tradesman or professional is in relationship with a wide range of people, and has opportunities to talk about his/her relationship with the Lord. The issues of role in the society make a powerful relational reason for some intercultural servants to be trained as market place professionals[285] rather than in full time Christian work.

Paul/Timothy Topic #11: Missionary team formation (Acts 20:4)

When it comes to selecting and sending missionaries, the relational paradigm again has a perspective to consider. Paul's procedure seems to have been to enter a community and share the Gospel. With time, he would teach as deeply as he could to the people there and then either right away or a little later, he named internal leaders for the group.

---

[285] With gratitude to Crossworld mission, Kansas City MO whose tagline includes these words <crossworld.org> accessed Dec 10, 2015.

From Acts 20:4, though, it appears that Paul did one other thing. He seems to have found one or two young men from each new Christian community whom he then invited to join him in mission to the next town.

In Acts 16:2 Paul made inquiry before inviting Timothy to join his team. He found Timothy to be sound in his own conversations, yet he also found through interviews with local Christian leaders that they gave a good report of Timothy. He had a good testimony. The references were not just a formality; Paul looked for missionary colleagues who had a history of healthy and appropriate relationships with others. Those same people he then invited to join his mission team.

Besides the issues of team member selection, Acts 20 implies another issue that is important to a relational paradigm. Paul and his team worked as a multicultural unit. They recognized the cultural differences between them. As Paul and this multicultural team traveled and worked together, without a doubt there was a training, teaching environment where these people from a diverse set of backgrounds interacted around the scriptural truths that they were hearing. From personal experience, I am sure that those diverse cultural perspectives gave rise to different understanding of the Scriptures and the Gospel. Paul used a multicultural team as both his ministry outreach and his training environment.

Paul/Timothy Topic #12: Doctrines and their application to Christian life (Rom 16:21, 1 Cor 4:17; 1 Thes 1:1; 2 Thes 1:1; Philemon 1:1)

The last point uncovered by this inductive review of the interaction between Paul and Timothy includes the fact that Timothy's name is present in just about every one of Paul's epistles. In other words, part of mission training is to give ongoing and in-depth teaching about God's truths as found in the Bible.

Relationally, the point is not to fill academic or intellectual desires. While that indeed can happen, the higher, primary purpose of these doctrinal discussions is to continue to grow in the grace and the knowledge of the Lord Jesus Christ; the issue is to deepen relationships between the Triune God, his people, and his Truth.

This point calls for deep content understanding of the Bible. As disciple-makers for the kingdom, the Bible is the source as well as the goal. Gospel messengers need to "grow in the grace and the knowledge of the Lord Jesus Christ," including in that a strong and ever-growing understanding of the Word of God.

When I entered into mission work in the late 1980s, many sending agencies put their entire focus on knowledge of the Word. It was expected that graduate studies in theology or ministry were completed before one moved towards intercultural ministry. There was little or no emphasis, though, on learning the culture to which one was sent. In our current milieu, we dare not lose the knowledge of God's Word as we add increasing sophistication in intercultural skill and knowledge. The missionary calling is to present God's truth to a people who have not yet received it. That interactive process requires a deep knowledge by the missionary of both the Word and the people. Neither one nor the other can be overlooked.

In fact, from a relational paradigm perspective the purpose of missions is to grow in relationship with a particular person/group of people in such a way that they develop a relationship with the Lord and his Word. It is not the missionary who should become the center of attention. Rather, it is the relationship between a group of people and the Lord that is key to mission work.

Knowledge of the Word is a basic foundational need for the training of missionaries. It is also a foundation that could be built by schools, tutors, or local churches. The important thing is not necessarily who does that teaching, but the importance is that the gospel messenger has solid knowledge and understanding of the Bible.

Summary

This chapter has sought to identify content areas that are important for mission training from a relational paradigm. The example of Paul and Timothy gave us a guide to understand topics to include in preparing a new generation of mission workers.

Section Four: Summary and Conclusions

Chapter Nine
Summary

Introduction

This book has looked at the assumptions that underlie training for intercultural Christian ministry. Our goal has been to introduce a new set of assumptions: a new paradigm that will be somehow superior to what is done now. We have called that paradigm "the Paradigm of Relational Realism." That paradigm, in the simplest of language, says that the basic reality of life is based on relationships: primarily relationships with the Triune God, and secondarily relationships between created beings. Chapter Nine will summarize the theological, theoretical, and practical concepts that have been presented in this book.

Theological Foundations

A new set of assumptions about ministry must start with theological foundations. We have built our paradigm of missionary training on the theological foundation of Trinitarian studies. That foundation provided valuable insights that apply to any Christian ministry: The Trinity is within themselves relational. It is a complex relationship that includes both equality and levels of hierarchy. It is a relationship that rejoices when one member is recognized, without any of the jealousy that marks our human relationships.

The theological assumptions of the Trinity also help us to better understand God's interactive relationship with creation (including yet not limited to humanity.) As we looked at this "economic Trinity" we saw a series of relationship pairs which became one of the strong organizing themes of the book. That review of Economic Trinity led to a simpler list of seven key missionary relationships:

1. Relationships within the Trinity
2. Relationships between the Trinity and the missionary that he sends to the nations
3. Relationships between the Trinity and the audience. God's active involvement is essential if a person or a people are going to come to faith.
4. Relationships between the Missionary and the audience. In one of the most amazing truths of the Bible, God seeks the involvement of his people to proclaim his message to others. We have responsibility to develop our skills and understanding as best we can: and yet our efforts are never independent of God's active involvement.
5. Relationships between the missionary and his/her home culture. The point of ministry is to bring people to a healthy, appropriate relationship with the Triune God. For people in that relationship, that idea includes, for instance, an attitude of dependence, our faith in the promises and

character of God, our faithfulness to what he has told us. We are called to be meek, poor in spirit, and to walk in love. Those are some of the areas where the Kingdom of God must replace the cultural assumptions of any of this world's cultures.

6. Relationships between the audience and his/her culture. Much as the messenger learns to live on the basis of the values and truths of the Kingdom instead of the assumptions of his/her culture, so too the call of discipleship is to help those of a new culture to be transformed in their thinking by learning to question the values and beliefs of their culture and replace those assumptions with the truths and values of the kingdom.

7. An appropriate relationship with evil spirits. Not all relationships are healthy nor appropriate. There are evil beings, and the only appropriate relationship for a believer of any culture with those evil beings is to recognize their wiles, actively choose God and his ways, and flee from the evil one.

Educational Principles

Since our primary focus in this book is on training for missionary service based on the paradigm of relational realism, it is obvious that not only do we need a foundational theological position, yet we likewise need a foundational educational approach.

Education is in the throes of enormous shifts. To the standard teaching/learning approaches of previous generations, we now see online options and increasing sensitivity to the needs of the learner. With that focus on the learner comes also awareness that individuals differ in their preferred learning styles, and there are likewise different cultural preferences in learning styles.

We also looked at matters of education that are specifically designed for adults. This is especially important to our question because the missionary candidates we wish to train are, after all, adults.

In the light of this review of educational approaches, the concept of "transformative education" took a particularly key role in our review. Transformative education is a type of adult education that encourages the learner to question basic assumptions. In our case, transformative education will call the missionary to reconsider assumptions about training and about ministry, arriving (we trust) at new understandings that more closely reflect scriptural patterns of relationships between Beings/beings. In our case, missionary training will ultimately prepare Gospel messengers to understand the underlying values and life assumptions of the people among whom they work, so that they can slowly and carefully suggest scriptural alternatives. The point of missionary work is to facilitate a relationship between their host people and the Triune God, and in doing that, Gospel workers need to identify the assumptions of the people, and then help people move from conformity with those cultural norms to a transformed set of assumptions that grow from God and his kingdom.

How might one undertake that kind of enormous transformational challenge? We looked at various approaches to mission training and at the literature to see what best practices for mission training can offer to us. The basic approach is not tied to methods and techniques, but to a goal of transformation through vertical and horizontal relationships.

Practical Implications

Finally, the Third Section of this book included practical suggestions: specific ideas for mission training presented within a relational paradigm. It is our perspective that mission is by nature relational, and if mission training is to be effective, it too needs to be relational. This stands in distinction to the technique/method approaches that can easily dominate. We are not contrary to methods; yet the methods must serve healthy, appropriate relationships, not the other way around.

With that perspective, we looked at relationships in light of the context and content of training. We considered areas as diverse as learning styles, training styles, and teaching approaches that favor relationship. We looked at training environments: how venues from internet to residential can work within a Paradigm of Relational Realism.

We also looked at the content of training with particular focus on 2 Timothy 2:2. In that passage, we identified what Paul taught to Timothy in the course of their 17 or so years together. That inductive review of biblical material gave a solid outline of the content of mission training.

The key factor in life is relationship: first of all, with Triune God, and secondarily between members of creation. This book has applied that seed thought to the practice of training for missionary work.

Summary

This short chapter has summarized the questions that we have wrestled with through the pages of this book. In the next chapter, we will summarize the conclusions that we have reached and the next steps that are called for.

Chapter Ten
Conclusions

What does it mean to train missionaries under a paradigm of relational realism? Based on the analysis of theological, theoretical, and practical material, this final chapter will suggest conclusions that we trust will lead to further discussion and practice.

What does it mean to train missionaries from a paradigm of relational realism?

It means that the organizing principle for training is relational. By "organizing principle" we mean the core question at every turn:

The program will understand that mission work is a series of relationships, with God first and secondarily with people.

The program will understand that the purpose of mission is relational: to facilitate a relationship between Triune God and the people who are being reached. The relationship with the missionary is normally a key to facilitating this healthy walk with the Lord, yet there are times (as in the example of Phillip and the Ethiopian) when the relationship with the missionary is short lived. The key is to see people growing in the Lord.

The program will strive to use good teaching and outreach methods, yet will always see those methods as serving relationship, not the other way around.

The evaluation of the program will be measured in terms of healthy relational patterns; first of all, with Triune God, and then between training staff, training cohorts, and members of a given ministry team.

It means that mission skills, attitudes, knowledge are designed for and evaluated on the basis of relational outcomes.
The content of teaching/learning is relational.
The context of teaching/learning is relational.
The methods of teaching/learning are relational.
The task of mission is relational.
It means that desired training outcomes are relational.

This will admittedly be less precise and less easily measured than traditional student-learning outcomes; but the ability to individualize training grows from theological as well as practical reflection. The Father is not the Son, nor are either of them the Spirit. We can come to God in his unity; but we can also know each of the three individually. In the same way, training that focuses on the class or cohort is not wrong; but it is not complete. Training in a relational paradigm will have expectations for the whole group; and will also individualize to the needs of a given learner.

A particularly important area of outcomes to keep in mind has to do with transformative education. The training of missionaries is not just a matter of cognitive, affective, and skill development: it is a process that challenges pre-conceived notions of life and our human condition. When we speak of challenging those pre-conceived notions, we are talking about presenting new ways of looking at the values and beliefs that shape the trainee. One clear distinction of training for mission work is that the outcomes are meant to challenge existing beliefs and values: in other words, it is a transformative process.

Similarly, mission training is distinctly relational. As mission trainer Ruth Wall points out, this is an area where outcomes are not simply "acquiring" new skills, knowledge or perspectives; mission outcomes are distinctly interactive with both God and humans as well. This interactive relational approach goes even further when we consider the contributions of Enoch Wan. Vertical relationship between God, the trainer, and the trainee are vital. Horizontal relationships are likewise important: between the trainer and trainee and within the larger Christian community as well.

It means that training is dependent on more than one person/Person to be effective.

The goal is to see healthy and appropriate relationships between all of the people involved, as well as each of those people in their walk with Triune God. Relationship requires at least two! And so if a relationship fails, how do we evaluate? In a skill-based paradigm of mission training the outcomes are easily identified and the methods can be assumed to lead to those outcomes. Yet if the goal is a series of healthy relationships between all of the various Beings and beings who are involved, then one person can do all that is "right" and still not see the goals accomplished.

Relational paradigm training is multidimensional and complex, unlike traditional training that is one-dimensional and simple. *It means that we assume relationships to be dynamic, not static.*

Given the dynamic nature of human relationships, this is very good news. If a given approach at training or ministry is not successful, this principle allows us to try a new approach. A relational paradigm approach to training will not create a single approach, yet will instead develop multiple approaches, and will vary methods until a good fit between trainer and trainee is found. *It means that training will not be seen as the mechanical following of a prepared curriculum, but as the flexible interaction of content, training methods, and training relationships within a flexible philosophy of education.*

This principle calls for flexibility in both content, relationship and method in order to achieve transformation. We could summarize this idea with the equation "TC = OC + PC" as developed by Wan.[286]

transformational change = ontological convergence + pedagogical convergence

OC is the ontological convergence where trainer and trainee grow to understand each other at the level of being, including elements of common humanity, cultural diversity, and role distinction.

---

[286] Wan, Enoch. *En-qing Theology: Interdisciplinary Studies and Practice.* (in Chinese) Hong Kong: TienDao Publisher. 2016: chapter 8. www.toelibrary.com.

PC is the pedagogical convergence where trainer and trainee understand each other at the level of teaching methods, location, thought processes, etc.

These two factors, each varying according to the specific needs and experiences of the specific people involved, are to be modified to maximize TC – the transformational change where not only behaviors but underlying assumptions about life are transformed because of the maximized impact of content, relationship and method. The transformation that is sought is to take on the mindset of the Spirit (Romans 8:5-6) and reject the mindset of the world.

Figures 3 and 4 graphically describe the same issues as we see in the OC + PC = TC equation. The training of missionaries seeks transformation, and that sort of desired outcome is far from mechanical or technical. Transformation occurs in a process and progress that is shaped by the interaction of vertical relationships and horizontal relationships which ultimately bring the learner, the trainers, the larger Christian community (church) together around the concepts and practice of theology, Bible, intercultural study, and ministry.

It means that the trainee is prepared to be transformed even as he/she takes a message of Gospel transformation to the unreached.

The transformation that is sought is not, as is so often assumed, only of the non-Christian. Seeing the unreached come to faith is one part of the multi-faceted work that God is doing in mission. He is also deeply involved in challenging the assumptions of his own children. As Christian witness spreads from one culture and language to another, the transformative process and progress that we are describing continues. A vertical relationship in the context of horizontal relationships in an unfamiliar culture bring about challenges to the assumptions of that Christian messenger. Life in a new context brings "disruptive dilemmas" to the intercultural Gospel messenger. The training process needs to prepare that worker to embrace a transformative process as she/he sees vertical truths in light of new horizontal contexts. *Training based on the Paradigm of Relational Realism is accepted, appreciated, and consistent with lifestyle patterns of most of the non-Western world as well as a growing number of Western civilization's younger generations.*

We realize that a focus on relationship as the organizing principle of mission training is not normal for Western schools or mission agencies. The previous decades of mechanistic training programs that grew from a modernity perspective do not tend to value relationship *per se*. Yet it is our belief that the growing mission sending impulse from Asia, Latin America, and Africa will be much more aligned with relational patterns, and not as tied to methods and techniques. In fact, this last point is the subject of a sequel that the authors have in mind, presenting case studies of missionary training approaches around the world that illustrate the paradigm of relational realism: training approaches that understand the essence of life to be first and foremost about a vertical relationship with God, and secondarily to be about the horizontal relationship between created beings.

The question we are answering in this chapter is, "What does it mean to train missionaries from a paradigm of relational realism?" We close with a final observation: it means that we are equipping a generation of leaders from Jesus's church who have developed relational skills and insights in vertical and horizontal directions, both within and across cultures.

In our globalized, multicultural world, leaders will not be those who master technique and method. Leaders will know the Lord in a deep relationship, and they will be able to form deep, healthy relationships with people across all kinds of cultures. Training for a relational paradigm has impact that goes much wider than preparation of missionaries, though that in itself is a great goal.

A paradigm of relational realism will train people who will ultimately lead churches, schools, missions, hospitals and businesses as those trained to walk wisely with God and with his diverse humanity.

To say that one uses a relational realism paradigm to train missionaries has many implications. This chapter has presented some answers to the question, "What does it mean to train missionaries through a paradigm of relational realism?" The answer to that question includes organizing training around relational concepts, forming outcomes, values, methods, training staff, daily schedules, and all other parts of the training around the conscious recognition that reality is based on relationships: first in priority is one's relationship with Triune God, and secondarily the relationship between created beings. Our prayer is that this book will begin a conversation that leads to increasing awareness of relational issues in ministry of all kinds, and especially ministry that raises up effective cross-cultural gospel messengers and wise, relational intercultural leaders.

Appendix 1 -

Transformative andragogy

Boyd, Robert D., and Myers, J. Gordon. "Transformative Education." *International Journal of Lifelong Education* 7, no. 4 (October–December 1988): 261–284.

Brookfield, S.D. (2000). "Transformative learning as ideology critique." In J. Mezirow & Associates (Eds.), *Learning as transformation. Critical perspectives on a theory in progress* (pp. 125–150). San Francisco, CA: Jossey-Bass.

Burbules, N.C. and Berk, R. (1999) "Critical Thinking and Critical Pedagogy: Relations, Differences, and Limits." In Thomas S. Popkewitz and Lynn Fendler, eds.: *Critical Theories in Education*. New York: Routledge. Available at http://faculty.ed.uiuc.edu/burbules/ncb/papers/critical.html.

Cragg, C.E., Plotnikoff, R.C., Hugo, K. & Casey, A. (2001) "Perspective transformation in RN-to-BSN distance education." *Journal of nursing education*, 40(7).

Cranton, Patricia. *Understanding and Promoting Transformative Learning: A Guide for Educators of Adults*. San Francisco, CA: Jossey-Bass, 1994.

Cranton, P. (1996) *Professional Development as Transformative Learning: New Perspectives for Teachers of Adults*. San Francisco, CA: Jossey-Bass Inc.

Cranton, Patricia, ed. *Transformative Learning in Action: Insights from Practice. New Directions for Adult and Continuing Education.* no. 74. San Francisco, CA: Jossey-Bass, Summer 1997.

Cranton, P. (2006) *Understanding and Promoting Transformative Learning: A Guide for Educators of Adults* (2nd ed.). San Francisco, CA: John Wiley & Sons, Inc.

Cranton, P. & King, K.P. (2003). "Transformative learning as a professional development goal." *New Directions for Adult and Continuing Education, 98,* 31–37.

Dirkx, J.M., Mezirow, J., & Cranton, P. (2006). "Musings and reflections on the meaning, context, and process of transformative learning: A dialogue between John M. Dirkx and Jack Mezirow." *Journal of Transformative Education, 4*(2), 123–139.

Elias, D. (1997) "It's time to change our minds: An introduction to transformative learning." *ReVision,* 20(1).

Fletcher, S. (2007). "Mentoring adult learners: Realizing possible selves." In M. Rossiter (Ed.), *Possible selves and adult learning: Perspectives and potential. New directions for adult and continuing education* (no. 114, pp. 75–86). San Francisco: Jossey-Bass.

Gagnon, Jr., G.W. & Collay, M. (1999) *Constructivist Learning Design.* Available at http://www.prainbow.com/cld/cldp.html.

Grabove, Valerie. "The Many Facets of Transformative Learning Theory and Practice." In: *Transformative Learning in Action: Insights from Practice. New Directions for Adult and Continuing Education.* no. 74, edited by P. Cranton, 89–96. San Francisco, CA: Jossey-Bass, Summer 1997.

King, Kathleen P. (2005). *Bringing transformative learning to life*. Malabar, FL: Krieger.

Kligyte, G. (2011). "Transformation narratives in academic practice." *International Journal for Academic Development, 16(3)*, 201–213.

Lee, M. (1999) "The Role of Cultural Values in the Interpretation of Significant Life Experiences. Conference Proceedings," Adult Education Research Conference (AERC).

Loughlin, Kathleen A. *Women's Perceptions of Transformative Learning Experiences Within Consciousness-Raising*. San Francisco, CA: Mellen Research University Press, 1993.

Lulee, Su-Tuan, et. al. "Transformative Learning" Created for EDDE 801, Ed D at Athabasca University, Canada on August, 2009. http://www.slideshare.net/susanlulee/introduction-to-transformative-learning (accessed Oct. 1, 2016).

Lysaker, J. & Furuness, S. (2011). "Space for transformation: Relational, dialogic pedagogy." *Journal of Transformative Education, 9(3)*, 183–187.

Mezirow, J. (1975). *Education for Perspective Transformation: Women's Reentry Programs in Community Colleges*. New York: Center for Adult Education Teachers College, Columbia University.

Mezirow, J. (1978). "Perspective Transformation." *Adult Education*, 100–110.

Mezirow, J. (1981). "A Critical Theory of Adult Learning and Education." *Adult Education* 32: 3–23.

Mezirow, J. (1991). *Transformative Dimensions of Adult Learning*. San Francisco, CA: Jossey-Bass.

Mezirow, J. (1995). "Transformation Theory of Adult Learning." In: *In Defense of the Lifeworld*, edited by M.R. Welton, pp. 39–70. New York: SUNY Press.

Mezirow, J. (1997). "Transformative Learning: Theory to Practice." *New Directions for Adult and Continuing Education, 74*, 5–12.

Mezirow, J. (2000). *Learning as Transformation: Critical Perspectives on a Theory in Progress*. San Francisco: Jossey Bass.

Miller, J.P. & Seller, W. (1990) *Curriculum: perspectives and practice*. Toronto: Copp Clark Pitman

O'Sullivan, E. (1999) *Transformative Learning: Educational vision for the 21st century*. Toronto, Canada: University of Toronto Press Inc.

O'Sullivan, E. (2003) "Bringing a perspective of transformative learning to globalized consumption." *International Journal of Consumer Studies*, 27 (4), 326–330.

Scott, Sue M. "The Grieving Soul in the Transformation Process." In: *Transformative Learning in Action: Insights from Practice. New Directions for Adult and Continuing Education*. no. 74, edited by P. Cranton, 41–50. San Francisco, CA: Jossey-Bass, Summer 1997.

Swanson, K.W. (2010). "Constructing a learning partnership in transformative teacher development." *Reflective Practice, 11*(2), 259–269.

Taylor, Edward W. *The Theory and Practice of Transformative Learning: A Critical Review*. Information Series no. 374. Columbus: ERIC Clearinghouse on Adult, Career, and Vocational Education, Center on Education and Training for Employment, College of Education, the Ohio State University, 1998. http://www.calproonline.org/eric/docs/taylor/taylor_02.pdf (access Oct. 1, 2016)

Tisdell, Elizabeth J. *Exploring Spirituality and Culture in Adult and Higher*. San Francisco, CA: Jossey-Bass. 2003.

Torosyan, Roben. (2007). *Teaching for Transformation: Integrative Learning, Consciousness Development and Critical Reflection*. Unpublished manuscript. http://www.faculty.fairfield.edu/rtorosyan/.

Appendix 2 –

ANDRAGOGY VS. PEDAGOGY

A. General Comparison[287]

1. "Andragogy" is a word coined by Malcolm Knowles from the Greek word *aner* (with the stem *andr-*) meaning "man" and means "the art and science of helping adults learn" as distinguished from "pedagogy" (from the Greek stem *paid—* meaning child) which is the art and science of teaching children.

2. The Andragogical Process
   - The establishment of a climate conducive to adult learning.
   - The creation of an organizational structure for participative planning.
   - The diagnosis of needs for learning.
   - The formulation of directions of learning (objectives).
   - The development of a design of learning activities (plan).
   - The operation of the learning activities (implementation).
   - The rediagnosis of needs for learning (evaluation).

3. A comparison of andragogy and pedagogy:

ELEMENTS	PEDAGOGICAL Teacher Directed Learning	ANDRAGOGICAL Self-Directed Learning
Climate	Formal authority-oriented Competitive Judgmental	Informal, mutually respectful Consensual Collaborative Supportive
Planning	Primarily by teacher	By participative decision-making
Diagnosis of Needs	Primarily by teacher	By mutual assessment
Setting Goals	Primarily by teacher	By mutual negotiation
Designing a Learning Plan	Content units Course syllabus Logical sequence	Learning projects Learning content sequenced in terms of readiness
Learning Activities	Transmit techniques Assigned readings	Inquiry projects, independent study, experimental techniques
Evaluation	Primarily by teacher	By mutual assessment of self-collected evidence

---

[287] L. Robert Kohls, *Training Know-how for Cross-cultural and Diversity Trainers.* Duncanville, TX: Adult Learning Systems. Inc. 1995, 64.

B. Assumptions and process elements of pedagogical and andragogical model of learning[288]

ASSUMPTIONS		
ABOUT	**PEDAGOGICAL**	**ANDRAGOGICAL**
Concept of the learner	Dependent personality	Increasingly self-directing
Role of learner's experience	Role of learner's experience	A rich source for learning by self and others
Readiness to learn	Uniform by age level and curriculum	Develops from life tasks and problems
Orientation to learning	Subject-centered	Task or problem centered
Motivation	By external rewords and punishment	By internal incentives, curiosity
PROCESS ELEMENTS		
ELEMENTS	**PEDAGOGICAL**	**ANDRAGOGICAL**
Climate	Tense, low trust Formal, cold aloof Authority-oriented Competitive Judgmental	Relaxed, trusting Mutually respectful Informal, warm Collaborative Supportive
Planning	Primarily by teacher	Mutually by learners and facilitator
Diagnosis of needs	Primarily by teacher	By mutual negotiation
Setting of objectives	Primarily by teacher	By mutual negotiation
Designing learning plans	Teacher's content plans Course syllabus Logical sequence	Learning contracts Learning projects Sequenced by readiness
Learning activities	Transmittal techniques Assigned readings	Inquiry projects Independent study Experiential techniques
Evaluation	By teacher Norm-referenced (on a curve) With grades	By learner-collected evidence validated by peers, facilitators and experts. Criterion referenced

---

[288] Kohls, L. Robert, and Brussow, Herbert L. *Training Know-How for Cross Cultural and Diversity Trainers*. Duncanville, TX: Adult Learning Systems, 1995, 63.

Appendix 3 –

Creating the Climate for Learning[289]

Purpose of all instruction: the intent to send students away from instruction with at least as favorable an attitude toward the subject taught as they had when they first arrived.

People learn to avoid things they are hit with. If conditions for learning are unpleasant, people will avoid the situation, avoid learning, and may learn to hate the subject.

Need is to accentuate positive conditions and consequences in the learning situation and eliminate the negative, aversive conditions and consequences.

Aversive conditions to be eliminated:

1. Conditions which cause students fear and anxiety, distress, tension, foreboding, worry or disquiet, anticipation of the unpleasant.
2. Conditions which cause frustration, blocking, or interference with student's desire to learn.
3. Conditions which cause humiliation and embarrassment, causing lowering of a student's self-respect and self-esteem, making him uncomfortable or self-conscious or shaming, debasing or degrading him/her.
4. Conditions which cause boredom.

Positive conditions which create a climate for learning:

1. Acknowledging students' responses, whether correct or incorrect, as attempts to learn and following them with accepting rather than rejecting comments.
2. Providing instruction in increments that will allow success most of the time.
3. Providing enough sign posts so that the student always knows where he is and where he is expected to go.
4. Giving the student some choice in selecting and sequencing the subject matter.
5. Relating new information to old, within the experience of the student.
6. Treating the student as a person.
7. Providing instructional tasks that are relevant to your objectives and letting your student know what the objectives are.

---

[289] Ibid, 62.

Appendix 4 -

Content and Sequencing of Cross-Cultural Training[290]

1. Sensitivity Awareness/ *ATTITUDE* CHANGE	• Breaking out of your ethnocentrism • Considering other Cultures as different but not inferior • GENERIC	Ethnocentrism Perception Stereotyping Development Concept Culture Concept Worldview Biculturalism Models for Comparing/Contrasting Cultures Culture Shock Acculturation Cycle Levels of Acculturation
2. *KNOWLEDGE/* INFORMATION DISSEMINATION	AREA STUDIES { A. re: Your Own Country — AMERICAN STUDIES - - - - - - - - - - B. re: Target Country — COUNTRY SPECIFIC } COVERAGE Political Economic Historical Social Philosophical Religious Aesthetic	Implicit Cultural Assumptions / Values / Cognitive Styles LANGUAGE STUDY

3. *SKILLS* Development	1. Managing Transitions
	2. Basic Survival Skills: e.g.
	   Finding a place to live
	   Buying things/bargaining
	   Ordering in a restaurant
	   Using public transportation
	3. Asking directions
	4. Replacing Old Stabilizers
		5. Value Determination
		6. Information Gathering and Validation
		7. Functioning According to New Culture
		8. Norms
		9. Dealing with Ambiguity
		10. Communicating in a New Language
		11. Non-Verbal Communication (Gestures)

---

[290] Ibid, 45.

Bibliography

Abbe, Allison. "Building Cultural Capability for Full-Spectrum Operations." Study Report 2008-04. U.S. Army Research Institute, 2008.

Abbe, Allison, Lisa M.V. Gulick and Jeffrey L. Herman. *Cross-Cultural Competence in Army Leaders: A Conceptual and Empirical Foundation*. Arlington, VA: United States Army Research Institute for the Behavioral and Social Sciences, 2007.

Adair, Wendi L., Ivona Hideg and Jeffrey R. Spence. "The Culturally Intelligent Team: the Impact of Team Cultural intelligence and Cultural Heterogeneity on Team Shared Values." *Journal of Cross-Cultural Psychology* 44.941 (2013): 941–962.

Ajith, Fernando. In *Global Missiology for the 21st Century*, Pasadena, CA: William Carey Library, 1999, 189–254.

Anderson, Dan. *Missiological Implications of Biblical Mentoring for Mentoring Duna Youth*. Paper Submitted in Partial Requirements for course DIS 780. Western Seminary. Portland, 2014.

Anderson, Ray S. *The Shape of Practical Theology*. Downers Grove, IL: InterVarsity Press, 2001.

Anthony, Michael J., ed. *Evangelical Dictionary of Christian Education*. Grand Rapids, MI: Baker Academics, 2001.

Ardiwardana, Margaretha. "Formal and Non-Formal Pre-Field Training, Perspective of the New Sending Countries." In *Too Valuable to Lose*. Taylor, William B. ed. Pasadena, CA: William Carey Library, 1995.

Argyis, C, and D.A. Schön. "Increasing Professional Effectiveness." In *Theory Into Practice*. San Francisco: Jossey-Bass, 1974.

Armstrong, Ruth M. "A Christian Approach to Learning Theory." In *Christian Approaches to Learning Theory, A Symposium.* De Jung, Norman, ed. Lanham, MD: University of America Press, 1984.

Arndt, William F. and F. Wilbur Gingrich. *A Greek-English Lexicon of the New Testament And Other Early Christian Literature.* 2nd Edition revised by F. Wilbur Gingrich and Frederick W. Danker. Chicago: University of Chicago Press, 1979.

Austin, Bill. *Austin's Topical History of Christianity.* Wheaton, IL: Tyndale House Publishers, Inc., 1983.

Aylward, Gladys and Christine Hunter. *Gladys Aylward, the Little Woman.* Chicago, IL: Moody Press, 1970.

Banks, Robert. *Reenvisioning Theological Education. Exploring a Missional Alternative to Current Models.* Grand Rapids. MI: William B. Eerdmans Publishing Company, 1999.

Barth, Karl. *Church Dogmatics. Vol 1, The Doctrine of the Word of God.* Trans. G. T. Thomson, Harold Knight. Edinburg: T & T Clark, nd, printed 1980.

Bavinck, J. H. *An Introduction to the Science of Missions.* Philadelphia, PA: Presbyterian and Reformed Pub. Co., 1960.

Beechick, Ruth. *The Language Wars and Other Writings for Home Schoolers.* Pollock Pines, CA: Arrow Press, 1995.

Bennett, Janet M. "Intercultural Competencies" handout sheet. 2010.

Bennett, Milton J. "Becoming Interculturally Competent," in J. Wurzel (ed). *Towards Multiculturalism: A Reader in Multicultural Education.* 2nd ed. Newton MA: Intercultural Resources Corp., 2004.

Berardo, Kate and Darla Deardorff, *Building Cultural Competence; Innovative activities and Models*. Sterling, VA: Stylus Publishing, LLC, 2012.

Bernard, H. Russell. *Social Research Methods. Qualitative and Quantitative Approaches*. Thousand Oaks, CA: Sage Publications, Inc., 2000.

Blaikiock, E. M. ed. *Zondervan Pictorial Bible Atlas*. Grand Rapids, MI: Zondervan Publishing House, 1969, 1972.

Bloecher, Detlef. "Missionary Training Makes Missionaries Resilient – Lessons From ReMAP II," 18 Oct, 2003, 1–14. <http://www.wearesources.org> Accessed Sept 12, 2005.

Bloom, Benjamin S. *Taxonomy of Educational Objectives. Book One: Cognitive Domain*. New York: Longman Inc., 1954, 1956.

Boff, Leonardo. *Holy Trinity, Perfect Community*. Translated by Phillip Berryman. Maryknoll, NY: Orbis Books, 2000. Originally published in Portuguese *Santisima Trindade e a Melhor Communidade,* 1988.

Bosch, David J. *Transforming Mission: Paradigm Shifts in Theology of Mission*. Maryknoll, NY: Orbis Books, 1991.

Brinkmann, Ursula and van Weerdenburg, Oscar. *Intercultural Readiness. Four Competences for working across cultures*. New York: Palgrave Macmillan, 2014.

Broucek, Dave. "An In-Service Training Idea for Church Planters." *Occasional Bulletin of the Evangelical Missiological Society,* Vol 10, no. 2, Spring, 1998.

_____. "Best Practice Standards for Missionary Training," paper presented at IFMA/EFMA Personnel Conference, International Mission Board of the Southern Baptist Convention Missionary Learning Center, Rockville VA: Dec 4–6, 2003.

Brown, Colin, ed. *The New International Dictionary of New Testament Theology*, Vol 1, s.v. "hypostasis." Grand Rapids, MI: Zondervan Corporation. 1975. Originally published in German under the title *Thologisches Begfiffslexikon Zum Neuen Testament*. Wuppertal: Theologischer Verlag Rolf Brockhaus, 1971.

Bruce, A. B. *The Training of the Twelve*. New Canaan, CT: Keats Publishing, 1979.

Bryan, C. Doug. *Relationship Learning. A Primer in Christian Education*. Nashville, TN: Broadman Press, 1990.

Brynjolfson, Rob. "Effective Equipping of the Cross-Cultural Worker." *The Journal of the WEA Missions Commission*, Jan.–April, 2004, 72–79. <www.globalmission.org> Accessed Sept. 12, 2005.

Cairns, Earle E. *Christianity Through the Centuries. A History of the Christian Church*. Revised and Enlarged Edition. Grand Rapids, MI: Zondervan Publishing House, 1981.

Calvin, Jean. *Institutes of the Christian Religion*. In *The Library of Christian Classics*, Vol XX edited by John T. McNeill, trans. by Ford Lewis Battles. Philadelphia, PA: The Westminster Press, 1960.

Carroll, James B. "Social Action and Evangelism: Envisioning a New Relational Paradigm for 21st Century American Christianity." July 2012. *www.globalmissiology.org*. 10 December 2015. <ojs.globalmissiology.org/index.php/english/article/view/1035>.

Caswell, Hollis L. and Doak S. Campbell. *Curriculum Development*. New York: American Book Co., 1935.

Center for Church Based Training. *Elders and Leaders, Field Guide*. Richardson, TX: CCBT, 2003.

Chang, Peter. "Steak, Potato, Peas and Chopsuey: Linear and Non-linear Thinking in Theological Education." *Evangelical Review of Theology*. Vol. V, no. 2, Oct. 1981.

Chafer, Lewis Sperry. *Major Bible Themes*. Revised by John F. Walvoord. Grand Rapids, MI: Zondervan Publishing House, 1974.

Chittum, Matthew. "Unmasking Consumerism for the Practice of Relational Discipleship within the Contemporary American Cultural Context." Dissertation, Dr. of Intercultural Studies. Western Seminary, 2014.

Cobb, John B. Jr. and David Ray Griffin. *Process Theology. An Introductory Exposition*. Philadelphia, PA: Westminster Press, 1976.

Cohen, Norman H. *Mentoring Adult Learners – A Guide for Educators and Trainers*. Malabar, FL: Krieger Publishing Company, 1995.

Coombs, Philip H. with Marzoor Ahmed. *Attacking Rural Poverty – How Nonformal Education Can Help*. Baltimore, MD: Johns Hopkins Univ. Press, 1974.

Copi, Irving M. *Introduction to Logic*, 6th ed. New York: Macmillan Publishing Co., Inc. 1982.

Corwin, Gary. "Reinventing Mission Training." *Evangelical Missions Quarterly,* Vol 32: no. 2, April 1996, 144–145.

Creswell, John W. *Qualitative Inquiry and Research Design. Choosing Among Five Traditions*. Thousand Oaks, CA: Sage Publications, 1998.

_____. *Research Design. Qualitative, Quantitative, and Mixed Methods Approaches*. 2nd edition. Thousand Oaks, CA: Sage Publications Inc., 2003.

Cummings, William K. "Evaluation and Examinations: Why and How Are Educational Outcomes Assessed." In *International Comparative Education – Practices, Issues And Prospects*. Thomas, R. Murray, ed. New York: Pergamon Press, 1990.

Cunningham, David. *These Three Are One. The Practice of Trinitarian Theology*. Malden, MA: Blackwell Publishers, 1998.

Dahms, John V. "Biblical Ecclesiology." *Global Missiology,* January 2005, <www.globalmissiology.net> Accessed Feb. 16, 2005.

_____. "Biblical Feelings and Emotions." *Global Missiology,* January 2005, <www.globalmissiology.net> Accessed Feb. 16, 2005.

Deardorff, Darla K. "Theory Reflections: Intercultural Competence Framework/Model." https://www.nafsa.org/_/File/_/theory_connections_intercultural_competence.pdf 2006, accessed Dec. 25, 2015.

_____. "Identification and Assessment of Intercultural Competence as a Student Ourcome of Internationalization." *Journal of Studies in International Education* 10.241 (2006): 241–266.

De Jung, Norman, ed. *Christian Approaches to Learning Theory, A Symposium*. Latham, MD: University of America Press, 1984.

_____, ed. *Christian Approaches to Learning Theory, Vol 2. The Nature of the Learner*. Latham, MD: University of America Press, 1985.

Dill, Dr. Stephen. Headmaster, Delaware County Christian Schools, personal interview. 7 July, 2005.

Driel, Marinus van, and William K. Jr. Gabrenya. "Organizational Cross-Cultural Competence: Approaches to Measurement." *Journal of Cross-Cultural Psychology*44, no. 874 (2013).

duBois, Cora. "The Dominant Value Profile of American Culture." *American Anthropologist* 57, no. 6 (December 1955): 1236.

Dunbar, Robin, 2015. socialsciencespace.com/2013/11/robin-dunbar-on-dunbar-numbers.

Elias, John L and Sharan B. Merriam. *Philosophical Foundations of Adult Education, 3rd Ed*. Malabar, FL: Krieger Publishing Company, 2005.

Elwell, Walter A. ed. *Evangelical Dictionary of Theology*. Grand Rapids, MI: Baker Book House Company, 1984.

Engel, S. Morris. *With Good Reason. An Introduction to Informal Fallacies*. New York: St. Martin's Press, 1976.

Erickson, Millard J. *Christian Theology*. 3rd Edition. Grand Rapids, MI: Baker Academic, 2013.

Escobar, Samuel. *The New Global Mission: The Gospel from Everywhere to Everyone*. Downers Grove, IL: InterVarsity Press, 2003.

———. "The Training for Missiologists for a Latin American Context." In *Missiological Education for the 21st Century*, 105, n.d.

Falker, William F. "Gaebelein, Frank E." in *Evangelical Dictionary of Christian Education*, Michael J. Anthony, ed. Grand Rapids, MI: Baker Academic, 2001.

Farley, Edward. *The Fragility of Knowledge. Theological Education in the Church And the University*. Philadelphia, PA, PA: Fortress Press, 1988.

_____. *Theologia: The Fragmentation And Unity of Theological Education*. Philadelphia, PA: Fortress Press, 1983.

Feenestra, Ronald J., and Cornelius Plantiga Jr., eds. *Trinity, Incarnation, and Atonement*. Notre Dame, IN: University of Notre Dame Press, 1989.

Fernando, Ajith. "Grounding Our Reflections in Scripture: Biblical Trinitarianism and Mission." In *Global Missiology for the 21st Century: The Iguassu Dialogue*. Taylor, William B., ed. Pasadena, CA: William Carey Library, 1999.

Ferris, Robert W., ed. *Establishing Ministry Training*. Pasedena, CA: William Carey Library, 1995.

_____. "Standards of Excellence in Missionary Training Centers," 1–7. <www.wearesources.org> Accessed Sept 12, 2005. First published in *Training for Cross-Cultural Ministries,* Vol 2000: no 1, January 2000.

Ford, Leroy. *Curriculum Design Manual for Theological Education: A Learning Outcomes Focus*. Nashville, TN: Broadman Press, 1991.

Freire, Paulo. *Pedagogy of the Oppressed*. Trans. Myra Bergman Ramos. New York: Continuum, 2002.

Gaebelein, Frank E. *Christian Education in a Democracy*. New York: Oxford University Press, 1951.

Garrison, D.R. "Online Community of Inquiry Review: Social, Cognitive, and Teaching Presence Issues." *Journal of Asynchronous Learning Networks* 11.1 (2007): 61 - 72.

Gava, Omar y Robert Strauss. *Manual de Capacitacion Transcultural*. Cordoba, Argentina: Recursos Estrategicos Globales, 2009.

Getz, Gene. *Elders and Leaders, God's Plan for Leading the Church.* Chicago: Moody Press, 2003.

Goncalves, Kleber D. "Missional Models of a Church for Postmoderns in Urban Contexts." *Journal of Adventist Mission Studies*10, no. 95 (2014): 82–99. http://digitalcommons.andrews.edu/cgi/viewcontent.cgi?article=1279&context=jams.

González, Justo L. *Mañana. Christian Theology from a Hispanic Perspective.* Nashville, TN: Abingdon Press, 1990.

_____. *The Story of Christianity, vol 1, The Early Church to the Dawn of the Reformation.* San Francisco, CA: Harper and Row, 1984.

Gunton, Colin E. *The One, The Three and the Many. God, Creation and the Culture of Modernity.* New York: Cambridge University Press, 1993.

_____. *The Promise of Trinitarian Theology,* 2nd Edition. New York: T & T Clark, 1997.

Guthrie, Donald. *The Pastoral Epistles.* In *Tyndale New Testament Commentaries.* Grand Rapids, MI: Wm. B. Eerdmans Publishing Company, 1957, reprinted 1984.

Hall, Edward T. *Beyond Culture.* New York: Anchor Books, 1977, 1989.

Harley, David. *Preparing to Serve. Training for Cross-Cultural Mission.* Pasadena, CA: William Carey Library, 1995.

Haynes, Stephen R. *Professing in the Postmodern Academy.* Waco, TX: Baylor Univ. Press, 2002.

Hedinger, Mark R. *Towards a Paradigm of Integrated Missionary Training.* Dr of Missiology Dissertation. Western Seminary. Portland, OR, 2006.

Hendricks, Howard and William Hendricks. *As Iron Sharpens Iron. Building Character in a Mentoring Relationship.* Chicago: Moody Press, 1995.

Hesselgrave, David. "A Missio-Relational Reading of Romans." *Occasional Bulletin* 23, no. 1 (Winter 2010): 1–8. https://www.westernseminary.edu/files/documents/faculty/wan/Missio_relational_Romans.pdf.

Hiebert, D. Edmond. *First Timothy.* Chicago, IL: Moody Press, 1957.

_____. *An Introduction to the New Testament. Vol. Two, The Pauline Epistles.* Chicago, IL: Moody Press, 1954, 1977.

_____. *Titus and Philemon.* Chicago, IL: Moody Press, 1957.

Hiebert, Paul G. *Anthropological Insights for Missionaries.* Grand Rapids, MI: Baker Book House, 1985.

_____. *Missiological Implications of Epistemological Shifts.* Harrisburg, PA: Trinity Press International, 1999.

Hodge, Charles. *Systematic Theology. Vol. One, Introduction. Part One, Theology.* Grand Rapids, MI: William B. Eerdmans Publishing Company. Reprint date 1982.

Hofstede, Geert, Geert Jan Hofstede and Michael Minkov. *Cultures and Organizations; Software of the Mind 3rd Ed.* USA: McGraw-Hill, 2010.

Hoke, Steve. "International Missionary Training Network (formerly "Fellowship") Gains Ownership Through Participation." *The Journal of the WEA Missions Commission,* October–December 2003, 43–47. <www.globalmission.org> Accessed September 12, 2005.

_____. "Missionary Training." *Connections.* August 2007. www.initialmedia.com accessed Dec. 24, 2015.

Hoke, Steve and Bill Taylor. *Send Me! Your Journey to the Nations*. Pasadena, CA: William Carey Library, 1999.

Horrell, J. Scott. "In the Name of the Father, Son and Holy Spirit: Constructing a Trinitarian Worldview," <http://www.bible.org> Accessed Nov. 26, 2005.

_____."Toward Clarifying a Biblical Model of the Social Trinity: Avoiding Equivocation of Nature And Order," *Global Missiology*, January 2004. <http://www.globalmissiology.net> Accessed Feb. 16, 2005.

Howard, Jiaying Zhuang. "Instructional Methods and Materials." In *International Comparative Education – Practices, Issues And Prospects*. Thomas, R. Murray ed. New York: Pergamon Press, 1990.

Hull, Bill. *The Disciple Making Pastor. The Key to Building Healthy Christians in Today's Church*. Old Tappan, NJ: Fleming H. Revell, 1988.

_____. *Jesus Christ, Disciplemaker*. Colorado Springs, CO: NavPress, 1984.

Hyman, Ronald and Barbara Rosoff. "Matching Learning and Teaching Styles: the Jug and What's in it." *Theory into Practice* 23.1 (1984): 35—43.

Illeris, Knud. *Transformative Learning and Identity*. New York: Routledge, 2014.

Jabbour, Nabeel T. *The Crescent Through the Eyes of the Cross*. Colorado Springs, CO: NavPress, 2008.

James, William. *Pragmatism*. New York: Meridian Books, 1955. Originally published Longmans, Green and Co., Inc., 1907.

Jarvis, Peter, ed. *Twentieth Century Thinkers in Adult and Continuing Education,* 2nd edition. Sterling, VA: Stylus Publishing Inc., 2001.

Jenkins, Philip. *The Next Christendom. The Coming of Global Christianity.* New York: Oxford Univ. Press, 2002.

Jeyaraj, Jesudason Baskar. *Christian Ministry. Models of Ministry And Training.* Bangalor: The J & P Print and Allied Industries, 2002.

Kaplan, Robert. "Cultural Thought Patterns in Intercultural Education." *Language Learning* 16 (1966).

Kent, Homer A. Jr., *Jerusalem to Rome, Studies in Acts.* Winona Lake, IN: BMH Books, 1972.

_____. *The Pastoral Epistles, Rev.* ed. Winona Lake, IN: BMH Books, 1958, 1982.

Kimel, Alvin F., ed. *Speaking the Christian God. The Holy Trinity And the Challenge of Feminism.* Grand Rapids, MI: William B. Eerdmans Publishing Company, 1992.

Kinsler, F. Ross, and James H. Emery. editors. *Opting for Change. A Handbook on Evaluation And Planning for Theological Education by Extension.* Pasadena, CA: William Carey Library, 1991.

Klafehn, Jennifer, Li Chenchen and Chi-yue Chiu. "To Know or Not to Know, is That the Question? Exploring the Role and Assessment of Metacognitiion in Cross-Cultural Contexts." *Journal of Cross-Cultural Psychology* 44 (2013): 963 - 991. 16 September 2014. <http://jcc.sagepub.com/content/44/6/963.refs.html>.

Knight, George R. *Philosophy and Education. An Introduction in Christian Perspective,* 4th edition. Berrien Springs, MI: Andrews Univ. Press, 2006.

Kohls, L. Robert with Herbert L. Brussow. *Training Know-How for Cross Cultural and Diversity Trainers*. Duncanville, TX: Adult Learning Systems, Inc., 1995.

Kohls, L. Robert and John M. Knight. *Developing Intercultural Awareness. A Cross-Cultural Training Handbook* 2nd ed. Yarmouth, ME: Intercultural Press, 1994.

Kolb, David A. *Experimental Learning: Experience as the Source of Learning and Development*. Englewood Cliffs; London: Prentice-Hall, 1984.

Kolb, David, and Simy Joy. "Are There Cultural Differences in Learning Styles?" Weatherhead School of Management, Case Western Reserve University, Dept of Organizational Research., n.d.

Konieczny, Richard J. and Enoch Wan. "An Old Testament Theology of Multiculturalism." *Global Missiology*, July, 2004. <www.globalmissiology.net> Accessed Sept. 21, 2004.

LaBelle, Thomas J., and Judy J. Sylvester. "Delivery Systems – Formal, Nonformal, And Informal." In *International Comparative Education – Practices, Issues And Prospects*. Thomas, R. Murray ed. New York: Pergamon Press, 1990.

LaCugna, Catherine Mowry. *God for Us. The Trinity And Christian Life*. San Francisco: Harper San Francisco, 1991.

_____. "God in Communion With Us – the Trinity" in *Freeing Theology. The Essentials of Theology in Feminist Perspective*. LaCugna, Catherine Mowry, ed. New York: HarperCollins Publishers Inc., 1993.

Landis, Dan and Rabi S. Bhagat, *Handbook of Intercultural Training, 2nd Ed*. Thousand Oaks, CA: SAGE Publications, Inc, 1996.

Leung, Angela K.-y., Sau-lai Lee and Chi-yue Chiu. "Meta-Knowledge of Culture Promotes Cultural Competence." *Journal of Cross-Cultural Psychology* (2013): 992 - 1006. 16 September 2014. <http://jcc.sagepub.com/content/44/6/992.refs.html>.

Lewis, Jonathan, "International Missionary Training Fellowship: What the Army Needs," *The Journal of the WEA Missions Commission,* February 2003, 46–48. <http://www.globalmission.org> Accessed September 12, 2005.

_____. "Internet Based Missionary Training." *Journal of the WEA Missions Commission,* October 2004 – January 2005, 60–61. <http://www.globalmission.org> Accessed September 12, 2005.

_____. "Teaching, Technology And Transformation," *Evangelical Missions Quarterly,* Vol 36: no. 4, Oct. 2000, 490-496.

Lister, J. Ryan. *The Presence of God: Its Place in the Storyline of Scripture and the Story of Our Lives*. Wheaton, IL: Crossway, 2015.

Lockerbie, D. Bruce. *Thinking And Acting Like a Christian*. Portland, OR: Multnomah, 1989.

Maffet, Gregory J. "A Scriptural Model of the Learner – A Van Tillian Perspective." In *Christian Approaches to Learning Theory. Vol Two, The Nature of the Learner*. De Jung, Norman ed. Lanham, MD: University of America Press, 1984.

Marshall, Howard I. *Acts*. In *Tyndale New Testament Commentaries*. Grand Rapids, MI: William B. Eerdmans Publishing Company, 1980.

Masemann, Vandra, and Anthony Welch, editors. *Tradition, Modernity, And Post-Modernity in Comparative*

Education. Boston, MA: Kluwer Academic Publishers, 1997.

Matsumoto, David and Hyisung C. Hwang. "Assessing Cross-Cultural Competence: A Review of Available Tests." *Journal of Cross-Cultural Psychology* 44 (2013): 849 - 873. 16 September 2014. <http://jcc.sagepub.com/content/44/6/849.refs.html>.

Matsuo, T. Dave. *The Person in Complete Context: The Whole of Theological Anthropology Distinguished*. TDM, 2014. <www.4X12.org>.

McKinney, Lois. "Contextualizing Instruction: ContriYetions to Missiology From the Field of Education," *Missiology*. Vol XII, no. 3, July 1984.

_____. "Missionaries in the Twenty-First Century. Their Nature, Their Nurture, Their Mission," *Missiology*. Vol. XXI, no. 1, Jan. 1993.

_____. "New Directions in Missionary Education." In *Internationalising Missionary Training: A Global Perspective*. William David Taylor, ed. Grand Rapids, MI: Baker Books, 1991.

McKinney-Douglas, Lois. "Learning Theories." In *Evangelical Dictionary of World Missions*. A. Scott Moreau, ed. Grand Rapids, MI: Baker Book House, 2000.

Mezirow, Jack and Associates. *Learning as Transformation. Critical Perspectives on a Theory in Progress*. San Francisco: John Wiley and Sons, 2000.

<http://www.mentorandmultiply.com> Accessed November 26, 2005.

Mitter, Wolfgang. "Challenges to Comparative Education – Between Retrospect and Expectation." In *Tradition, Modernity and Post-Modernity in Comparative*

Education. Maseman, Vandra and Anthony Welch, eds. Boston: Kluwer Academic Publishers, 1997.

Molinsky, Andy. *Global Dexterity*. Boston: Harvard Business Review Press, 2013.

Moltmann, Jürgen. *The Trinity And the Kingdom*. Minneapolis, MN: Fortress Press, 1993.

Moreau, A., ed. *Evangelical Dictionary of World Missions*. Grand Rapids, MI: Carlisle, Cumbria, UK: Baker Academic, 2000.

Moreland, J.P. and William Lane Craig. *Philosophical Foundations for a Christian Worldview*. Downers Grove: InterVarsity Press, 2003.

Müller, Roland. *The Messenger, The Message, and the Community*. 2nd Ed. Canada: CanBooks, 2010.

Nash, Ronald, ed. *Process Theology*. Grand Rapids: Baker Book House, 1987.

Nisbett, Richard E. *The Geography of Thought. How Asians and Westerners Think Differently, and Why*. New York: Simon and Schuster Inc, 2003.

Orr, James, General Editor. "Titus." *International Standard Bible Encyclopedia*. <http://www.bible-history.com-ISBE, 1915> Accessed November 26, 2005.

Paige, R. Michael. *Education for the Intercultural Experience*. 2nd Edition. Yarmouth, ME: Intercultural Press, 1993.

Patterson, George, with Galen Currah and Enoch Wan. "Classroom Instruction and Mentoring Compared." *Globalmissiology*, Sept 2003, <http://www.globalmissiology.net.> Accessed February 16, 2005.

<http://www.paul-timothy.net> Accessed November 26, 2005.

Pauw, Amy Plantinga. *The Supreme Harmony of All – The Trinitarian Theology of Jonathan Edwards*. Grand Rapids, MI: William B. Eerdmans Publishing Co., 2002.

Pazmiño, Robert W. *Foundational Issues in Christian Education,* 2nd edition. Grand Rapids, MI: Baker Books, 1997.

_____. *God Our Teacher. Theological Basics in Christian Education*. Grand Rapids, MI: Baker Academic, 2001.

_____. *Principles and Practices of Christian Education. An Evangelical Perspective*. Eugene, OR: Wipf and Stock Publishers, 2002

Pearcey, Nancy. *Total Truth. Liberating Christianity From its Cultural Captivity*. Wheaton, IL: Crossway Books, 2004.

Peter, Jarvis, ed. *20th Century Thinkers in Adult & Continuing Education*. 2nd Revised ed. edition. London: Routledge, 2001.

Peters, Ted. *God As Trinity. Relationality And Temporality in Divine Life*. Louisville, KY: Westminster Knox Press, 1993.

Peterson, Michael L. *Philosophy of Education: Issues And Options*. In series *Contours of Christian Philosophy*, C. Stephen Evans general editor. Downers Grove, IL: InterVarsity Press, 1986.

Pierson, Paul Everett, John Dudley Woodberry, Charles Edward van Engen, and Edgar J Elliston. *Missiological Education for the Twenty-First Century: The Book, the Circle, and the Sandals: Essays in Honor of Paul E. Pierson*. Maryknoll, NY: Orbis Books, 1996.

Piper, John. *Let the Nations be Glad! The Supremacy of God in Missions*. Grand Rapids, MI: Baker Books, 1993.

Plueddemann, James E. "Culture, Learning and Missionary Training." In *Internationalising Missionary Training*.

Taylor, William B. ed. Grand Rapids: Baker Book House, 1991.

Poythress, Vern S. "Reforming Ontology And Logic in the Light of the Trinity: An Application of Van Til's Idea of Analogy." *Westminster Theological Journal,* Vol 57:1 Spring, 1995, 187–219.

Rahner, Karl. *The Trinity.* Trans by Joseph Donceel. New York: Herder and Herder, 1970.

_____. *The Trinity.* Trans by Joseph Donceel. With Introduction, index and glossary by Catherine Mowry LaCugna. In series *Milestones in Catholic Theology.* New York: Crossroad Publishing Company, 1997.

Ramirez, Alonzo and Enoch Wan. "A Biblical Theology of Multi-Ethnicity and Multi-Culturality. Diversity in Unity And God's Ultimate Purpose for Humanity." *Global Missiology,* July 2004. <www.globalmissiology.net> Accessed September 21, 2004.

Reed, Jeff. "Church Based Missions: Creating a New Paradigm." Paper presented at 3rd Annual Conference, BILD International, Oct 1992. <www. BILD.org> Accessed June 1, 2005.

_____. "Church Based Theological Education: Creating a New Paradigm." Paper presented to North American Professors of Christian Education, 1992. <www. BILD.org> Accessed June 1, 2005.

Sawyer, James M. "Establishing a Doctrinal Taxonomy: A Hierarchy of Doctrinal Commitments." <http://www.bible.org> Accessed Nov. 26, 2005.

Schaff, Philip. *The Creeds of Christendom,* 3 volumes. Grand Rapids, MI: Baker Book House, 1931 (reprinted 1985).

Schultz, George. "The BEST Missionary Training Model?" *Evangelical Missions Quarterly,* vol 39: no. 1, January 2003, 90–95.

Scollon, Ron, Suzanne Wong Scollon and Rodney H. Jones. *Intercultural Communication A Discourse Approach, 3rd Ed.*. West Sussex, UK: John Wiley & Sons, Inc., 2012.

Sharp, Larry W. "A Mission Agency Director's Perspective on the Changing Relationship Between UFM, the Church, Training Institutions and the Mobilizers of Mission." Presented at the Evangelical Missiological Society Meeting, March 19–20, 1999, Lancaster, PA.

Shaules, Joseph. *The Intercultural Mind: Connecting Culture, Cognition, and Global Living*. Boston: Intercultural Press, 2015.

Shedd, William G. T. *Dogmatic Theology* 2nd edition. Nashville, TN: Thomas Nelson, reprinted 1980.

Shenk, Sara Wenger. *Anabaptist Ways of Knowing. A Conversation About Tradition-Based Critical Education*. Telford, PA: Cascadia Publishing House, 2003.

Sills, Michael David. "Training Leaders for the Majority World Church in the 21st Century," *Global Missiology*, April, 2004.<http://www.globalmissiology.org> Accessed August 13, 2005.

Simy, Joy and David A. Kolb. *Are there Cultural differences in Learning Style?* paper. Case Western Reserve University. Cleveland, OH: n.d.

Smallman, William H. *Able To Teach Others Also. Nationalizing Global Ministry Training*. Pasadena, CA: Mandate Press, 2001.

Smith, Donald K. *Creating Understanding. A Handbook for Christian Communication Across Cultural Landscapes.* Grand Rapids, MI: Zondervan Publishing House, 1992.

_____. "Training Within Non-Western Thought Patterns. A Relevant Educational Methodology for Two-Thirds World Leaders." Unpublished seminar notes, Portland, OR: Western Seminary, Feb. 6, 2005.

Smith, Ralph. *Paradox And Truth. Rethinking Van Til on the Trinity.* Moscow, ID: Canon Press, 2002.

_____. "The Trinitarian Covenant in John 17." *Global Missiology,* January 2005, <http://www.globalmissiology.net> Accessed February 16, 2005.

_____. *Trinity And Reality. An Introduction to the Christian Faith.* Moscow, ID: Canon Press, 2004.

_____. "Van Til's Insights on the Trinity." *Global Missiology,* January 2005, <http://www.globalmissiology.net> Accessed February 16, 2005.

Stanley, Paul D. and J. Robert Clinton. *Connecting: The Mentoring Relationships You Need to Succeed in Life.* Colorado Springs, CO: NavPress, 1992.

Steffen, Tom. "Missiological Education for the 21st Century." *Evangelical Missions Quarterly.* April, 1993, 178 – 183.

Stevens, David E. *God's New Humanity: A Biblical Theology of Multiethnicity for the Church.* Eugene OR: Wipf and Stock Publishers, 2012.

Street, Brian V. "Culture Is a Verb." In ., *Language and Culture, Papers from the Annual Meeting of the British Studies in Applied Linguistics.*, Vol. 7. Towanda NY: British Assoc of Applied Linguistics in association with Multilingual Matters, Ltd., 1993.

Taylor, William David, ed., *Global Missiology for the 21st Century. The Iguassu Dialogue*. Grand Rapids, MI: Baker Academic, 2000.

_____, ed. *Internationalising Missionary Training, A Global Perspective*. Grand Rapids, MI: Baker Book House, 1991.

_____, ed. *Too Valuable to Lose*. Pasadena, CA: William Carey Library, 1997.

The NET Bible. Biblical Studies Press, LLC, 1996 - 2009.

Thomas, R. Murray, ed. *International Comparative Education – Practices, Issues And Prospects*. New York: Pergamon Press, 1990.

Ting-Toomey, Stella. *Communicating Across Cultures*. New York, NY: The Guilford Press, 1999.

Tira, Sadiri Joy and Enoch Wan, *Missions in Action in the 21st Century*. Quezon City: Lifechange Publishing Inc and Global Diaspora Network, 2012.

Tisdell, Elizabeth J. *Exploring Spirituality and Culture in Adult and Higher Education*. San Francisco: Jossey-Bass, 2003. http://public.eblib.com/choice/publicfullrecord.asp x?p=158016.

Tozer, A. W. *The Knowledge of the Holy, the AttriYetes of God; Their Meaning in the Christian Life*. San Francisco: Harper and Row, 1961.

_____. *The Pursuit of God*. Harrisburg, PA: Christian Publications, Inc., 1948.

Tradition, Modernity, and Post-Modernity in Comparative Education. Dordrecht Netherlands   : Boston: Kluwer Academic Publishers published in cooperation with UNESCO Institute for Education, Hamburg, 1997.

van der Zee, Karen and Jan Pieter van Oudenhoven. "Culture Shock or Challenge? The Role of Personality as a Determinant of Intercultural Competence." *Journal of Cross-Cultural Psychology* 44 (2013): 928-940.

van Driel, Marinus and William K., Jr. Gabrenya. "Organizational Cross-Cultural Competence: Approaches to Measurement." *Journal of Cross-Cultural Psychology* 44 (2013): 874 - 899. 16 September 2014. <http://jcc.sagepub.com/content/44/6/874.refs.html>.

Van Til, Cornelius, *A Christian Theory of Knowledge.* Philadelphia, PA: Presbyterian and Reformed Publishing Co., 1969.

_____. *The Defense of the Faith.* Philadelphia, PA: Presbyterian and Reformed Publishing Company, 1955.

_____. *Essays on Christian Education.* Phillipsburg, NJ: Presbyterian and Reformed Publishing Co., 1974.

Vella, Jane. *Learning to Listen, Learning to Teach.* Revised ed. San Francisco, CA: Jossey-Bass. 2002.

_____. *On Teaching and Learning.* San Francisco: Jossey-Bass. 2008.

Verduin, John R., Jr., Harry G. Miller, and Charles E. Greer. *Adults Teaching Adults. Principles And Strategies.* Austin, TX: Learning Concepts, Inc., 1977.

Wall, Ruth M. "Equipping the Whole Person. Bulletin 1." *International Missionary Training Network* (2015).

Walvoord, John F and Roy B. Zuck, *The Bible Knowledge Commentary Old Testament.* SP Publications, Inc., 1988.

Wan, Enoch. "A Missio-Relational Reading of Romans: A Complementary Study to Current Approaches." 1 April 2010. *www.globalmissiology.org.* 10 December 2015.

<ojs.globalmissiology.org/index.php/english/article/view/104>.

_____. "A Warm, Yet Empty Voice? Reflections on Face-to-Face Interactions." 2 December 2013. *www.gospel-life.net/A-Warm-Yet-Empty-Voice.* Wheaton College. 10 December 2015. <www.gospel-life.net/a-warm-Yet-empty-voice-reflections-on-face-to-face-interactions>.

_____. "Christianity in the East And the West. Article Two Christianity in the Eye of Traditional Chinese." *Missiology.org.* < http://www.missiology.org> Accessed July 24, 2004.

_____. "Christianity in the East and the West. Article Four. Practical Contextualization: A Case Study of Evangelizing Contemporary Chinese," *Missiology.org,* <http://www.missiology.org> Accessed July 24, 2004.

_____. "Christianity in the East and the West. Article Five. Theological ContriYetions of Sino-theology to the Global Christian Community (Part One)." *Missiology.org.* <http://www.missiology.org> Accessed July 24, 2004.

_____. "Critiquing the Method of Traditional Western Theology and Calling for Sino-Theology." *Chinese Around the World,* November 1999, 12–17. Also published <http://www.missiology.org> Accessed July 24, 2004.

_____. "Ethnohermeneutics: Its Necessity and Difficulty for All Christians of All Times." *Global Missiology,* January, 2004. <http:// www.globalmissiology.net> Accessed July 24, 2004.

_____. "Exploring Sino-Spirituality." *First Evangelical Church Association Bulletin.* December, 1999, 16–21. <http://www.christianityinchina.org> Accessed July 24, 2004.

_____. "Rethinking Missiological Research Methodology: Exploring A New Direction." *Global Missiology.* <http://www.globalmissiology.net> Accessed June 16, 2004.

_____. "Spiritual Warfare. Overcoming Demonization." *Alliance Family,* Winter 1988, Manilla, Philippines, CAMACOP. 8–15.

_____. "Spiritual Warfare. Understanding Demonization." *Alliance Family,* Summer, 1988, Manilla Philippines, CAMACOP 6–18.

_____. "Spiritual Warfare. What Chinese Christians Should Know and Do." *First Evangelical Church Association,* December 1999. <http://www.feca.org> Accessed July 24, 2004.

Wan, Enoch and Johnny Yee-chong Wan. "A Relational Study of the Trinity and the Epistle to the Philippians." 1 April 2010. *www.globalmissiology.net.* 10 December 2015. <ojs.globalmissiology.org/index.php/english/article/view/102/294>.

Wan, Enoch and Mark Hedinger. "Missionary Training for the Twenty First Century: Biblical Foundations." July 2011. *globalmissiology.org.* Ed. Enoch Wan. 10 December 2015. <http://globalmissiology.org/index.php/english/issue/view/56>.

Wan, Enoch and Narry Santos. "A Missio-Relational Reading of Mark." Spring 2011. *www.emsweb.org.* <http://www.emsweb.org>.

Wan, Enoch and Tin V. Nguyen. "Towards a Theology of Relational Mission training - an Application of the Relational Paradigm." 1 January 2014. *www.globalmissiology.org.* 10 December 2015. <ojs.globalmissiology.org/index/php/english/article/view/1626>.

Wan, Enoch. *Diaspora Missiology: Theory, Methodology and Practice*. Portland OR: IDS-US@Western Seminary, 2011.

_____. "Relationship in the 21st Century: Theory and Practice." 7 March 2014. *www.gospel-life.net/relationship-in-the-21st-century-theory-and-practice/*. Billy Graham Center for Evangelism. 10 December 2015. <www.gospel-life.net>.

_____. "The Paradigm of "Relational Realism"." Spring 2006. *www.westernseminary.edu*. 10 December 2015. <www.westernseminary.edu/files/documents/faculty/Wan>.

Ware, Bruce A. *Father, Son, & Holy Spirit. Relationships, Roles, & Relevance*. Wheaton, IL: Crossway, 2005.

Welsh, Claude. *In This Name. The Doctrine of the Trinity in Contemporary Theology*. New York: Charles Scribner's Sons, 1952.

Whiteman, Darrell L. "Integral Training Today for Cross-Cultural Mission." *Missiology: and International Review* 36.1 (2008): 5 - 16.

Wilkinson, Bruce and Kenneth Boa. *Talk Thru the New Testament, Vol. Two*. Nashville, TN: Thomas Nelson Publishers, 1983.

Wilson, Jessie, Colleen Ward and Ronald Fischer. "Beyond Culture Learning Theory: What can Personality Tell us about Cultural Competence?" *Journal of Cross-Cultural Psychology* 44 (2013): 900—927.

Woodberry, Dudley J. *Missiological Education for the 21st Century. The Book, The Circle, and the Sandals*. Maryknoll NY: Orbis Books, 1996.

Wright, Christopher J.H. *The Mission of God*. Downers Grove, IL: InterVarsity Press, 2006.

About the Authors

Enoch Wan, Ph.D. (www.enochwan.com)

- Research Professor of Intercultural Studies and Director, Doctor of Intercultural Studies Program, Western Seminary (2001-present)
- Founding Director - Ph.D. Intercultural Studies Program, Reformed Theological Seminary (1993-2001)
- Past President of Evangelical Missiological Society ; VP-Publications, EMS (2015-present)
- Founder/Editor, multi-lingual e-journal www.GlobalMissiology.org

Mark Hedinger, DMiss

- Executive Director of Institute of International Christian Communication (WorldView), Portland, OR (2011-present)
- Intercultural Trainer with a network of international partner organizations (2008-present)
- Adjunct Professor, Western Seminary (2013-present)
- International Director with Crossworld (2002-2008)
- Missionary with Crossworld (1989-present)

www.ingramcontent.com/pod-product-compliance
Lightning Source LLC
Chambersburg PA
CBHW070018100426
42740CB00013B/2539